My Mother's Southern Kitchen

Also by James Villas

American Taste (1982)

The Town & Country *Cookbook* (1985)

James Villas' Country Cooking (1988)

Villas at Table (1988)

The French Country Kitchen (1992)

My Mother's Southern Kitchen

Recipes and Reminiscences

James Villas
with Martha Pearl Villas

MACMILLAN • USA

MACMILLAN
A Prentice Hall Macmillan Company
15 Columbus Circle
New York, NY 10023

MACMILLAN is a registered trademark of Macmillan, Inc.

Library of Congress Cataloging-in-Publication Data

Villas, James.
My mother's southern kitchen / James Villas.
p.   cm.
Includes index.
ISBN 0-02-622015-6
1. Cookery, American—Southern style.   I. Title.
TX715.2.S68V55   1994
641.5975—dc20   94-2627
CIP

Book design: Jennifer Dossin

Manufactured in the United States of America
10 9 8 7 6 5 4 3 2 1

To Patricia Sigrid, my sister, "Hootie,"
who carries on Mother's proud cooking tradition
and who makes the most sinful desserts in the South

Contents

When my sister's son, Charles Royal, was baptized back in the early sixties, Mother honored the occasion with an elaborate lunch buffet attended, left to right, *by my Aunt Mary Frances; my Swedish grandmother, Mama Sigrid; and my Georgia grandmother, Maw Maw.*

Introduction

"Son," Mother begins in frustration, grabbing a handful of flour from the five-pound sack while gazing at the label, "if I've told you once, I've told you a thousand times you can't make good biscuit with this Northern flour. It's just too hard." She pushes it around in the mixing bowl with her chubby fingers, a look of disgust on her face as she feels the texture. "Yankee flour! There's no way on God's green earth . . ." she huffs. "You've gotta have Red Band or White Lily or some other good soft *Southern* flour." She glances at the big cast-iron skillet on top of the stove. "Are you watching that chicken? I *knew* I should have brought my own flour."

The subject is hot buttermilk biscuits, or, if you talk true Rebel like my mother, biscuit—in the singular and referring to one or two or a dozen of this wondrous Southern staple to be included on a wholesome fried chicken dinner we're preparing for three hungry guests having cocktails at my home in East Hampton on Long Island. Reconciled to having to use inferior flour, she proceeds to teach me, to explain to me in detail, to show me for the millionth time why my biscuits never, ever come out as fluffy and light, as smooth and even, as golden and sumptuous as hers. When she reaches for another handful of flour, I ask her for the approximate measure so I can jot it down for the perfect recipe I'm forever questioning, changing, modifying.

"I have no earthly idea how much," she mumbles impatiently. "Two good handfuls—maybe a little more. You can tell when you've got the right amount—everybody in the South knows that!" Quickly she shakes unmeasured amounts of baking powder, salt, and baking soda into the flour, oblivious to the measuring spoon I'm holding over the bowl. "How fresh is this baking powder?" she asks with a frown, sticking her little finger down into the yellow box. "Feels hard."

While she shakes off the excess flour from her hand into the sink and looks around for a large soup spoon, I begin opening a can of shortening, the supermarket's own brand I found on sale. "You know, honey," she comments, "you'll never get through that thick skull of yours that you can't make good biscuit with those cheap shortenings. How many times do I have to tell you to buy Crisco and noth-

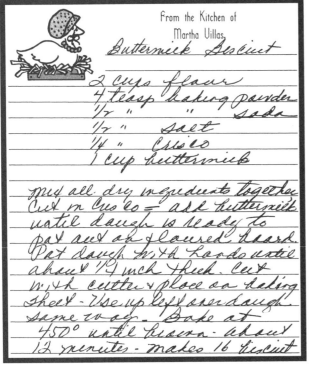

From the Kitchen of
Martha Villas,

Buttermilk Biscuit

2 cups flour
4 teasp baking powder
1/2 " " soda
1/2 " salt
1/4 " Crisco
1 cup buttermilk

Mix all dry ingredients together.
Cut in Crisco — add buttermilk
until dough is ready to
pat out on floured board.
Pat dough with hands until
about 1/4 inch thick. Cut
with cutter & place on baking
sheet. Use up left over dough
same way. Bake at
450° until brown. about
12 minutes. makes 16 biscuit

Here are Mother's inimitable butter-milk "biscuit" that I've never really mastered. Never would she tamper with a single ingredient in the old family recipe or modify the mixing technique, which she firmly believes is part of the secret.

ing but Crisco?" She digs the spoon four times into the can, scrapes the fat off with a finger into the bowl, wipes her finger on her apron, then hands me the pastry cutter. "Here," she directs, "now you cut in the shortening." I begin hacking away at the pale gobs. "No, no, no," she corrects, taking my hand and guiding the blade in more gentle strokes. "Don't crush those lumps so much! They're what makes the biscuit flaky."

"By the way, Missy," I ask with genuine curiosity, expecting some learned revelation, "why do you always use buttermilk for biscuits? Why not just whole milk?"

"Because buttermilk's better," she proclaims, deftly popping open the container and taking a sniff, then a sip.

"But why is it better?"

"It just is—every Southerner knows that."

Just as one guest appears in the kitchen and quickly cows away as he hears Mother and me goading one another as we always do when cooking together, I beg, plead with her to measure out at least the liquid.

"Honey, I swear to goodness," she moans in real exasperation, pouring a little milk into the dry ingredients before stirring to test the consistency of the dough. "You might know how to fix all those fancy French dishes and write those cook-books . . . but I'm telling you, you *still* don't understand Southern cooking." She pours more milk and stirs, never once taking her eyes off the mixture till it looks and feels perfect. "I don't have time to fool around with all those measuring cups and things you people use. I just add the milk as it's needed. Why such a to-do over something like biscuit?"

Working fast as ever, she gathers a big ball of dough in her strong hands and plops it on a sheet of waxed paper. "Now, you do the kneading—but not too much." I begin pushing it as I would my French country bread. "I said not too much!" she exclaims, coaxing my hands away and taking over. "Mercy, you want tough biscuit? Now, just pat the dough out about half an inch thick . . . but gently." She pats, and I imitate, not daring to ask still again why she would never use a rolling pin. "Now here, cut 'em out," she then directs, handing me the biscuit cutter while she uses a juice glass. "No, no, don't twist the cutter, for heaven's sake; just press straight down. You want lopsided biscuit?" She takes my large baking sheet and, fast as lightning, begins to arrange the biscuits in three rows. "Always remember to leave plenty of room between biscuit so the sides will get crusty."

I slide the sheet into the 450°F oven. "Twelve minutes, isn't it?" I ask, remembering the latest recipe she had dictated over the phone from North Carolina and setting the timer.

"You can't say that," she counters, taking a big slug of Jack Daniel's and soda before moving over to begin draining the fried chicken on a paper sack. "Just watch those biscuit till they're done—you can tell."

Before the timer rings, Mother peeps through the glass on the oven door and commands "Take 'em out, they're done." To my eye, the biscuits don't appear near browned enough, so we argue back and forth. "I'm telling you to take them out *this second* or they'll be hard as rocks," she insists before commenting on whether there might be something wrong with my eyesight. "Honey, I can see without asking that one of your big problems is you overcook your biscuit." Out they come, and, sure enough, despite the Yankee flour and unmeasured ingredients and my ever so wounded pride, the biscuits, puffy and golden and even, are exemplary as ever.

Over the years, I guess I've managed to hold my own with my mother over the best preparations of such dishes as French *coq au vin*, Italian *osso bucco*, Greek *spanakopita*, Swedish *limpa* bread, and other international favorites we've so often shared together around the world. But when it comes to authentic Southern cooking, the food on which I was weaned, I'm forced to admit that I'm still no match for the lady known to family as Martha Pearl, to friends simply as Martha, and to me as Mother, Missy, Big Mama, and, when she gets particularly overbearing, Brunhilde. It's an infuriating, embarrassing, lamentable fact of life I've simply come to accept—almost. Sure, I can turn out pretty good pork barbecue, squash soufflé, hush puppies, and peach cobbler, but even these classics always lack that indefinable master touch, that knack, that native instinct that characterize virtually any Southern dish that Mother produces. "Maybe you've just lived up North too long," she quips.

I realize that the image of the old-fashioned, homespun Southern cook has become almost a cliché in the minds of most Americans, not the least of whom would include such outspoken champions of Mom's home cooking as Tom Wicker, Reynolds Price, Charles Kurault, and Craig Claiborne. The irony, of course, is that during this anemic age stigmatized more and more by kitchen illiterates playing with microwaves, counting calories, and bowing to the egregious dictates of cholesterol, the only genuine regional American food that is still not being overly threatened by technology, culinary trends, and health fanaticism is the traditional Southern style of cooking that my mother learned from her parents and grandparents and that she has spent a lifetime mastering. "Listen," she says

whenever anyone mentions diets, fats, sugar substitutes, and the like, "I never think about all that mess, and I'll soon be eighty—and my mama lived into her nineties. All I care about is whether food *tastes* good or not, and real Southern food does taste good. And I'll tell you something else: it's healthy food—I don't care what anybody says."

Creamy cheese and eggs with slabs of cured country ham; poppy seed chicken and baked spareribs; earthy Brunswick stew

Mother loves watermelon more than life itself, and when she spots a perfect wedge on one of our shopping sprees, she wastes no time cutting a first slab to taste seconds after we return home.

and spicy gumbos; bowls of butterbeans and collards and black-eyed peas simmered with lean salt pork, as well as okra and tomatoes, succotash, squash soufflé, and fresh corn pudding; satiny spoonbread and corn muffins; luscious fruit cobblers, Kentucky whiskey cake, buttermilk pie, and syllabub—this is the food I've known my whole life, dishes Mother knew how to elevate to the highest level of quality, and, whether in my home or hers, the fare people still beg us to prepare on any given occasion. Every dish smacks of virtuosity, wisdom, and Mother's unalterable devotion to sacred Southern principles that must be respected and upheld. She has cooked for Craig Claiborne, Pierre Franey, Jay Jacobs, Paul Bocuse, and a few dozen other chefs and notable food authors, all of whom stand in awe of her creative talents, her technical expertise, and often her severe if friendly manner. "Honey, you might be Craig Claiborne and from Mississippi," she once scoffed lovingly at the food editor of *The New York Times* when he kept nagging her about how she was making giblet gravy, "but if you don't get out of my kitchen this minute and let me finish what I'm doing, there's not going to be any Thanksgiving dinner." Another time at an elaborate Southern breakfast on my deck, my old friend and colleague Paula Wolfert asked if we didn't soak our salty Carolina country ham before frying it and making red-eye gravy. "I should say not," exclaimed Mother. "Do that, honey, and you not only don't have one ounce of flavor left but you can't make good gravy. Besides, a little salt never hurt anybody."

As far back as I can remember, there's been virtually no aspect of my mother's life that hasn't revolved around preparing the same vast depository of victuals that nourished my grandparents and great grandparents in Georgia, South Carolina, North Carolina, and heaven knows how many other Southern states. When the large family still included small children, grandparents (of three different nationalities), aunts and uncles, and a sprinkling of other relatives and close friends, it was not unusual for Mother's holiday tables to groan with tureens of oyster stew, twenty-five-pound roasted turkeys with sausage and pecan dressing, mammoth country hams lugged periodically from the mountains of North Carolina, bowls of dirty rice and field peas and corn pudding and two or three other vegetables, platters of freshly baked cornbread, all sorts of homemade pickles, fresh cakes and cookies of every description, and crystal containers of ambrosia. Breakfast every morning might include (and still does) the likes of brains and eggs with country sausage, baked cheese grits, fried apples, hobotee (curried meat custard), fried spots or salt mackerel, batter cakes, pecan waffles, Mother's peach and strawberry preserves, and, of course, piping hot buttermilk biscuits. While other children at school had to make do with processed meat sandwiches and peanut butter crackers or cafeteria muck, my and my sister's colorful lunch boxes always contained items such as fried chicken, ham or cheese biscuits, spiced apple slices, jelly cookies, a few watermelon-rind pickles, and a small thermos of buttermilk. Lord only knows what all Mother fed us at those important and bountiful evening meals, but to this day my favorite standard dinner is a bowl of fresh vegetable soup followed by her father's short ribs of beef baked slowly with tomatoes and potatoes, her inimitable squash soufflé, green snap beans simmered with cooking meat, my grandmother's skillet cornbread, and a nice helping of hot blackberry cobbler topped with vanilla ice cream.

In addition, one of Mother's greatest pleasures has always been—in old Southern tradition—cooking for others outside the family (at church functions, for patients in hospitals and nursing homes, when friends and neighbors die), and at no time are her delicacies in greater demand and more appreciated than around Christmas. Unlike most of today's younger generation of Southern cooks, Mother still practices religiously the old ritual of collecting just the right pecans and candied fruits in early fall, making numberless fruitcakes of different sizes, aging them carefully, and sending them all over the country to a discriminating network of friends and distant relatives and new acquaintances and even perfect strangers with whom she might have had a single talk on the phone. There are also those who would be utterly distraught if, in place of an ordinary and impersonal gift, a

LEFT: *Mother picking raspberries intended for preserves.*

RIGHT: *No summer scene is more traditional and typical around the house than that of Mother putting up the season's fresh fruits and vegetables. Here she pours hot paraffin over strawberry preserves.*

tin of nutty fingers, pecan-studded cheese biscuits, preserves, jellies, and marmalade (all with her personal "From Martha's Kitchen" label) were not delivered in time for Christmas. "It's so ridiculous giving people things they don't really want or need," she proclaims every year, "but I've never met anybody who didn't like something good to eat."

Equally important to Mother as her holiday food-making is the canning she and I do all summer long, a hobby that never fails to betray her utter obsession with fresh ingredients right at their prime. No sooner has the first perfect strawberry been plucked from the field than we haul out the gigantic sterilizing kettle, boxes of empty jars saved over the year, fat packages of new sealing lids, bottles of alum and pectin, and all kinds of spices. While other Southern cooks might settle for supermarket products, Mother still prefers to pick her own strawberries and raspberries; she drives across the border deep into South Carolina just to buy Elberta peaches by the peck in the orchard; and she always makes sure I've planted plenty of squash, tomatoes, and tiny pickling cucumbers in the East Hampton garden just like my grandfather always did in our large plot in Charlotte. She wouldn't dream of canning corn relish with any variety but *white* Silver Queen,

and often we've sat patiently at roadside vegetable stands for who knows how long till the next wagonload of fresh-picked corn pulled up. Mother gets very irritated if told she shouldn't pull back the husks on corn to check for quality, but the fur really flies when a farmer or vendor refuses to allow her to "plug" a watermelon with her small penknife to determine the rind's depth ("I hope you don't expect me to make watermelon-rind pickle with thin rind," I've heard her snap more than once at startled mongers.)

As a result of all the planning and searching and time-consuming work, our shelves remain well stocked with strawberry, peach, blueberry, fig, pear, and damson plum preserves; blackberry, apple, and hot pepper jelly; pickled peaches, artichokes, green tomatoes, okra, and watermelon rind; and a daunting array of cucumber pickles, relishes, chow chows, chutneys, and marmalades. Just as I have never once seen in my mother's kitchen packages of processed meats and cheeses, canned vegetables, or, heaven forbid, storebought cakes or cookies, the very idea of opening a jar of commercial bread-and-butter pickles is as inconceivable to us both as buying one of those plastic tubs of Kentucky Fried Chicken ("Not fit for human consumption," in Mother's lingo).

Having been subjected year after year to various professional cooking schools and innumerable hotshot young chefs and foodies boasting all their wizardly kitchen equipment, boutique mustards and vinegars, ultra-exotic herbs and spices, prepubescent organic veggies, and outlandish cooking techniques and food combinations, I never cease to be utterly amazed at Mother's almost unself-conscious ability to whip up fresh mayonnaise and virtually any style sauce without glancing even at her sacred but impossibly jumbled black recipe book, to turn out homemade bread and pastry with the same ease as she does needlepoint, to butcher anything from a chicken to a thirty-pound pig, and to transform the most rudimentary of ingredients into sumptuous feasts with no more than her time-tested pots and pans. "Why do people have to mess around so much with food?" she questions innocently. "All those special machines and gadgets . . . a little herb here and spice there . . . combine this with that just for novelty—no wonder half of what you find in magazines and restaurants tastes so awful. The problem is that most cooks today don't know the basics, and that there're lots of dishes you just shouldn't fool around with."

As many people know, my mother is a real character, basically a fun-loving, selfless lady but also a highly opinionated one for whom certain rules are simply not to be broken—or even modified. So that a prized pully-bone (wishbone) can

A happy Southern lady is Mother returning home from the market with armloads of freshly picked Silver Queen corn.

be cut out for fried chicken, for instance, the bird must be bought whole, soaked briefly in seasoned milk, fried in no more than about one inch of vegetable shortening, turned no more than once in the pan for ideal crispness, and drained on a paper sack—period. Peas or green beans (preferably Kentucky Wonder snaps) boiled till they're just toothy in the trendy modern manner? "Not in my kitchen!" Mother declares forcefully. "I'd just as soon eat cardboard as hard, bland beans that haven't simmered two hours with a little piece of fat." Once, when she wasn't looking, I figured that adding a few fresh herbs and green olives to our beloved short ribs of beef might give the dish an interesting new dimension. "You've been playing around again, and you've absolutely ruined these ribs," she almost cried after the first bite. "You know, son, you still haven't gotten through your thick head that the secret to great Southern food is its natural simplicity and flavors. Southern short ribs is *not* French *pot-au-feu.*" Another time I suggested that we prepare a nice wine sauce for a beautiful whole flounder we planned to broil, only to be lectured about how that was not Southern, and that anything more than salt, pepper, butter, and lemon would destroy the sweet flavor of the fish, and that if I had to be so creative she just might decide to eat something else. And why waste time recording her reaction when, thinking the old-fashioned cornbread we were planning to serve one Thanksgiving could use a little zip, I began chopping a few jalapeño peppers.

"You two are certainly cut from the same cloth," friends have been known to mutter in dazed wonderment when the scene of Mother and me cooking together becomes particularly hairy and I start "messing around." Yes, we do argue constantly in the kitchen, just as I remember Mother arguing with her mother about how to pull Christmas mints correctly, and my grandfather arguing with his wife over the frying of salt mackerel for breakfast, and my mother and her sister holding forth on the proper texture of pimiento cheese and chocolate pound cake. I suppose it's in our nature as Southerners to be forever "discussing" our native cooking, questioning it, debating it, and, indeed, defending it; and if others fail to understand how, over the decades, the preparation and sharing of food has always served to reinforce strong bonds of family love and respect, they fail to understand the very spirit of Southern cooking.

"It was Mama's usual light touch—the turkey with cornbread dressing and cranberry sauce, country ham, corn pudding, snaps and little butterbeans she'd put up last July, spiced peaches, cold crisp watermelon-rind pickle, macaroni and cheese, creamed potatoes and gravy, then her own angel food cake and ambrosia. Every mouthful made the only way, from the naked pot upward by hand . . . Whenever I compliment her on it, she just says, 'It's the only way I know to cook.'"

That is Reynolds Price in the novel *Good Hearts* recalling his Southern mother and her food, the details of which apply almost exactly to

This is actually my sister's white chocolate pound cake—a perfect example of the way she takes a recipe over the phone. Needless to say, she knows exactly what every step in the directions means.

my own mother and the gastronomic legacy she is currently passing down to me and my sister and to anyone who cares to question and learn and even argue a bit. Hers is a proud heritage that champions age-old traditions and defies change, and who knows, if one day I stop challenging her art and "messing around," I may eventually turn out that perfect batch of buttermilk *biscuit.*

1

Breakfast and Brunch

When I'd return home from college, a familiar early morning sight was always Mother in the kitchen preparing to whip up still another hearty Southern breakfast for the whole family.

A recipe from

Martha Villas

For Daddy's Cheese & Eggs —
½ stick butter or marg.
4 slices white bread, trimmed
about 1 cup milk
¾ lb A&P N.Y. Sharp cheddar cheese
5 large eggs —
Melt butter in skillet, crumble the bread
& add; start adding milk, mashing with
fork until well blended & no lumps but
soft. add the finely cut up cheese gradually, over low heat until the mixture
is well blended & smooth. Beat eggs
& add to cheese mixture stirring constantly
until eggs set up — add salt & pepper
to taste — Serve in heated bowl.

Usually serve country ham or sausage
with the, especially on Christmas morning

Since this is one of Mother's most cherished recipes, she hits the ceiling when I tell people they can use something other than A&P New York State cheddar and when I spice up the cheese and eggs with a dash or so of cayenne.

Of all the meals that Mother prepared when I was growing up, none was more important than the lavish, hot, ritualistic breakfasts shared each and every morning by everyone in our large family. The idea of my sister or me going to school, or my father and grandfathers leaving for work, without first stoking our systems with eggs and sausage or country ham, hash or creamed chipped beef on toast, fluffy batter cakes or pecan waffles, some form of fresh fruit, buttery grits, and, of course, biscuits with homemade preserves was simply unheard of. Sometimes my Georgia grandmother, Maw Maw, would offer to fix her brains and eggs, or Paw Paw would decide to fry up his smelly but delicious salt mackerel; and it was always a special weekend treat when my Swedish grandmother, Sigrid, agreed to make her native small pancakes served with lingonberries or her sumptuous vegetable omelette. Breakfast was always such a joyous occasion in our home, a time of true leisure when Paw Paw would test us children on our spelling, or my Greek grandfather, Papa, would tell hilarious stories about raising goats in the Old Country, or Mother and Daddy would debate on and on what we should have for dinner that evening. In those days, there was no talk of diets and fats and salt and cholesterol, only whether the quality of the country ham was up to snuff, or which itinerant farmer might show up at the back door with fresh eggs and chickens, or when Mother and Maw Maw should begin putting up preserves and pickle or making fruitcakes. I suppose that politics and taxes and school were also discussed over those momentous Southern breakfasts, but there were few topics that, somehow, didn't always manage to revert back to the subject of what we were eating, what we planned to eat, and what might be interesting to eat.

Except for the fact that Mother now prepares more brunches than in days when the concept was virtually unknown in the South, nothing has changed today with regard to what we eat in the morning. Neither she nor I could conceive of beginning any day without a wholesome Southern breakfast, and neither we nor most of our guests pay any mind to diets, fats, salt, and cholesterol. We're just too busy eating Mother's cheese and eggs and buttering biscuits.

Paw Paw's Cheese and Eggs

No breakfast dish goes back further in our family than this luscious preparation that has inspired the acclaim of everyone from Craig Claiborne to Paula Wolfert to dozens of less famous guests who've shared one of our hearty early-morning repasts. Mother traces the dish back to at least her Georgia grandfather and thinks it likely that it evolved as a means to stretch eggs for a large family. Whatever its humble origins, today Mother is so proud of her cheese and eggs that she serves them at breakfast and brunch buffets and over holidays in her finest silver chafing dish.

½ cup (1 stick) butter
8 slices white bread, trimmed and cubed
1½ cups milk
1½ pounds extra-sharp cheddar cheese, coarsely grated
10 large eggs, beaten
Salt and black pepper to taste
Dash of cayenne pepper

In a large, heavy skillet, melt the butter, then add the bread and milk and mash steadily and thoroughly over moderately low heat with a heavy fork till the mixture has the consistency of a soft, smooth roux, adding more milk if necessary. Add the cheese and continue mashing and stirring till the cheese is well incorporated and the mixture is very smooth. Add the eggs, salt, pepper, and cayenne and stir slowly and steadily with a large spoon till the eggs are set and the mixture is

Martha Pearl Says:

"Never skimp on the cheese in this dish, and don't use just any old cheddar. Probably my best cheese and eggs ever were made with a blend of aged English farmhouse cheddar and double Gloucester, but since that's not very practical, I generally use only A & P's New York State extra-sharp cheddar. Also, this dish takes patience. If you rush the roux or stir the eggs quickly over heat that's too high, you'll end up with a lumpy mess."

creamy. (If the mixture seems to be sticking to the bottom of the skillet, lower the heat while stirring.)

Serve the cheese and eggs in a chafing dish or large heated bowl.

Yield: 6 to 8 servings

Scrambled Eggs with Feta Cheese

After my mother and father were married during the Depression, they lived with Daddy's Greek father and Swedish mother for a short while. Normally, Mama Villas cooked hearty Swedish, Greek, or American dinners, but Mother remembers that when everybody knew Papa would be coming home from work particularly late, what he loved most were eggs scrambled with lots of ripe feta, a big Greek salad, and homemade bread. Today, Mother still not only serves these wonderful eggs at breakfasts and brunches but also fixes them for dinner, along with a pot of buttery grits—a cross-cultural combination if there ever was one!

3 tablespoons butter
10 large eggs, beaten
Freshly ground black pepper to taste
$\frac{1}{2}$ pound feta cheese, crumbled
1 tablespoon chopped fresh parsley

In a large omelette pan or nonstick skillet, melt the butter over low heat, then add the eggs and pepper. When the eggs have just begun to set, sprinkle on the feta

Martha Pearl Says:

"I don't make these eggs if I can't find genuine Greek feta stored in its own brine—preferably in a barrel. Domestic feta is like moist cardboard. Also, the cooking of these eggs simply cannot be rushed. The finished dish should be delicately soft, almost runny."

and slowly but steadily stir with a wooden spoon till the eggs are softly scrambled and the cheese has almost melted. Transfer to a heated serving bowl and serve immediately.

Yield: 4 to 6 servings

Baked Cheese Omelette

When we don't care to take the time to make individual omelettes, this is one of the simplest and most attractive dishes for a small breakfast group. Also, we often use feta cheese instead of cheddar.

1 dozen large eggs, separated
¼ cup heavy cream
½ teaspoon salt
Freshly ground black pepper to taste
3 ounces extra-sharp cheddar cheese, grated
Dash of cayenne pepper
¼ cup (½ stick) butter
1 tablespoon minced fresh chives

Preheat the oven to 375°F.

In a large mixing bowl, combine the egg yolks, cream, salt, and pepper and beat till well blended. In another bowl, whisk the egg whites with a pinch of salt till they form stiff peaks. Gently stir the yolk mixture into the egg whites, add the cheese and cayenne, and stir just till combined.

Melt the butter in a large stainless-steel omelette pan or skillet just till it begins to sizzle. Pour in the egg mixture, stir for a few seconds, place the pan on the center rack of the oven, and bake till the omelette is puffy, about 8 minutes. Slide the omelette onto a large heated platter, fold it in half, and sprinkle the minced chives over the top.

Yield: 4 servings

Sigrid's Breakfast Vegetable Omelette

Where in heaven's name my father's Swedish mother ever came up with this delicious omelette remains a mystery to this day, but when I was growing up (with Mama in the house), both she and Mother would often satisfy Daddy's craving for the omelette by serving it on Sunday mornings after we'd all returned from early church. Today, Mother will also turn out one large single omelette when two or three of us want something different for lunch.

$\frac{1}{2}$ cup (1 stick) butter
2 cups chopped celery
1 cup chopped onion
2 large ripe tomatoes, peeled and chopped
1 medium-size green bell pepper, seeded and chopped
1 cup frozen peas, thawed
Salt and black pepper to taste
8 slices bacon
8 jumbo eggs

In a large saucepan, melt half the butter, then add the celery, onion, tomatoes, and bell pepper, stir slightly, cover, and simmer the vegetables over low heat about 45 minutes. Add the peas, salt, and pepper, stir, cover, simmer 10 minutes longer, and remove from the heat.

Meanwhile, fry the bacon in a large skillet till crisp and drain on paper towels.

Break two eggs into a small bowl and beat. Melt 1 tablespoon of the remaining butter till sizzling in a medium-size omelette pan or skillet, add the eggs, let set slightly, and spoon one quarter of the vegetables over half the eggs. Flip the other half over the mixture and turn out the omelette immediately onto a heated plate, making sure not to overcook. Repeat the procedure with the remaining eggs and vegetables.

Garnish the top of each omelette with two strips of bacon and serve immediately.

Yield: 4 servings

Brains and Eggs

As a child, Mother remembers well how, when a certain Mr. and Mrs. Norwood made their biweekly house delivery of farm-fresh eggs, butter, milk, sausage, and chickens, there was often included a container of hog's brains which her mother and grandmother loved to scramble with eggs for breakfast. The one time I tasted Maw Maw's brains and eggs, I hated the strong flavor, but once, years later, I learned about the much milder and more delicate calves' brains (often available frozen in specialty food markets), I became hooked on the dish. Remember that all brains are very perishable and fragile, so don't order fresh ones from the butcher until you're ready to prepare them, and be sure to trim them as carefully as possible to avoid tearing.

1 pound calf brains
1 tablespoon fresh lemon juice
1 tablespoon bacon grease
1 cup water
1 teaspoon salt
Black pepper to taste
6 tablespoons (¾ stick) butter, cut into pieces
8 large eggs, beaten

To prepare the brains in advance, rinse them carefully under cold water, place in a bowl, add water to cover plus the lemon juice, and let soak about 2 hours in the refrigerator. Drain, gently peel off and discard as much of the thin outer membrane as possible, and dry the brains carefully with paper towels.

In a large skillet, heat the bacon grease, add the brains, water, salt, and pepper and simmer, uncovered, over moderately low heat till the water has evaporated, about 20 minutes. Remove from the heat.

When ready to serve, add the pieces of butter to the pan and, when melted around the brains, add the eggs, stir gently, and scramble over low heat just till the eggs are set and still slightly soft. Transfer to a bowl and serve immediately.

Yield: 4 servings

Ham Hash with Baked Eggs

Guests really love this homey dish for either breakfast or brunch, and Mother likes to serve it since the hash can be baked in advance and easily reheated before breaking the eggs into the depressions. We've also made the hash from well-trimmed end pieces of country ham—delectable! We serve the dish with little more than a big bowl of fresh fruit compote, biscuits, and homemade preserves.

2 pounds cooked ham
4 medium-size potatoes, boiled in water to cover until tender
1 medium-size onion, finely chopped
½ cup finely chopped fresh parsley
¼ teaspoon ground sage
⅛ teaspoon ground nutmeg
Salt and black pepper to taste
Tabasco sauce to taste
½ cup heavy cream
3 tablespoons butter
8 large eggs
Finely chopped fresh parsley for garnish

Trim the ham of any fat and gristle, chop the meat finely, and place in a large mixing bowl. Peel the potatoes, cut them into small dice, and add to the ham. Add the onion, parsley, sage, nutmeg, salt, pepper, and Tabasco and stir till the ingredients are well blended. Add the cream and stir till the mixture is moist.

Preheat the oven to 375°F.

Transfer equal amounts of the mixture to two buttered 1-quart baking dishes and press the mixture down with your fingers. Make four depressions with a large spoon on the top of each mixture, dot the top of each with pieces of butter, and bake 20 minutes.

Remove the dishes from the oven, break an egg into each depression, and bake till the eggs are cooked but still soft, about 5 minutes longer. Sprinkle the hash with chopped parsley and serve.

Yield: 8 servings

Fresh Country Sausage

A major thrill for my sister and me when we were children was piling into the old Ford with Mother and Daddy and Maw Maw and Paw Paw on Saturday mornings and driving out to Morrocroft Farms in Charlotte (owned by ex-North Carolina governor Cameron Morrison) to buy fresh eggs, butter, poultry, buttermilk, and, without doubt, the best country sausage ever made. (Mother is still convinced that the reason that sausage was so good was because it contained every unmentionable part of the hog from the offal to the ears and feet to the snout, and I tend to agree with her.) The next best sausage was that made and given to us every fall by none other than the family dentist shortly after the pigs were slaughtered. Today, we eat as much sausage for breakfast as we did fifty years ago, usually resorting to grinding and blending our own when the eternal search for great sausage proves futile. I am *never* without stacks of wrapped patties in the freezer, and even Mother says I eat too much sausage.

2 pounds boneless pork shoulder, chilled
1 pound fresh pork fat, chilled
1 tablespoon salt
1 teaspoon freshly ground black pepper
2 teaspoons ground sage
1 teaspoon dried red pepper flakes
3 tablespoons cold water

Cut the pork and pork fat into 2-inch chunks and pass the chunks first through the coarse blade, then through the fine blade of a meat grinder into a large mix-

Martha Pearl Says:

"Most of the commercial sausage you find in supermarkets is either too lean, too fatty, or underseasoned—a disgrace—and Southerners hate that Yankee Italian-style sausage. The only cut of pork on today's market acceptable for sausage-making is the shoulder and, for both flavor and tenderness, the ratio of lean and fat must be two to one. Don't ask me why, but fresh chopped sage never works as well as powdered in making sausage."

ing bowl. Add the remaining ingredients, moisten both hands with water, and knead the mixture with your hands till well blended and smooth. Form the sausage meat into 3-inch patties, wrap the patties tightly in plastic wrap, and refrigerate at least 2 hours before frying. (The sausage freezes well up to 2 months.)

Yield: 3 pounds sausage meat

Country Ham with Red-Eye Gravy

Mother and I value genuine country ham the way others prize fresh Russian caviar or white truffles. Come spring or summer every year, we're in the car to Glendale Springs in the mountains of North Carolina to rummage through Clayton Long's aromatic ham house, watch him ice-pick a few well-aged specimens for soundness, and make our choices. It's all a real production (hauling the heavy hams back to Charlotte, cleaning off the mold, taking them to the butcher to be sliced, and separating the various cuts for storage in the freezer), but, as a result, we have enough of some of the country's finest old-fashioned, home-cured country ham to last us all year. Center slices are fried up only for special breakfasts (and special friends), semicenter for ham biscuits, and the end pieces used in cooking beans, turnip greens, and other vegetables. The main thing to remember about frying country ham is never to overcook it—the ham becomes hard and tough.

Martha Pearl Says:

"Yes, real country ham is salty, but nothing gets my goat more than people who destroy the flavor of good ham (including Smithfields) by soaking it in water. If you want to stuff a country ham and bake it with lots of seasonings, that's another story; but I never soak ham I intend to fry. As for the red-eye gravy, Jimmy thinks coffee is best for deglazing the pan; I prefer water."

Three ¼-inch-thick center slices cured country ham
1 cup brewed coffee or water

Score the fatty edges of the ham slices and place them in one or two cast-iron skillets. Heat to moderately low, slowly fry the slices till they are just slightly browned on each side, and transfer with a spatula to a heated platter just large enough to hold the slices.

Increase the heat to high, pour the coffee into the skillet, scrape the bottom of the skillet with the spatula, and let boil till the liquid is reduced almost to a glaze. Pour the gravy over the ham slices and cut the slices widthwise into 2-inch serving pieces.

Yield: 8 servings

Creamed Chipped Beef

My father loved nothing more for breakfast than creamed chipped beef on toast or English muffins, and since we had it so much at home, it used to make Mother furious when he'd order it in hotels. Sadly, the dish doesn't seem to be as popular as it was twenty or thirty years ago, but whenever we serve it at breakfast or brunch buffets, the chafing dish is always spooned clean.

6 ounces chipped beef
6 tablespoons (¾ stick) butter
4 to 5 tablespoons all-purpose flour
2½ cups milk
⅛ teaspoon black pepper
6 English muffins, toasted

Separate the beef slices and tear into bite-size shreds. Place the shreds in a colander, rinse under hot running water, and drain well.

In a saucepan, heat the butter till moderately hot,

Martha Pearl Says:

"The quality of the chipped beef is what counts most in this dish, and the best is sold in jars. Be very careful adding the flour; if there's too much, the mixture will be heavy as lead."

then add the beef and toss till curly, about 2 minutes. Remove the pan from the heat, gradually add the flour, stirring, then add the milk and pepper. Return to the heat and cook, stirring constantly, till the mixture is thickened and smooth.

Serve the chipped beef over the English muffins.

Yield: 6 servings

Pan-Fried Spots

When my sister and I were very young, we were taken every summer to the legendary Patricia Inn at Myrtle Beach, South Carolina, known throughout the South for its formal dining room and its superlative Southern cooking. Occasionally at breakfast, our loyal waiter, Joseph, would approach the table with a big grin on his face, lean down to my father, and whisper, "Mr. Villas, I caught a few spots earlier this morning," the implication being that Daddy's order was already in the kitchen. Some years later, when we had our own cottage and surf-fished for spots and blues each and every day, it became routine for Mother to clean the fish and fry them for breakfast in the exact way she remembered Joseph directing. Fishing in the South, of course, we throw back as many of these tender, sweet spots as we keep, something that sparks Mother's fury when she sees them selling for six dollars a pound in East Hampton. If you can't find spots, small red mullets or snappers make a nice substitute. Remember not to overcook the fish, and serve them with plenty of hot grits and biscuits.

1 cup cornmeal
1 teaspoon salt
Black pepper to taste
1 cup vegetable shortening
3 pounds small spots, dressed with heads off and rinsed

In a baking dish, combine the cornmeal, salt, and pepper and mix well.

In a large, heavy skillet, melt the shortening over moderately high heat. Dredge the fish in the cornmeal, place in the skillet, and pan-fry till golden brown, about 3 minutes on each side. Drain on brown paper bags.

Yield: 4 to 6 servings

Crusty Green Tomatoes

Son, go pick me a couple of tomatoes," my grandmother would dictate while frying the bacon on those chilly, early fall mornings. Every year at season's end, I think Maw Maw lost sleep worrying that every single green tomato left on the vines might not be used up before frost hit; but, my, those tomatoes she'd fry up in bacon grease were something to marvel at. Eventually, both Mother and I began frying our tomatoes in a more sensible fat, but rest assured that if there's any bacon grease on hand (and there always is), we still might drop a tablespoon into the less flavorful oil.

5 unripened green tomatoes
2 large eggs
½ cup milk
1½ cups cornmeal
Salt and black pepper to taste
Vegetable oil for frying

Cut out and discard the stems of the tomatoes and cut the tomatoes into ¼-inch-thick slices.

In a shallow dish, beat the eggs with the milk. Combine the cornmeal, salt, and pepper in another shallow dish. Dip the tomato slices in the egg mixture, dredge them lightly in the cornmeal, place the slices on a baking sheet, cover with plastic wrap, and chill for about 30 minutes.

In a large cast-iron skillet, heat ½ inch of oil over moderately high heat. In batches, fry the tomatoes till golden, about 1 minute on each side, drain on paper towels, and keep warm on a platter till ready to serve.

Yield: 8 servings

Real Grits

What can I say about the paramount role of grits in my mother's life? For her (and for her parents and my father), no breakfast was ever complete without a mess of buttered grits. ("Fried potatoes!" she huffs while in the North. "Why can't these people learn to cook a few grits?") Today, she loves them in the morning, not the quick variety but the long-simmered real McCoy she knew as a child. She'll reinforce them with butter and reheat them for lunch, and when she's not feeling up to snuff, her idea of a therapeutic supper is grits with string beans and cornbread. As to why I've never shared her unadulterated passion for grits, perhaps it's because she always forgets to soak the pot after cooking and leaves me to clean up the caked mess.

5 cups water
1 teaspoon salt
1 cup regular hominy grits
2 tablespoons butter

In a heavy saucepan, bring the salted water to a brisk boil and slowly sift the grits through the fingers of one hand into the water while stirring with the other. Stirring constantly, reduce the heat to a gentle simmer. Continue cooking till the grits are thick, 30 minutes, stirring frequently to prevent sticking.

To serve, scrape the grits into a heated bowl, add the butter, and stir till well blended. (Save leftover grits to make Fried Grits, below.)

Yield: 6 servings

Fried Grits

I called my maternal grandfather Paw Paw, and Mother still talks about how, in Monticello, Georgia, he would get up in the morning, remove from the icebox a ball of leftover grits wrapped in waxed paper, fry them in small squares, and put them on the table with fried eggs and sausage. Years later, Paw Paw and Maw Maw were doing the same thing at the house in Charlotte, and I'm still convinced that the reason I prefer my grits fried is because theirs were so delicious.

1 recipe Real Grits (page 15)
1 large egg
½ cup milk
½ cup all-purpose flour
¼ cup bacon grease

Grease a large, shallow baking dish, scrape hot grits into the dish, smooth the top with a rubber spatula, and let cool. Cover with plastic wrap and chill the grits in the refrigerator at least 3 hours or overnight.

When the grits are firm, cut into 2-inch squares. In a shallow dish, beat the egg and milk together till well blended, dip the squares into the batter, then dredge lightly in the flour.

Heat the bacon grease to moderately hot in a large cast-iron skillet, add the squares to the fat, fry till golden brown, about 5 minutes on each side, and drain on paper towels. Repeat with the remaining squares.

Serve the fried grits on a heated platter.

Yield: 4 to 6 servings

Martha Pearl Says:

"You know why these are so good? Because they're fried in bacon fat. I'll have you know that my mama lived to be ninety-two, and she fried everything *in either bacon fat or lard."*

Cheese Grits Soufflé

Here's one time when Mother thinks that quick grits work just as well as regular ones, and I defy anyone to detect the difference. What's so nice about serving this dish at a late weekend breakfast or elaborate brunch is that it can be assembled the night before and simply baked off the next day. As with any Southern "soufflé" (i.e., any baked dish that contains eggs), don't expect this to be puffy like a classic soufflé.

4 cups water
1 cup quick grits
2 teaspoons salt
3 cups milk
6 tablespoons (¾ stick) butter, at room temperature
1 tablespoon Worcestershire sauce
4 large eggs, beaten
¾ cup grated extra-sharp cheddar cheese
Black pepper to taste
Paprika to taste

In a large saucepan, bring the water to a roaring boil, add the grits and salt, and stir. Reduce the heat slightly and cook the grits till thick, about 5 minutes, stirring often. Add 2 cups of the milk, stir well, return the mixture to a boil, and continue cooking the grits till thickened, about 5 minutes, stirring. Add the remaining milk, the butter, Worcestershire, eggs, cheese, and pepper and stir steadily till the butter and cheese are well incorporated. Pour the mixture into a buttered 2-quart soufflé dish, cover with plastic wrap, and chill overnight.

When ready to bake, preheat the oven to 350°F, sprinkle paprika liberally on top of the mixture, and bake 1 hour.

Yield: 8 servings

Mashed Potato Cakes

Needless to say, my forever frugal mother first made these crusty cakes when she once had lots of mashed potatoes left over from dinner the night before. Ever since, she often purposely whips up extra potatoes in the evening, forms the cakes, and refrigerates them overnight between sheets of waxed paper. The cakes are best piping hot, but even cold they're never any left on the breakfast or brunch serving platter.

¼ cup (½ stick) butter
3 large onions, finely chopped
4 large eggs
3 cups mashed cooked potatoes
½ cup all-purpose flour
Salt and black pepper to taste
Tabasco sauce to taste
2 tablespoons water

Preheat the oven to 375°F.

In a large skillet, melt the butter, then add the onions, and cook over moderate heat 3 minutes, stirring. Remove the skillet from the heat.

In a large mixing bowl, whisk three of the eggs till well blended, then add the cooked onions, the potatoes, flour, salt, pepper, and Tabasco and stir till the mixture is firm. Form the mixture into sixteen round cakes and place on a large greased baking sheet.

In a small bowl, whisk the remaining egg with the water, brush the top of each cake with the egg wash, and bake the cakes till golden brown, 20 to 25 minutes. Transfer to a heated platter and serve.

Yield: 8 servings

Pecan Sour Cream Waffles

2 large eggs, separated
1 cup sour cream
1 cup all-purpose flour
2 teaspoons baking powder
½ teaspoon salt
½ cup finely chopped pecans
Maple syrup or strawberry preserves

In a mixing bowl, beat the egg yolks well, then add the sour cream and blend thoroughly. In another bowl, whisk the egg whites till stiff peaks form and fold into the sour cream mixture. Fold in the flour, baking powder, salt, and pecans and stir till well blended and smooth.

Pour the mixture into a hot waffle iron about one third full, cover, and cook till the waffles are browned and crisp. Repeat till all the batter is used, keeping the waffles warm.

Serve the waffles with maple syrup or strawberry preserves.

Yield: About 1 dozen waffles (depending on size of waffle iron)

Martha Pearl Says:

"I don't care what people say about using pure maple syrup on waffles, I still think it's just too heavy—strong compared with the blended—and more than one breakfast up in Vermont has convinced me. I use Log Cabin or Aunt Jemima."

Cornmeal Batter Cakes

These are the batter cakes that Mother and the other ladies used to prepare in vast quantities at the church pancake suppers held every Tuesday night before Ash Wednesday in symbolic preparation for fasting at Lent. And you never saw such food: giant platters of fluffy cornmeal cakes and pancakes, bacon and country sausage, scrambled eggs, and grits; big bowls of fresh macerated fruit; slabs of butter and pitchers of maple syrup and honey—no wonder we were all ready the next day to deny ourselves!

1 cup cornmeal (preferably white)
1 tablespoon sugar
½ teaspoon baking powder
½ teaspoon salt
1½ cups milk
2 large eggs
½ cup (1 stick) butter, melted
Maple syrup or honey

In a bowl, sift together the cornmeal, sugar, baking powder, and salt. Add the milk and beat vigorously with a large spoon till well blended. Add the eggs and continue beating till the batter is smooth.

Heat a griddle or skillet till quite hot, lightly brush with butter, ladle about ¼ cup batter onto the griddle for each cake, and cook till nicely browned, 2 to 3 minutes on each side. Stir the batter again, and continue brushing the griddle with butter and ladling batter till all is used up, keeping the cakes covered with aluminum foil on a heated platter.

Serve the batter cakes with syrup or honey.

Yield: At least 1 dozen cakes

Buttermilk Pancakes

1½ cups all-purpose flour
2 tablespoons sugar
1 teaspoon baking powder
¾ teaspoon baking soda
½ teaspoon salt
1 large egg, beaten
1⅓ cups buttermilk
¼ cup (½ stick) butter, melted
Maple syrup

Sift the dry ingredients together into a mixing bowl, add the egg, buttermilk, and butter, and mix quickly with a few strokes of a wooden spoon.

Martha Pearl Says:

"One reason you find so many awful pancakes is because people mix the batter too much. All you need is a few strokes with the spoon, just enough to incorporate the ingredients. Also, don't flip the pancakes but one time unless you want them to be tough as leather."

Grease and heat a griddle or large frying pan till a few drops of water sputter. Using a large soup spoon, drop batter onto the griddle to make cakes about 4 inches in diameter and cook till bubbles appear on top and the bottom is browned, 2 to 3 minutes. Turn the cakes with a spatula and let cook till slightly browned, about 1 to 2 minutes. Repeat with the remaining batter.

Serve the cakes at once with maple syrup.

Yield: About 12 pancakes

Swedish Pancakes

These are the feather-light pancakes my Swedish grandmother, Sigrid, used to prepare for the family on Saturday mornings and the ones my father in particular relished. Mama kept a special bowl and big flat wooden spoon just for beating her pancake batter, but today Mother and I use a blender with good results. No matter where we travel, Mother is always on the lookout for jars of lingonberries, but when we run out, we serve either raspberry or strawberry preserves.

4 large eggs
2 cups milk
1 cup half-and-half
1½ cups all-purpose flour
½ cup (1 stick) butter, melted
½ teaspoon salt
Lingonberries or fresh fruit preserves
Heavy cream
Confectioners' sugar

In a blender, combine the eggs, milk, and half-and-half and blend for 5 seconds. Add the flour and blend till the batter is smooth, about 30 seconds. Add the butter and salt and blend 5 seconds longer. Scrape the batter into a mixing bowl, cover with plastic wrap, and let stand 1 hour.

Grease lightly a heavy cast-iron griddle or skillet, heat till very hot, and drop on enough batter to make 3-inch pancakes. Cook till the edges of the pancakes are lightly browned, about 1 minute, turn the pancakes with a spatula, and cook till lightly browned, 1 minute longer. Stack each batch of pancakes on a platter and keep warm in the oven till ready to serve. Allowing about three pancakes per person, place one tablespoon of lingonberries on one edge of each pancake, fold over, and serve with a pitcher of heavy cream and a shaker of confectioners' sugar.

Yield: 24 pancakes

French Toast

I judge that the origins of this quintessentially Southern breakfast dish is the Creole *pain perdu* found in New Orleans. For some reason, French toast in our home has always been a special treat usually reserved for cold Saturday mornings and involving Canadian bacon, fried apples, and hot chocolate.

3 large eggs
1 cup milk
$\frac{1}{4}$ teaspoon salt
1 tablespoon sugar
$\frac{1}{2}$ teaspoon ground cinnamon
$\frac{1}{2}$ teaspoon pure vanilla extract
$\frac{1}{4}$ cup ($\frac{1}{2}$ stick) butter
Eight to ten $\frac{1}{2}$-inch-thick slices day-old bread, preferably homemade (page 212)
Maple syrup

In a bowl, beat the eggs well, add the milk, salt, sugar, cinnamon, and vanilla, and beat till well blended and frothy.

In a large, heavy skillet, heat half the butter till moderately hot. Dip half the bread slices into the egg mixture, transfer them with a spatula to the skillet, and cook, turning once, till the slices are lightly browned. Transfer to a heated platter and repeat with the remaining butter and bread slices, keeping the cooked slices warm.

Serve the toast with maple syrup.

Yield: 4 to 5 servings

Fried Apple Rings

Mother still shivers when she thinks about having to eat Maw Maw's fried apples as a child, namely because her mother neither cored nor seeded the apples before cutting and frying them. "Mama was a little lazy about things like that," she admits, "but, you know, those were the best-tasting apple rings I ever put in my mouth." Here, no cooking fat but bacon grease will do.

6 firm, tart cooking apples
1/2 cup firmly packed light brown sugar
3 teaspoons ground cinnamon
Bacon grease

Core the apples and slice them crosswise into 1/2-inch rings. In a small bowl, combine the brown sugar and cinnamon.

In a large, heavy skillet, heat till moderately hot about 1/2 inch of bacon grease till a cube of bread tossed in browns. Using a slotted spatula, slide a quarter of the apple rings into the fat and cook 2 minutes. Turn the rings over, sprinkle with a little of the sugar-cinnamon mixture, cook till tender, about 2 minutes longer, and drain on paper towels. Repeat with the remaining rings till all are fried, keeping the apples warm till ready to serve.

Yield: 6 servings

Spiced Dried Fruit Compote

Mother says she came up with this practical compote one year when someone gave her and Daddy a gigantic Christmas basket of dried fruits that she didn't think she had any earthly use for. It makes a great brunch buffet dish.

½ pound each dried apricots, figs, pears, and peaches
3 cups water
1 cup dry white wine
4 thin lemon slices, seeded
One 3-inch stick cinnamon
½ cup honey
¼ cup dark rum
¼ teaspoon ground allspice

Combine the fruits in a large saucepan, add the water, wine, lemon slices, and cinnamon stick, and stir. Bring to the boil, reduce the heat to low, and simmer till the fruits begin to swell, about 20 minutes. Transfer the fruits to a plate.

Add the honey, rum, and allspice to the saucepan, increase the heat to high, and cook, stirring, till the liquid is reduced by half. Return the fruits to the saucepan, stir well, and let cool. Transfer the fruits and liquid to a serving dish, cover with plastic wrap, and chill overnight. Bring the fruits back to room temperature before serving with a slotted spoon.

Yield: At least 8 servings

Cinnamon Walnut Coffee Cake

A neighbor brought this coffee cake to the house on Christmas morning over fifty years ago, and once Mother got the recipe, it not only became almost a staple on our breakfast table—eaten with preserves, curiously enough, *after* we had finished all the eggs and sausage and biscuits—but was also served midmorning at my Swedish grandmother's ritual coffee break. Today, our appetites even at breakfast are just not what they used to be, so, unless we're planning to serve coffee cake at an upcoming brunch, we always have a sufficiency frozen and ready to heat up quickly on a moment's notice.

2½ cups all-purpose flour
1¼ cups sugar
1 tablespoon baking powder
1 teaspoon salt
1 cup milk
¼ cup vegetable shortening
1½ teaspoons pure vanilla extract
2 large eggs
1½ cups coarsely chopped walnuts
1 teaspoon ground cinnamon
3 tablespoons butter, cut into pieces

Into a large mixing bowl, sift together 2 cups of the flour, 1 cup of the sugar, the baking powder, and salt. Add the milk, shortening, and vanilla and beat 3 minutes with an electric mixer. Add the eggs, beat 2 minutes longer, and pour the batter into a buttered 9- or 10-inch round baking pan. Distribute the chopped walnuts evenly over the top.

Preheat the oven to 350°F.

In a bowl, combine the remaining flour and sugar and the cinnamon, add the butter, and work with your fingertips till the mixture becomes mealy. Distribute the mixture evenly over the walnuts and bake the cake till a straw inserted in the middle comes out clean, about 45 minutes. Cool the cake, transfer to a round serving dish, and cut into wedges.

Yield: One 9- or 10-inch cake; 8 to 10 servings

Martha Pearl Says:

"This coffee cake makes a wonderful gift, especially during the Christmas holidays. I also like to take one to funeral receptions. I know I probably shouldn't make the cake for sick friends in the hospital, but I do—and they love it."

2

Canapés, Appetizers, and Snacks

In my East Hampton kitchen, Mother explains the Southern dinner menu to Craig Claiborne while Daddy nurses his first cocktail of the evening before canapés and appetizers are served.

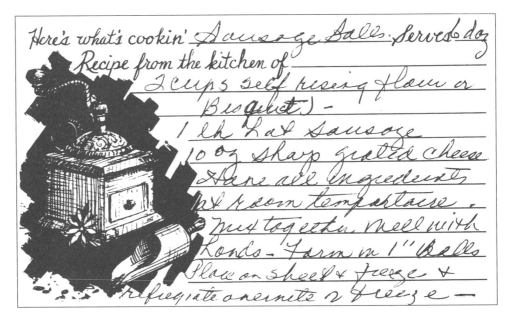

Here's what's cookin' *Sausage Balls. Serves doz*

Recipe from the kitchen of _____

2 cups self rising flour or
Bisquick) -
1 lb Hot Sausage
10 oz sharp grated cheese
Have all ingredients
at room temperature.
Mix together well with
hands - Form in 1" balls
Place on sheet & freeze &
refrigerate overnite or freeze —

Notice that Mother would have used self-rising flour or Bisquick to make her sausage balls 40 years ago ("I was just too busy raising a family to worry about such things in those days"). And note her detailed cooking directions.

Southerners don't go in much for formal first courses at meals, the most probable reason being that, given our age-old proclivity for strong drink, we like to serve plenty of good canapés and appetizers with our ritual cocktails (and by cocktails I don't mean meager glasses of wine and mineral water). When we were expecting guests and Daddy used to ask Mother "What are we going to serve tonight?", he was hardly referring to the short ribs of beef and squash soufflé waiting to go into the oven. What he was wondering about was what tasty dip or spread or puff or morsels of seafood she'd prepared to accompany drinks before dinner. Today, Mother would never dream of putting out merely a bowl of peanuts or wedge of innocuous cheese with crackers, and when friends come to either her home or mine, they know they can expect cocktail food that is every bit as original and good as what they'll savor later at the table when the truly serious eating begins.

Hot Pecan Beef Dip

Both Mother and my sister love to serve this delicious dip at cocktail parties, and guests always wolf it down faster than we can mix bourbon Manhattans and whiskey sours. The dip should not be made too long in advance since the pecans will get too soggy.

2 tablespoons butter
1 cup finely chopped pecans
Two 8-ounce packages cream cheese, at room temperature
¼ cup milk
1 small onion, minced
4 ounces dried beef, finely shredded
1 teaspoon garlic salt
Freshly ground black pepper to taste
1 cup sour cream

Preheat the oven to 350°F.

   Heat the butter in a small skillet, add the pecans, and toss over low heat about 3 minutes. Remove from the heat.

In a mixing bowl, combine the cream cheese and milk and mash well with a heavy fork. Add one quarter of the hot pecans, the onion, dried beef, garlic salt, and pepper and mix well. Add the sour cream and stir till well blended. Scrape the mixture into a small baking dish, top with the remaining pecans, and bake 20 minutes.

Serve the dip with small crackers or melba toast rounds.

Yield: About 3 cups

Martha Pearl Says:

"Packaged dried beef is okay, but the variety put up in jars always seems to have better flavor and texture."

Spicy Clam Dip

One 8-ounce can minced clams, drained
Two 3-ounce packages cream cheese, at room temperature
1 small onion, minced
1 to 2 tablespoons bottled clam juice
1 teaspoon fresh lemon juice
1 teaspoon Worcestershire sauce
½ teaspoon salt
Cayenne pepper to taste

In a mixing bowl, combine the clams, cream cheese, and onion and mix with a wooden spoon till blended. Add the remaining ingredients and mix till well blended and smooth.

Transfer the dip to a ceramic crock and serve with melba toast rounds or corn chips.

Yield: 8 to 10 servings

Artichoke and Almond Dip

Mother got the original recipe for this dip about ten years ago from her old friend Nancy Bates (with whom she still exchanges recipes constantly), then proceeded to add her own touches. Today when she prepares it in East Hampton and my herb garden is flourishing, she might include a little minced tarragon or summer savory.

One 6-ounce jar artichoke hearts
3/4 cup homemade (page 305) or Hellmann's mayonnaise
2 teaspoons fresh lemon juice
1 cup grated Parmesan cheese
Black pepper to taste
1/2 cup slivered almonds

Preheat the oven to 350°F.

Drain the artichoke hearts, place in a mixing bowl, and mash well with a heavy fork. Add the mayonnaise, lemon juice, cheese, and pepper and continue mashing and mixing till the mixture is well blended. Transfer the mixture to an ovenproof crock, top with the almonds, and bake till bubbly, about 20 minutes.

Serve the dip with toast rounds or English water biscuits.

Yield: 6 to 8 servings

Pimiento Cheese Spread

Ask any Southerner to name the most nostalgic preparations of his or her youth and I guarantee that pimiento cheese will be listed right along with fried chicken, turnip greens, grits, and pecan pie. Never once have I found this rich, delectable spread outside the South, and never once have I tasted pimiento cheese that can equal that prepared by my maternal grandmother and great grandmother in a meat grinder and the one that Mother still makes on a regular basis. This recipe has been in the family for generations, and to compare it with that awful processed stuff you find today in Southern supermarkets is like comparing fresh and canned lima beans.

½ pound extra-sharp cheddar cheese
One 4-ounce jar pimientos, drained and finely chopped
½ cup finely chopped green olives (optional)
½ cup homemade (page 305) or Hellmann's mayonnaise
1 tablespoon fresh lemon juice
1 teaspoon Worcestershire sauce
Black pepper to taste
Tabasco sauce to taste

Grate the cheese into a mixing bowl, add the pimientos and optional olives, and mix well. Add the mayonnaise, lemon juice, Worcestershire, pepper, and Tabasco and, using a fork, stir and mash the mixture till blended and almost a chunky paste.

Scrape the mixture into a crock and serve with crackers as a canapé. (Spread keeps up to a week tightly covered in the refrigerator.)

Yield: 8 to 10 servings

Martha Pearl Says:

"Jimmy puts olives in his pimiento cheese; I don't. To use diet mayonnaise in this pimiento cheese—or in any other dish—is a sacrilege and abomination. The only thing good about those fake, watery mayonnaises are the jars that might be used for canning. If you can't make fresh mayonnaise, real Hellmann's is the one acceptable substitute."

Vegetable Sandwich Spread

Back in the fifties when I was in high school and Mother did volunteer office work for the priest at Holy Comforter Episcopal Church in Charlotte, more often than not she ended up in the kitchen helping the ladies produce any number of special fund-raising feasts that church was known for. One day, a friend whom Mother had gone to school with as a child commenced to turn out large containers of this vegetable spread, and I remember well Mother coming home waving the recipe in the air and declaring that she would serve it with soup at her next bridge club luncheon. Since the sandwiches are so attractive and colorful, she prepares them not only for various social lunches but also for large cocktail parties.

2 medium-size ripe tomatoes, cored and peeled
1 small green bell pepper, seeded
1 medium-size onion, peeled
1 medium-size cucumber, peeled
1 teaspoon salt
Freshly ground black pepper to taste
1½ cups homemade (page 305) or Hellmann's mayonnaise
1 tablespoon unflavored gelatin
¼ cup warm water

On a cutting board, chop finely the tomatoes, bell pepper, onion, and cucumber, add the salt and pepper, and stir well. Let the vegetables drain in a colander about 15 minutes, transfer to a large mixing bowl, add the mayonnaise, and mix well.

In a small saucepan, combine the gelatin and water, stir, and dissolve over low heat. Add the gelatin to the vegetables, stir till well blended, and chill in the refrigerator till firm. (Spread can be kept tightly covered in the refrigerator up to 1 week.)

To serve with cocktails, make small 2 x 1-inch sandwiches using white bread for the tops and whole-wheat for the bottoms (crusts trimmed). For a buffet or informal luncheon, make larger sandwiches.

Yield: About 2½ cups

Martha Pearl Says:

"The secret to this particular spread—as well as similar ones made with finely chopped, loose seafood, poultry, and meats—is the tablespoon of gelatin, which keeps the sandwiches from becoming soggy."

Chicken Liver and Pecan Spread

I remember the night over twenty years ago when Mother, Daddy, and I had dinner in New York at my Virginia-born friend Pearl Byrd Foster's small, intimate restaurant (Mr. and Mrs. Foster's Place) and Mother begged for this recipe. Dear Pearl was always loathe to part with the secrets of even her simplest dishes, but a few weeks later, the recipe arrived in Charlotte scribbled on her stylish blue-rimmed Tiffany stationery. Mother likes to keep one or two small crocks of this spread available at all times in the freezer.

6 tablespoons (¾ stick) butter
1 pound chicken livers, trimmed
2 medium-size onions, thinly sliced
½ cup chopped pecans
½ cup Marsala
¼ teaspoon ground mace or nutmeg
Salt and cayenne pepper to taste

Heat the butter in a medium-size skillet, add the livers and onions, and stir over low heat till the livers are no longer pink inside and the onions are translucent, about 10 minutes. Transfer to a blender, add the remaining ingredients, and blend on high speed till the spread is velvety. Scrape the spread into a crock, cover with plastic wrap, and chill 1 hour. Serve with small toasted bread rounds or melba toast with cocktails.

Yield: 8 to 10 servings

Salted Pecans

Nothing is more Southern than to serve salted pecans with cocktails, and nothing is more sacred to Mother than the twenty-five-pound case of nuts she receives every fall from Atwell Pecan Company in Wrens, Georgia, not too far from where she was born. I truly think my mother would be helpless in the kitchen without her vast stash of pecans, the majority of which go into fruitcakes, cheese biscuits, cookies, pies, cakes, and all sorts of main courses.

4 cups (about 1½ pounds) pecan halves
6 tablespoons (¾ stick) butter, melted
1 tablespoon salt

Preheat the oven to 300°F.

Place the nuts in a large, shallow baking dish and pour the butter over them. Sprinkle on the salt, toss the nuts well with a fork to coat evenly, then spread them out evenly in one layer. Bake, uncovered, till golden brown, about 30 minutes, tossing the nuts from time to time (do not overcook). Drain on paper towels, let cool, and serve with cocktails. (Nuts may be stored in an airtight container up to 2 weeks or frozen up to about 6 months.)

Yield: 4 cups pecans

Martha Pearl Says:

"Both pecans and walnuts begin to turn rancid even in the refrigerator after a few weeks—and nothing is worse than a rancid nut! I freeze my pecans in double freezerproof plastic bags, and what's so nice is that—like country ham—they really don't require thawing when needed."

Cheese Biscuits

These are the famous, sacred, inimitable little biscuits that Mother has been making since I was a child and that those around the country who receive one of her tins of Christmas goodies always rave about. She still makes her biscuits not with just any old cheddar but exclusively with A & P New York State extra-sharp cheese. The addition of genuine Parmigiano is a fairly recent idea of mine (one of which she halfheartedly approves), so if you want her classic original, forget the lavish Italian touch and use 8 ounces of the cheddar. Stored in tightly closed tins, the biscuits keep at least a month without turning slightly stale.

1 cup (2 sticks) butter, at room temperature
5 ounces extra-sharp cheddar cheese, finely grated and brought to room temperature
3 ounces imported Parmigiano-Reggiano cheese, finely grated and brought to
    room temperature
¼ teaspoon salt
Big dash of cayenne pepper
2 cups all-purpose flour
Pecan halves

Preheat the oven to 350°F.

In a large mixing bowl, combine the butter, cheeses, salt, and cayenne and mix with your hands till well blended. Add the flour gradually and mix with your hands till firm and smooth, adding a little more flour if necessary.

Roll the pieces of dough in the palms of your hands into balls the size of large marbles and place on ungreased baking sheets about 1 inch apart. Press a pecan half into the center of each and bake till slightly browned but still fairly soft, about 20 minutes. Store the biscuits in tightly sealed tins and serve with cocktails.

Yield: About 75 biscuits

 ## Martha Pearl Says:

"When people tell me these biscuits turned out much grainier than mine, I know without asking that they haven't brought the butter and cheese to room temperature before mixing and have tried instead to heat them. There are no shortcuts with these biscuits."

Country Ham Biscuits

Since at home it's a rare time that there are no biscuits stored in a plastic bag and leftover end pieces of country ham in the refrigerator, we think nothing of eating plain ham biscuits as a snack any time of day—and Lord, are they good! This age-old, dressed-up family recipe, however, is something truly special, especially when the biscuits are served as the bread item on a traditional Southern luncheon buffet with cold fried chicken or sliced turkey, a congealed salad, pickled peaches, a fruit cobbler, and heaven knows what else. If you want to serve these with cocktails (which guests always love), I do suggest you bake a batch of bite-size biscuits no bigger than about one inch in diameter so they can be popped into the mouth.

½ cup (1 stick) butter, at room temperature
2 teaspoons Creole mustard
2 teaspoons Worcestershire sauce
2 tablespoons toasted (page 38) sesame seeds
16 buttermilk biscuits (page 217)
Two 8-ounce slices aged country ham, fried and cut into 1-inch pieces
6 ounces aged Swiss cheese, cut into 1-inch slices

Preheat the oven to 350°F.

In a small bowl, combine the butter, mustard, Worcestershire, and sesame seeds and mix till well blended.

Open the biscuits and spread the mixture on both interior surfaces. Place a piece of ham and a slice of cheese on the bottom of each biscuit, add the tops, and heat in the oven till the cheese melts, about 10 minutes.

Serve the biscuits as snacks or on a luncheon buffet.

Yield: 16 biscuits; 8 servings

Benne Bits

All along the Carolina coastal Low Country, sesame seeds have always been called benne seeds after their African heritage and used in numerous regional dishes, savory and sweet. Since the family had a summer beach cottage at Garden City, South Carolina, we often drove down to stately Middleton Plantation outside Charleston for lunch just to eat real she-crab soup and some of the best shrimp pilau in the entire area. On one occasion, when the waitress placed a bowl of these zesty little nuggets on the table with our drinks, Mother wasted no time quizzing the black cook about the recipe. Suffice it that since that day, benne bits have been a staple at our many cocktail parties. They keep for weeks in a tightly closed tin.

¼ cup benne (sesame) seeds
1 cup all-purpose flour
¼ teaspoon salt
Cayenne pepper to taste
¼ cup (½ stick) butter, chilled and cut into pieces
1 tablespoon milk
1 tablespoon water

Preheat the oven to 350°F.

Scatter the benne seeds evenly on a baking sheet and toast in the oven, stirring, till golden brown, about 10 minutes. Let cool.

In a mixing bowl, combine the flour, salt, and cayenne, add the butter in pieces, and work with your fingertips till the mixture resembles coarse meal. Add the benne seeds, milk, and water and mix with your hands till the dough is smooth.

Roll out the dough on a floured surface about ¼ inch thick and cut into 1-inch rounds. Place the rounds on an ungreased baking sheet and bake till golden, about 12 minutes. Let cool, then serve with cocktails.

Yield: About 40 benne bits

Martha Pearl Says:

"When toasting any seeds or nuts, you have to watch them like a hawk to make sure they don't burn. Overtoasted seeds and nuts will destroy the taste of any dish."

Shrimp Toast

Rarely do I recall visiting our friends down in Charleston that we were not served these delectable strips of toast on any given occasion and at any time of day or night. In the old days, Mother and Maw Maw would grind the ingredients in a meat grinder, and, in all honesty, I must say that shrimp paste always seemed to taste better than the mixture we process today in a blender. I doubt that Charlestonians would ever include water chestnuts in their paste, one of Mother's innovations that adds lots to the texture. We do not freeze these toasts.

½ pound fresh shrimp
1 small lemon, cut in half and seeded
2 green onions (green leaves included), rinsed thoroughly and cut in half
5 whole water chestnuts
1 teaspoon prepared horseradish
Pinch of ground nutmeg
½ teaspoon salt
Black pepper to taste
1 large egg white, at room temperature
10 slices toast, crusts trimmed

Place the shrimp in a saucepan, add enough water to cover, squeeze one lemon half into the water, then drop it in. Bring the water to a boil, drain the shrimp in a colander, and, when cool enough to handle, peel and devein them.

Place the shrimp in a blender or food processor, add the juice of the remaining lemon half, the green onions, water chestnuts, horseradish, nutmeg, salt, and pepper and blend till the ingredients are finely ground. Scrape into a mixing bowl.

In a small bowl, beat the egg white with an electric mixer till stiff peaks form, then fold into the shrimp mixture.

Preheat the oven to 400°F.

Cut each slice of toast into three strips, spread each strip with shrimp mixture, place strips on one of two ungreased baking sheets, and bake till lightly browned, about 5 minutes. Serve the toast hot or at room temperature with cocktails.

Yield: 6 to 8 servings

Cheese Grits Squares

This is still another way Mother utilizes all her leftover breakfast grits—she always overestimates our appetites (on purpose?), and I've never seen her discard even a half cup of cooked grits. Even non-Southerners take to these little squares like pigs to peanuts, one reason being that Mother urges everyone to eat them while they're still hot and crispy.

2 cups cooked grits (page 15)
4 ounces extra-sharp cheddar cheese, grated
1 tablespoon Tabasco sauce
$\frac{1}{2}$ teaspoon salt
2 tablespoons butter
2 tablespoons vegetable oil
1 large egg, beaten
1 cup fine plain bread crumbs

Grease an 8-inch-square baking pan and refrigerate till cold.

In a saucepan, reheat the grits, add the cheese, Tabasco, and salt, and stir till well blended. Spread the grits in the prepared pan and place in the freezer 30 minutes.

Heat the butter and oil in a heavy frying pan. Cut the grits into $1\frac{1}{2}$-inch squares, dip the squares into the egg, dredge both sides in the bread crumbs, and fry till crisp, about 2 minutes on each side.

Serve the squares with cocktails.

Yield: 8 to 10 servings

Olive Puffs

People have always begged Mother as much for this recipe as for her sausage balls, and there's literally never a time when part of her crowded freezer is not taken up with a large plastic bag of olive puffs ready to pop into the oven at the last minute. For the first five or so minutes after baking, these little devils do retain heat like no appetizer I know, so warn cocktail guests accordingly.

$^2/_3$ cup sifted all-purpose flour
$^1/_4$ cup ($^1/_2$ stick) butter, at room temperature
1 cup grated sharp cheddar cheese
1 teaspoon paprika
$^1/_4$ teaspoon dry mustard
30 stuffed olives, drained

In a mixing bowl, combine all the ingredients except the olives and knead briefly with your hands till well blended and smooth.

Pinch off pieces of dough and flatten them with your hand to make small circles just large enough to wrap around an olive. Enclose the olives in circles of dough and roll each with the palms of your hands to form olive balls. Arrange the balls on a baking sheet, cover tightly with plastic wrap, and freeze. Place the frozen balls in a plastic bag in the freezer till ready to use.

To cook, preheat the oven to 400°F and bake the olives on an ungreased baking sheet till golden brown, about 15 minutes. Serve with cocktails.

Yield: 30 olive puffs

Hot Cheese Puffs

Mother says that she remembers eating these puffs as a child, usually a few days after bread had been baked. Why her mother always used both grated onion and minced chives remains a mystery.

One 3-ounce package cream cheese, at room temperature
$^1/_4$ cup grated Parmesan cheese
1 teaspoon grated onion
1 tablespoon minced fresh chives
$^1/_8$ teaspoon cayenne pepper
$^1/_4$ cup homemade (page 305) or Hellmann's mayonnaise
4 to 5 slices homemade bread (page 212)

In a mixing bowl, combine the cheeses, onion, chives, and cayenne and mix well with a wooden spoon. Add the mayonnaise and mix till well blended and smooth. (Or combine all the ingredients in a blender and blend just till smooth.)

Preheat the oven to 350°F.

Cut the bread into 1½-inch rounds, spread each round with cheese mixture, place the rounds on a large ungreased baking sheet, and bake till golden, about 15 minutes. Serve the puffs with cocktails.

Yield: About 25 puffs

Three-Cheese Triangles

Since my paternal grandfather was Greek, and since Charlotte probably has the largest Greek community between New York City and Tarpon Springs, Florida, there has always been a pronounced Greek influence on my mother's Southern kitchen. One of my earliest memories is going downtown with my father to buy briny feta cheese and kalamata olives direct from the barrels at our Greek delicatessen, and one of the first Greek specialties I learned to love were the small feta, spinach, or ground meat triangles that Mother would carefully and lovingly prepare and bake as a first course or for cocktail parties. Today, still, there's never a time when her freezer doesn't contain at least a dozen of these delicious little pastries ready to pop into the oven.

½ pound feta cheese
½ pound ricotta cheese
¼ cup grated Parmesan cheese
2 large eggs, well beaten
½ pound phyllo pastry (available frozen in supermarkets), thawed according to
    package instructions
1 cup (2 sticks) butter, melted

In a mixing bowl, combine the three cheeses, add the eggs, and stir till well blended.

Preheat the oven to 350°F.

Lay the phyllo pastry out on a counter and keep covered at all times with a damp tea towel. Place one sheet of pastry on a working surface and cut width-wise into 2½- to 3-inch strips. Brush a strip with melted butter and spoon 1 teaspoon of the cheese mixture into the center, about 1 inch away from the edges. Fold one corner over into a triangle, then continue folding like a flag to the end of the strip, brushing each triangle with melted butter. Repeat with the remaining strips, placing each triangle on an ungreased baking sheet. Bake till golden brown, 20 to 25 minutes, turning once, and serve piping hot with cocktails or as a first course. (Triangles may be stacked between sheets of waxed paper and frozen in airtight containers up to 3 months. When ready to serve, separate the triangles while still frozen and bake an extra 10 minutes.)

Yield: About 50 triangles

Martha Pearl Says:

"When working with phyllo pastry, I not only keep the sheets covered with a damp tea towel to prevent drying out, but I also keep my fingertips moist while forming the triangles."

Spinach Tarts

Mother created these little tarts many years ago, and although she doesn't remember how or why, I'm certain she must have been inspired either by the boxes of delicious fresh *spanakopita* (a feta cheese and spinach pie) that my paternal Greek grandfather would often bring home from his small restaurant in Charlotte or by a similar dish she tasted at one of the many bazaars we attended at the Greek Orthodox church. The tarts freeze well—minus the Romano and pimientos, which should be added only before baking.

For the patty shells

One 3-ounce package cream cheese, at room temperature
½ cup (1 stick) butter, at room temperature
1½ cups all-purpose flour

For the filling

1 pound fresh spinach, trimmed of tough stems, rinsed well, and finely chopped
    (or one 10-ounce package frozen spinach, thawed and finely chopped)
1 small onion, finely chopped
1 cup crumbled feta cheese
¼ cup (½ stick) butter
1 large egg, beaten
¼ teaspoon ground nutmeg
¼ teaspoon salt
Black pepper to taste
2 tablespoons grated Romano cheese
2 ounces diced pimiento

To make the patty shells, combine the cream cheese and butter in a mixing bowl and cream with an electric mixer till smooth. Gradually add the flour and mix till well blended. Shape the dough into twenty-four 1-inch balls, place the balls in two greased muffin pans with 1¾-inch cups, and shape each ball into a shell.

Preheat the oven to 350°F.

To make the filling, place the spinach on paper towels, squeeze till barely moist, and transfer to a mixing bowl. Add the remaining ingredients, except the Romano cheese and pimiento, and mix well.

Fill each patty shell with a generous spoonful of the spinach mixture, sprinkle the tops with the Romano, and bake 30 minutes. Garnish the tops with the diced pimiento.

Yield: 2 dozen tarts

Summer Tomato Pie

On a fairly recent trip that Mother and I took to Houston to visit friends and eat Texas barbecue, we sampled a tomato pie in some restaurant or another that kept her exclaiming for days. Not long after she returned home, my phone rang in East Hampton: "Well, honey, I've been working on a tomato pie," she related excitedly, "and I can't wait for you to try it." Try it I did—with my own tomatoes, my own green onions, my own herbs, even my own fresh Parmigiano I'd hauled back from Parma—and suffice it that not a soul who has tasted the pie has failed to ask for the recipe. It's nothing less than criminal to make the pie without fresh summer tomatoes and herbs, and, if you can afford the luxury, genuine imported Parmigiano does make a difference.

One 9-inch pie crust, homemade (page 234) or storebought, unbaked
5 medium-size ripe tomatoes, sliced
1 cup chopped green onions (part of leaves included)
1 tablespoon chopped fresh oregano
1 tablespoon chopped fresh basil
Salt and black pepper to taste
2 cups grated sharp cheddar cheese
1 cup homemade (page 305) or Hellmann's mayonnaise
½ cup grated Parmesan cheese

Preheat the oven to 400°F.

Prick the pie crust with a fork, bake 10 minutes, and remove from the oven. Reduce the heat to 325°F.

 ## Martha Pearl Says:

"It's nonsense the way highfalutin' chefs dump rice and beans and tacks into pie shells to make them bake evenly. Like any sensible Southern cook, I just prick the shell all over with a fork. The crust may not be the most even and beautiful in the world, but it tastes good."

Cover the bottom of the crust with two layers of tomatoes. Sprinkle on half the scallions, oregano, and basil and season with salt and pepper. In a bowl, combine the cheddar cheese and mayonnaise, mix till well blended, and spread half the mixture over the tomatoes. Repeat the layering with the remaining tomatoes, scallions, oregano, basil, salt, pepper, and mayonnaise spread, top with the Parmesan, and bake till golden and firm, about 45 minutes.

Let the pie cool slightly and cut into slices as a first course or wedges as canapés with cocktails.

Yield: One 9-inch pie; 4 first-course servings

Hootie's Pickled Shrimp

Originally, this was a dish my sister served when she and her family lived in Wilmington, North Carolina, and would throw elaborate oyster roasts and fish dinners under gigantic live oaks festooned with Spanish moss. On the coast we always simply jabbed the shrimp with toothpicks and washed them down with iced beer while the oysters were steaming in the burlap or the fish was on the grill, but today Mother serves the elegant shrimp on very proper small plates with cocktail forks.

2½ pounds medium-size fresh shrimp
4 medium-size onions, sliced
4 lemons, thinly sliced
1 cup olive oil
1 cup red wine vinegar
1 tablespoon prepared horseradish
1 tablespoon Worcestershire sauce
2 tablespoons sugar
1 teaspoon salt
2 tablespoons capers, drained
4 bay leaves, crushed
Tabasco sauce to taste
¼ cup finely chopped fresh parsley

Place the shrimp in a large pot with enough water to cover. Bring to a boil, remove from the heat, cover, and let stand 1 minute. Drain the shrimp, let cool, then peel and devein.

In a large baking dish, layer the shrimp, onions, and lemons. In a bowl, whisk the oil and vinegar together till frothy, add the remaining ingredients except the parsley, stir well, and pour over the shrimp mixture. Cover with plastic wrap and chill at least 12 hours.

Remove the shrimp from the marinade, arrange on a platter, and sprinkle with the chopped parsley.

Yield: 6 to 8 servings

Martha Pearl Says:

"The one and only way fresh shrimp can be frozen successfully is in a container full of water. You can use plastic containers, but I prefer well-rinsed milk cartons cut in half since all you have to do when ready to cook the shrimp is pull away the paper. This takes up lots of room in the freezer, but the frozen shrimp are just like fresh."

Sausage Balls

Both Mother and I are obsessed with making or finding great sausage, and she simply will not make these balls if the sausage does not contain the right cuts of pork, the correct proportion of fat, and the proper seasonings. Our homemade version is, of course, ideal, but when the supply is exhausted and Mother is "just not up to grinding sausage," there are always a few packages of Reese's or Jamaison's (North Carolina), Owen's (from our source in Houston), and Jimmy Dean (the one acceptable national brand). Also, make sure that the cheddar is extra sharp—and preferably New York State.

½ pound Fresh Country Sausage (page 10), at room temperature

5 ounces extra-sharp cheddar cheese, grated and brought to room temperature

2 tablespoons minced fresh chives

1 cup all-purpose flour

In a mixing bowl, combine all the ingredients and mix thoroughly with your hands. Form into balls about 1 inch in diameter, place on a large baking sheet, and either refrigerate overnight or freeze and store in a plastic bag till ready to use.

Preheat the oven to 400°F.

Bake the balls till golden, about 12 minutes if chilled, 15 if frozen. Serve with cocktails.

Yield: About 3 dozen balls

Daphne's Cocktail Meatballs

Just as she still does today when called upon, Mother used to help cook at any number of special events at our Episcopal church in Charlotte. Naturally, all the ladies loved to exchange recipes, and this one she got about twenty years ago from her old friend Daphne Gatlin after they'd prepared a lavish buffet at the church (with cocktails!). Don't snicker at the jar of grape jelly—it truly does add to the distinct flavor of the meatballs.

One 12-ounce bottle chili sauce

One 19-ounce jar grape jelly

¼ cup water

1½ pounds ground beef sirloin

1 medium-size onion, minced

1 celery rib, minced

1 garlic clove, minced

3 tablespoons finely chopped fresh parsley

1 teaspoon prepared mustard

2 teaspoons chili powder

½ teaspoon salt

¼ teaspoon freshly ground black pepper
Chopped fresh parsley for garnish

In a large saucepan, combine the chili sauce, jelly, and water, bringing to a low simmer, and stir till well blended.

In a mixing bowl, combine the remaining ingredients except the chopped parsley for garnish, and mix with your hands till well blended and smooth. Shape the mixture into 1-inch balls and place them in the jelly sauce. Return the heat to a simmer and cook the balls till no longer pink inside, about 30 minutes.

To serve with cocktails or on a small buffet, transfer the meatballs to a silver chafing dish, sprinkle with chopped parsley, and serve with toothpicks.

Yield: About 3 dozen meatballs

Martha Pearl Says:

"For these meatballs, I really prefer to buy a nice lean rump or bottom round roast, cut off a big chunk, and grind the meat myself through a fine blade. Never use ground chuck for this recipe, it's just too fatty."

Baked Wing Drumettes with Tangy Sauce

When guests exclaim over Mother's spiffy little baked drumettes glistening in their elegant chafing dish, she still delivers the same lecture about how, to a true Southerner, the humble chicken wing has always been the sweetest and most important part of the chicken, as are certain portions of the back. She must have a dozen different versions of these wings, but this is her most classic and the way she serves them when children or young people are expected at one of our buffets.

15 chicken wings (about 3 pounds)
⅓ cup soy sauce
3 tablespoons granulated sugar
3 tablespoons firmly packed light brown sugar
3 tablespoons cider vinegar
1 teaspoon ground ginger
1 small onion, minced
1 garlic clove, minced
Black pepper to taste

Cut the wing tips from the chicken wings, place the tips in a large saucepan, and add water to cover. Bring to a simmer, cover, cook 30 minutes, and discard the tips.

In a large baking dish, combine ½ cup of the chicken stock (reserve the remainder for another use) plus the remaining ingredients and stir well. Add the chicken wings, cover with plastic wrap, and marinate for 2 hours, turning frequently.

Preheat the oven to 325°F.

Place the baking dish in the oven and bake the wings till most of the marinade is gone, about 1½ hours. Serve in a hot chafing dish with cocktails or on a buffet.

Yield: 15 drumsticks

Hobotee

Hobotee, an unusual curried meat custard indigenous to the Low Country of South Carolina and Georgia, was a dish my grandmother loved to eat for lunch but one we prefer to serve (with small glasses of dry sherry) as a stylish appetizer at fish dinners. Charlestonians enjoy the ramekins even at breakfast.

3 tablespoons butter
1 medium-size onion, finely chopped
1 tablespoon curry powder
1½ cups finely chopped cooked beef, veal, or pork
1 slice bread, soaked in milk and squeezed dry
2 tablespoons chopped almonds

2 tablespoons fresh lemon juice
3 large eggs
½ teaspoon sugar
Salt to taste
1 cup half-and-half
Dash of white pepper
Small bay leaves

In a skillet, heat the butter, then add the onion and cook over low heat 2 minutes. Stir in the curry powder and cook 2 minutes longer. Transfer the mixture to a mixing bowl, add the meat, bread, almonds, lemon juice, one egg, the sugar, and salt and blend thoroughly.

Preheat the oven to 300°F.

Butter six ½-cup ramekins and divide the meat mixture among them. In another bowl, combine the half-and-half, remaining eggs, and pepper and whisk well. Pour equal amounts of the cream mixture into each ramekin, garnish the tops with a bay leaf, and bake 25 minutes.

Yield: 6 servings

3
Soups and Stews

Okra & Tomato Soup

1 soup bone –
about 1½ lb beef roast –
2 onions, chopped
celery
6 cups ~~to~~ water

3-4 tomatoes –
1½ lb okra
salt & pepper

In large soup pot put soup bone,
trimmed piece of beef, onions & about
1 cup celery, chopped add water
add salt
Let come to boil & simmer about
2 hours until beef is tender. Remove
soup bone & beef & cut beef into small
pieces – Strain the liquid into another
Pot & add the chopped tomatoes,
sliced okra & beef – test seasoning &
add more salt, some pepper & dash of
Worchester if desired – Simmer for about
another hour & serve hot –

One of the many dishes from Mother's jumbled recipe book that, for some unknown reason, was recorded on the back of a torn envelope. As her original recipe shows, she disapproves of my adding a bay leaf and Worcestershire.

Plenty of prep time goes into making a good Southern soup or stew.

Except for desserts and cookies, no section of Mother's sacred black recipe book is more extensive and treasured than that devoted to the various soups, chowders, gumbos, and bisques that she's been concocting for half a century. Pure nostalgia for me is the memory of fresh hot tomato soup or chicken and okra gumbo that Mother would serve with sandwiches when my sister and I were sick with colds as children, and many were the times when uncles and aunts and close neighbors invited for one of Mother's potluck dinners would find on the table a large tureen of her beloved marrow-bone vegetable soup or oyster stew to be consumed with no more than some elaborate salad and plenty of fresh cornbread. My father especially loved a good soup more than life itself, and while he could hardly chop vegetables, his keen ability to judge any potage in restaurants and, when enthused, to negotiate recipes often led to some of Mother's most successful efforts.

"Don't you dare pour out that chicken stock!" Mother still harps after I've boiled an old bird for chicken salad or hash. No matter that the freezer already holds at least four large containers of stock. "I don't care," she'll pursue. "I never know when I'll need plenty of stock for soup or stew." Chicken and beef stock, ham and marrow bones, peanuts and dried beans, turnips, carrots, potatoes, and beets almost over the hill—the ingredients for her soup-making are virtually endless and account for some of the most delicious dishes in her repertory.

Chicken Stock

One 4- to 5-pound fowl, neck and giblets included
4 quarts cold water
2 medium-size onions, cut in half
2 carrots, cut in half
2 celery ribs (leaves included), broken in half
Salt and black pepper to taste

Place the fowl, neck, and giblets in an 8- to 10-quart stockpot or large kettle and add the water. Bring to the boil, reduce to moderately low heat, and simmer 30 minutes, and skimming off any scum. Add the onions, carrots, celery, and salt and pepper and continue simmering 3 to 3½ hours, adding more water if necessary to keep the contents barely covered.

Strain the stock through cheesecloth into a large bowl, let cool, chill (preferably overnight), and remove most of the fat from the top. (Remove meat from the fowl and reserve for chicken salad or hash.) Keeps 1 week in the refrigerator and up to 3 months in the freezer.

Yield: About 2 quarts

Unca' Charlie's Creamy Peanut Soup

This luscious soup can be traced back to my grandmother's Unca' Charlie Malone, who raised peanuts on his large farm in Jasper County, Georgia, and would send Maw Maw and other relatives sacks of raw nuts to be roasted, made into peanut butter, and used in all sorts of dishes. Mother remembers eating this same soup as a child, and I can remember having my greedy hands slapped when I'd grab more than my fair share of ground nuts to sprinkle into my bowl. (I, uh, still do.)

6 tablespoons (¾ stick) butter
4 green onions, finely chopped
2 celery ribs, finely chopped
3 tablespoons all-purpose flour
4 cups fresh chicken stock (page 55)
1 cup creamy peanut butter
½ teaspoon salt
2 teaspoons fresh lemon juice
1 cup half-and-half
½ cup finely chopped peanuts

In a large, heavy pot, melt the butter, then add the onions and celery and cook over low heat 5 minutes, stirring. Sprinkle in the flour and stir till well blended. Add the stock and bring the mixture to a boil. Add the peanut butter, salt, and lemon juice, stir well, reduce the heat to low, and simmer, stirring till the mixture is smooth, about 20 minutes. Add the half-and-half and heat, never allowing the soup to boil.

Serve the soup with the chopped peanuts to be sprinkled on top.

Yield: 6 servings

Bell Pepper Soup

This is one of the simplest but subtlest soups Mother has ever come up with, mainly because of the contrast in flavors of the sweet peppers, tart buttermilk, and racy sherry. The soup is just as good chilled as hot, depending on the season.

½ cup (1 stick) butter
2 medium-size onions, chopped
2 green bell peppers, seeded and chopped
2 large red bell peppers, seeded and chopped
2 cups fresh chicken stock (page 55)
⅛ teaspoon ground nutmeg
Salt and black pepper to taste
3 cups buttermilk
1 tablespoon dry sherry

In a large saucepan, melt the butter, then add the onions and bell peppers and cook over low heat 3 minutes, stirring. Add the stock, nutmeg, salt, and pepper, bring to a boil, reduce the heat to low, cover, and simmer 30 minutes. Let cool slightly.

Transfer the mixture to a blender and process till smooth, then return to the saucepan. Add the buttermilk and sherry, stir till well blended, and heat thoroughly but do not boil.

Yield: 4 to 6 servings

Broccoli Soup

1 large head broccoli
3 tablespoons butter
1 medium-size onion, chopped
2 garlic cloves, minced
1 medium-size potato, peeled and diced
3 cups fresh chicken stock (page 55)
1 cup milk
Salt and black pepper to taste
Tabasco sauce to taste

Cut the florets from the broccoli stalks and place in a saucepan with 1 inch of water. Bring to the boil, reduce the heat to moderate, cover, and steam the florets till tender, about 10 minutes. Drain and set aside.

Trim, peel, and cut the stalks into dice. In a large, heavy saucepan, melt the butter, then add the onion, garlic, and diced stalks, and cook slowly over low heat about 10 minutes. Add the diced potato and stock, bring to a boil, reduce the heat to low, and simmer till the stalks and potatoes are tender, about 25 minutes. Add the milk, salt, pepper, and Tabasco, stir, and simmer 5 minutes longer.

Transfer the mixture in batches to a blender and reduce to a smooth puree. Return to the saucepan, add the reserved florets, heat thoroughly, check the seasoning, and serve.

Yield: 6 servings

Cold Herbed Tomato Soup

This is strictly a summertime soup that depends on the finest ripe tomatoes and fresh herbs you can grow or find. Mother throws a fit when I refuse to peel my tomatoes, but since the soup is processed in a blender, I can't see it makes that much difference. Although we usually serve the soup as a first course, it's also a great luncheon dish accompanied by something like pimiento cheese sandwiches followed by leftover fruit cobbler topped with ice cream.

3 tablespoons butter
1 medium-size onion, chopped
1 garlic clove, minced
8 large ripe tomatoes, peeled, seeded, and chopped
1 tablespoon chopped fresh sage
1 tablespoon chopped fresh basil
Salt and freshly ground black pepper to taste
Tabasco sauce to taste
Worcestershire sauce to taste
2 tablespoons all-purpose flour
6 cups fresh chicken stock (page 55)
1½ cups half-and-half
Fresh sage leaves for garnish

In a large stainless-steel or enameled saucepan, melt the butter, then add the onion and garlic and cook over moderate heat 3 minutes, stirring. Add the tomatoes, sage, basil, salt, pepper, Tabasco, and Worcestershire, increase the heat slightly, stir, and cook 10 minutes longer, stirring from time to time. Sprinkle the flour on top, stir, and continue cooking 10 minutes longer, stirring from time to time. Add the stock, stir, remove the pan from the heat, and let the soup come to room temperature.

Transfer the soup to a blender in batches, reduce to a smooth puree, and check the seasoning. Transfer to a stainless-steel or glass bowl and chill thoroughly, preferably overnight. When ready to serve, add the half-and-half and stir till well blended. Ladle the soup into wide soup bowls and float a sage leaf in the center of each.

Yield: 8 servings

Okra and Tomato Soup

Come August in East Hampton when our juicy beefsteak and Big Boy tomatoes are hanging heavy on the vines, Mother can be seen scurrying from one roadside vegetable stand to the next trying to find small, tender okra to make this and numerous other soups. I've never known anyone with her passion for okra, and whether it's in one of her many gumbos, in chicken and rice soup, or in her inimitable vegetable soup, okra's role as a thickener and flavor enhancer can never be overestimated. She wouldn't dream of making this soup without fresh, ripe homegrown tomatoes, nor does she ever fail to make enough extra to freeze for the winter.

1 soup bone
One 1½-pound piece boneless beef chuck, trimmed of excess fat
2 medium-size onions, chopped
2 celery ribs (leaves included), chopped
1 bay leaf
6 cups water
3 large ripe tomatoes, peeled and coarsely chopped
1½ pounds fresh okra, sliced
½ teaspoon Worcestershire sauce
Salt and black pepper to taste

In a large, heavy pot, combine the soup bone, beef, onions, celery, and bay leaf. Add the water, bring to a boil, reduce the heat to low, and simmer till the beef is tender, about 2 hours. Transfer the beef to a cutting board, cut it into small dice, and set aside. Discard the soup bone.

Strain the liquid in the pot and discard the solids. Skim the fat from the liquid, rinse out the pot, and return the liquid to the pot. Add the diced beef, tomatoes, okra, Worcestershire, salt, and pepper, return the soup to a simmer, and cook about 1 hour. Check the seasoning and serve very hot.

Yield: 4 to 6 servings

Martha Pearl Says:

"I always use water as the liquid base for this type of soup since, with the beef, chicken, or beef stock would make it just too rich and heavy. Jimmy sometimes wants to add some of his fresh basil, but I think that overwhelms the other flavors."

Marrow Bone Vegetable Soup

Handed down on Mother's side of the family for at least four generations, this recipe illustrates the monumental role that hearty soups have always played on our Southern table. When fresh vegetables are at their summer peak, she loves nothing more than to simmer a big pot of vegetable soup and invite lots of people over to the house to share it; and come late fall, one of her major projects is to make and freeze enough soup in plastic containers to last her and her close friend, Nancy Bates, most of the winter. Never use an inferior cut of meat in this soup, and by no means cheat by substituting ground beef for shoulder, top round, or rump roast.

3 quarts water
One 2-pound beef shoulder roast (bone-in), fat trimmed
2 marrow bones
Two 28-ounce cans whole tomatoes with juice
6 medium-size onions, coarsely chopped
6 celery ribs, coarsely chopped
4 carrots, scraped and cut into ½-inch rounds
2 cups fresh or frozen lima beans
2 cups fresh or frozen corn kernels
1 cup fresh or frozen green beans, snapped into thirds
1 pound fresh or frozen okra, cut into thirds
1 tablespoon salt
Black pepper to taste
1 cup long-grain rice
Tomato paste as needed

Pour the water into a large, heavy pot, add the beef and marrow bones, and bring to a boil. Add the tomatoes, cutting each into halves or quarters, depending on size. Add all the remaining ingre-

Martha Pearl Says:

"If you're planning to serve this soup immediately, it's fine to substitute 2 cups diced potatoes for the rice, but since potatoes don't freeze well, I never use them in my winter version."

dients except the rice and tomato paste, reduce heat to moderately low, cover, and simmer gently till the beef is tender, about 2½ hours. Remove the beef and marrow bones from the soup, discarding the bones. Cut the beef into small dice and return to the pot. Add the rice plus more water if needed, return the soup to a simmer, and cook till the rice is cooked, 30 minutes longer. If the soup is too thin, stir in tomato paste by the spoonful for desired consistency.

Yield: 10 to 12 servings

Sea Captain She-Crab Soup

I thought that my family's eternal search for perfect she-crab soup prepared with the delicate roe of blue female crabs had ended some twenty years ago in Murrel's Inlet, South Carolina, at a restaurant called The Sea Captain. Well, there also happens to be another Sea Captain up the coast at Myrtle Beach, and just recently Mother called from down there to announce that she'd just revisited both places and that "the she-crab at Myrtle is now definitely superior to the one at Murrel's Inlet—thicker, more crabmeat, and, for once, plenty of sherry." In any case, this is the recipe that she obtained originally, and I still say it can't be beat.

¼ cup (½ stick) butter
2 small onions, minced
3 tablespoons all-purpose flour
2 cups milk
2 cups heavy cream
1 teaspoon ground nutmeg
1 teaspoon white pepper
2 teaspoons salt
2 tablespoons Worcestershire sauce
2 tablespoons cornstarch
1 pound fresh lump crabmeat, picked over carefully for shells
½ cup crab roe (available in specialty food shops)
Dry sherry to taste

In the top of a double boiler, melt the butter over low direct heat, add the onions, and cook till just soft. Add the flour gradually and stir till the mixture thickens. Place the pan over the bottom of the double boiler half filled with boiling water and slowly add 1½ cups of the milk, stirring. When the milk is hot, add the cream, nutmeg, pepper, salt, and Worcestershire and cook for 5 minutes. Dissolve the cornstarch in the remaining milk, remove the pan from the hot water, and stir in the cornstarch mixture. Return the pan to the top of the double boiler and cook the mixture till hot, 5 minutes longer. When ready to serve, add the crabmeat and roe, heat the soup thoroughly over boiling water, and lace with sherry.

Yield: 4 to 6 servings

Martha Pearl Says:

"The real secret to this soup is preparing it in a double boiler over a water bath. I've tried making it several times in just a saucepan, and, trust me, it's never right."

Clam Chowder Bruno

Although this is the hearty clam chowder that Mother has been making for decades, it's not her favorite. Her (and my) favorite is the clam chowder served at Gosman's restaurant at Montauk on eastern Long Island, the recipe for which she has begged and pleaded for for almost ten years but which remains a closely guarded secret of the Gosman family. The diligent campaign continues to this day, so until she manages somehow to sweet-talk or bribe Roberta Gosman into revealing the mystery of that Platonic chowder, you'll have to settle for second best.

½ cup (1 stick) butter
2 tablespoons ¼-inch pieces salt pork
1 medium-size onion, chopped
5 tablespoons all-purpose flour
4 cups bottled clam juice
1 medium-size potato, peeled, cut into ½-inch dice, and boiled in water to cover
    till just tender
1 pound fresh clams, coarsely chopped
1 cup half-and-half
½ cup heavy cream
Salt and freshly ground black pepper to taste
Oyster crackers

In a large, heavy saucepan, melt the butter, add the salt pork, and cook, stirring occasionally, till the pork turns light brown, over low heat about 5 minutes. Add the onion and cook another 5 minutes, stirring. Sprinkle the flour on top, stir, and cook 5 minutes, stirring. Increase the heat to moderate, add the clam juice, stirring, and continue stirring till the mixture is smooth. Add the potato and clams, stir, and cook 5 minutes. Add the half-and-half, cream, salt, and pepper, reduce the heat to low, and simmer the chowder 15 minutes, stirring occasionally and adding a little more clam juice if a thinner chowder is desired.

To serve, ladle the chowder into heated soup plates or bowls and pass a bowl of oyster crackers to be sprinkled on top.

Yield: 6 servings

Martha Pearl Says:

"My husband, Harold (whom we nicknamed Bruno), loved full-bodied clam chowder more than life itself, and he's the one who taught us the trick of going to seafood restaurants as late as possible so that we'd be served thick chowder from the bottom of the pot. He liked lots of potatoes in his chowder; I don't."

Christmas Oyster Stew

Although most people no longer worry about eating fresh oysters in spring and summer, when I was growing up Mother wouldn't dream of making this stew except during the "r" months when our delectable Carolina and Virginia oysters were deemed safe. Of course no family Christmas dinner was complete without it, and today she still serves it very ceremoniously in the same exquisite gold-and-white Bavarian china tureen that her mother first used three quarters of a century ago. Accompanied by hot buttered biscuits and a green salad, the stew is also perfect for a casual lunch.

¼ cup (½ stick) butter
2 tablespoons all-purpose flour
3 cups milk
1 cup half-and-half
1 tablespoon grated onion
Salt and black pepper to taste
1 quart fresh shucked oysters, plus their liquor
Paprika for garnish
Oyster crackers

In a saucepan, melt the butter, then add the flour and stir over moderately low heat till blended and smooth. Gradually add the milk, stirring constantly, then add the half-and-half, onion, salt, and pepper, stirring.

Place the oysters and their liquor in another large saucepan and bring to a boil. Reduce the heat to moderate, add the milk mixture, and heat well without boiling till the oysters curl, about 5 minutes.

Serve the stew in heated soup bowls, sprinkle each with a little paprika, and pass a bowl of oyster crackers to be sprinkled into stew.

Yield: 4 to 6 servings

Martha Pearl Says:

"The reason most oyster stew you find in restaurants is so awful is because the oysters are overcooked and tough. Remember that you really don't want to cook the oysters completely, just warm them well in the liquid. Some people like to add a little sherry to oyster stew, but I think that's overkill."

Shrimp Bisque

Just the way Southerners classify any hot composed dish containing egg whites a "soufflé," so do they often confuse the terms "bisque" and "chowder," as in this chunky potage that my sister first concocted when she lived in Wilmington, North Carolina, and that Mother quickly adopted in her kitchen. Although Mother has served cups of this bisque with various congealed citrus salads at her bridge club, both she and Hootie generally consider it a meal in itself to be accompanied by crusty bread and a light green salad. When I make the bisque, I like to add a pinch of powdered fennel and about a tablespoon of dry sherry.

½ cup (1 stick) butter
5 medium-size onions, chopped
4 large potatoes, cut into small dice
2 cups water
3 cups milk
1 pound medium-sharp cheddar cheese, grated
1½ pounds fresh shrimp, peeled and deveined
Salt and black pepper to taste
½ cup chopped fresh parsley

In a large saucepan, melt the butter, then add the onions and cook over moderately low heat 5 minutes, stirring. Add the potatoes and water, increase the heat to moderate, and cook till the potatoes are tender, about 10 minutes.

In another small saucepan, combine the milk and cheese and heat over low heat, stirring, till the cheese is melted. Add to the onions and potatoes and stir well. Add the shrimp, salt, and pepper, stir, and simmer gently over moderately low heat for 10 minutes.

To serve, sprinkle a little chopped parsley on the bottom of each soup bowl and fill with bisque.

Yield: 8 servings

Shrimp and Corn Chowder

Shrimp and corn chowders are found throughout the Carolina and Georgia Low Country, as well as in the Gulf states, but none has ever equaled this downright elegant version that our beloved Pearl Byrd Foster from Virginia taught Mother and me how to make well over a decade ago. We generally offer it as a first course, but it also makes a superb luncheon dish served with a congealed salad, biscuits or hush puppies, and iced tea.

6 cups strong fresh chicken stock (page 55)
3 pounds fresh shrimp, shelled and deveined
2 tablespoons bacon grease
1 tablespoon butter
1 medium-size onion, minced
2 celery ribs, minced
½ large green bell pepper, seeded and minced
8 ears fresh corn (about 4 cups kernels)
2 tablespoons arrowroot dissolved in 1 cup cold milk
Salt and black pepper to taste
Tabasco sauce to taste
1 cup heavy cream
2 carrots, scraped and sliced paper thin
½ red bell pepper, seeded and cut into small dice
4 slices bacon, fried crisp and crumbled

Bring half the chicken stock to a boil in a large, heavy saucepan, add the shrimp, return to a boil, remove from the heat, and let stand 3 minutes. Reserve 24 shrimp, place the remainder in a blender with the remaining cold stock and process, till almost pureed, then add the liquefied shrimp to the hot stock.

In a skillet, heat the bacon grease and butter, add the onion, celery, and green pepper, and cook over low heat about 3 minutes, stirring. Set aside.

Slit the corn kernels by running the tip of a sharp knife down each row of kernels. With the back of the knife, scrape the pulp and juice into a bowl. Add the corn pulp and juice to the shrimp mixture, and cook over moderate heat 1 minute, stirring. Add the cooked vegetables and arrowroot mixture, stir, bring to a brisk boil, and cook 2 minutes. Remove from the heat, add the seasonings, cover, and let stand 30 minutes.

When ready to serve, bring the chowder to a boil, add the cream, carrots, and red pepper, and stir well. Pour into wide soup bowls and add 4 to 6 whole shrimp plus a sprinkling of crumbled bacon to each portion.

Yield: 6 servings

Wilmington Fish Chowder

Mother truly learned to make genuine coastal fish chowder when my sister lived in Wilmington, North Carolina, and we would talk with the fishermen while buying fish on the docks at Wrightsville Beach every summer. As always, it was Mother who cleaned all the fish back at the house, and, as always, the big bowls of chowder were served with coleslaw, hush puppies, and ice-cold beer.

1 large potato, peeled and cut into small dice
2 celery ribs, cut into small dice
2 carrots, scraped and cut into small dice
3 tablespoons butter
1 large onion, chopped
2 pounds bass, red snapper, grouper, or other firm white fish, heads and tails
    removed, dressed, and cut into 1-inch chunks
2 teaspoons Worcestershire sauce
2 teaspoons salt
Freshly ground black pepper to taste
2 cups milk

Martha Pearl Says:

"If you clean your own fish (which I always do), one secret of a great chowder is to toss the bits and pieces of fish not cut into chunks into the pot to cook with the vegetables. They almost disintegrate, but in doing so, they add lots of flavor and texture. As for the chunks of fish themselves, for heaven's sake do not overcook them."

In a large pot, combine the potato, celery, and carrots and add enough water to cover. Bring to a boil, reduce the heat to moderate, cover, and cook about 15 minutes. Drain the vegetables in a colander and set aside.

Melt the butter in the pot, add the onion, and cook over low heat about 5 minutes. Add the reserved vegetables, the fish, Worcestershire, salt, pepper, and enough water to cover. Bring almost to a boil, reduce the heat to low, and simmer till the fish is tender, 10 to 15 minutes. Add the milk, stir gently, and cook till the chowder is piping hot, about 5 minutes.

Yield: 8 servings

Chicken and Okra Gumbo

This was the soup that my grandmother Maw Maw always fixed for her children and grandchildren when they were sick, a custom that my sister, Hootie, followed when she was raising children and one she still observes when she herself catches a bad cold, calls Mother, and pleads "I hope you have a little chicken gumbo in the freezer." I'm not sure that modern medicine would endorse the remedy, but I can assure you that nothing tastes better on a cold winter night than this gumbo with hot potato yeast rolls.

8 cups fresh chicken stock
   (page 55)
1 cup finely chopped onion
1 cup chopped celery
2 cups fresh or frozen (and
   thawed) sliced okra
One 28-ounce can whole
   tomatoes with juice
Salt and black pepper to taste
1 cup long-grain rice
2 cups bite-size pieces cooked
   chicken

Martha Pearl Says:

"Since this gumbo is not thickened with a roux, it's absolutely essential to include both the okra and rice to get the right texture. Leave one out and you'll end up with a watery soup."

Pour the stock into a large pot, add the onion, celery, okra, tomatoes, salt, and pepper. Bring to a boil, reduce the heat to low, cover, and simmer till the vegetables are tender, about 20 minutes, stirring occasionally. Add the rice, stir, and cook till the rice is very tender, about 20 minutes. Add the chicken, stir gently, simmer 10 minutes, and ladle into individual bowls.

Yield: 8 servings

Chicken and Ham Chowder

Here is the perfect example of the way Mother not only utilizes the hocks she saws off ham shanks but also takes multiple advantage of whole chickens selling dirt cheap (forty-nine cents a pound) in the supermarket. From a simple chicken, she can produce a savory chowder, make a little chicken salad, and use whatever's left over in combination with other ingredients to concoct a hash.

6 slices bacon, cut into 1-inch pieces
One 3½-pound chicken, disjointed
1 small meaty ham hock
1 large onion, studded with 3 cloves
3 celery ribs (leaves included), broken in half
½ teaspoon dried tarragon
½ teaspoon dried thyme
Salt and black pepper to taste
3 quarts cold water
2 medium-size red potatoes
1 medium-size red bell pepper, seeded and finely diced

In a large, heavy skillet, fry the bacon till cooked but not crisp and drain on paper towels. Add the chicken pieces to the fat and cook over moderate heat till nicely browned, turning. Meanwhile, in a large, heavy pot, combine the ham hock, onion, celery, tarragon, thyme, salt, pepper, and water and bring to a boil. When the chicken has browned, add it to the pot along with the bacon, return the mixture to a boil, reduce the heat to low, cover, and simmer 1 hour. With a slotted spoon, remove the chicken to a plate and continue simmering the stock about 45 minutes.

When cool enough to handle, skin the chicken breasts and wings, remove the meat from the bones, cut into small dice, and reserve the dark meat for hash or salads. Peel the potatoes and cut into dice. Transfer the ham hock to a cutting board, strain the stock through a fine sieve into another large pot, and discard all the solids. Shred the ham finely and add to the stock. Add the potatoes, bell pepper, and, if the mixture is too thick, more water. Bring to a simmer over moderate heat and cook till the potatoes are just tender, about 15 minutes. Add the chicken, stir well, taste for salt and pepper, and ladle the chowder into heated soup plates.

Yield: 6 servings

Ham-Bone Bean Soup

Mother and I have some of our most intense spats as a result of her crowding my freezer with all sorts of weighty, space-consuming ham bones, but she'd just as soon throw away her precious cooking stocks as toss out a ham hock. Although she'll sometimes pick off part of the meat if she intends to make a certain casserole or salad that calls for a little ham, she really prefers a meaty bone when it comes to making soup. Traditionally in our family, this soup is served as a main course with plenty of cornbread and perhaps a mess of string beans or collard greens. Like most of Mother's soups, this one freezes well.

1 pound dried Great Northern beans, picked over
1 meaty ham bone, trimmed of excess fat
2 medium-size onions, chopped
2 celery ribs, chopped
2 carrots, scraped and chopped
1 garlic clove, minced
1 bay leaf
Salt and black pepper to taste

Place the beans in a large bowl, add enough cold water to cover by 1 inch, and let soak overnight.

Pick over the beans for loose, hard shells, drain in a colander, and transfer to a large pot. Add the remaining ingredients and enough water to cover. Bring to a boil, reduce the heat to low, cover, and cook about 2 hours. Remove the ham bone, clean off and dice the meat, return the meat to the soup, and cook about 1 hour longer, until the beans are tender. Taste for seasoning and serve.

Yield: 6 to 8 servings

Martha Pearl Says:

"If you prefer to use split peas instead of white beans, you may have to thicken the soup at the end of cooking with a cup or so of mashed potatoes. In any case, don't even think of substituting stock for water in this or any Southern bean soup, and never get any bright ideas about maybe adding a little wine to fancy things up."

Cold Buttermilk Soup

One of Mother's earliest memories is sitting on her cousin Berta's back porch in Monticello, Georgia, churning butter with the black maid Hattie, and drinking the cool buttermilk. And one of my earliest memories is Mother feeding me buttermilk with crumbled saltines as a child when I had intestinal problems and there were no antibiotics. "If everyone drank pure buttermilk," she remembers our family doctor saying, "there would be no stomach problems," a suggestion she still takes to heart everytime she makes this soup and every time she takes a slug of buttermilk straight from the carton while making buttermilk biscuits. "Lord, there's nothing as good on a hot summer day as a little cold buttermilk."

6 medium-size cucumbers
3 tablespoons butter
1 medium-size onion, chopped
1½ cups fresh chicken stock (page 55)
3 cups buttermilk
Salt and black pepper to taste

Dash of Tabasco sauce
Chopped fresh mint leaves for garnish

Peel and seed the cucumbers, cut five of them into chunks, chop the sixth finely, and reserve the chopped cucumber. Place the chunks in a colander, sprinkle lightly with salt, let stand 1 hour in the sink, then pat dry with paper towels.

In a large saucepan, melt the butter, then add the onions and cook over low heat 2 minutes. Add the cucumber chunks, stir, and cook till the vegetables are soft, about 2 minutes. Add the stock, stir, increase the heat to moderate, and simmer 5 minutes. Remove from the heat and let cool.

Transfer the mixture in batches to a blender, reduce to a puree, and scrape into a bowl. Add the buttermilk, salt, pepper, Tabasco, and reserved chopped cucumber, stir well, cover with plastic wrap, and chill at least 1 hour. Serve in glass soup bowls garnished with chopped mint leaves.

Yield: 6 to 8 servings

Peach Soup

Of all the fresh fruits of summer, none plays a bigger role in Mother's cooking or inspires her creativity more than the nectar-sweet, freestone pink Elberta peaches she has bought directly by the peck or bushel from Mr. and Mrs. Smith for over twenty years at The Peach Tree orchard at Filbert, South Carolina. I find nothing wrong with the large local peaches grown on the eastern end of Long Island, but she won't touch them, insisting that they have no taste and are too pulpy compared with the juicy Southern varieties. As a result, when she comes to visit in August for one of her extended stays, the car trunk is overflowing

Martha Pearl Says:

"Although white-fleshed peaches like Georgia Belles are probably the most delicious on earth, never use them for cooking or preserving since they're far too delicate and will simply fall apart."

with baskets of "real peaches" intended for pickling and to make everything from preserves to cobblers to bread to this unusual chilled soup she came up with some years ago and loves to serve at casual lunches around the pool.

3 cups peeled, pitted, and sliced fresh peaches
Fresh lemon juice
1½ cups water
1½ cups dry white wine
3 thin slices peeled fresh ginger
½ cup sugar
3 tablespoons bourbon
1½ tablespoons cornstarch mixed with 1½ tablespoons cold water
3 teaspoons grated lemon rind
¼ cup sour cream

Set aside four to six peach slices for garnish, sprinkling with lemon juice to prevent discoloration.

In a large saucepan, combine the remaining peaches, the water, wine, and ginger. Bring to simmer over moderate heat, cover, and cook 15 minutes. Add the sugar, bourbon, and cornstarch mixture, bring to a boil, and stir till well thickened. Let cool slightly.

Transfer the mixture in batches to a blender, add the lemon rind and sour cream, and blend till smooth. Cool the soup completely, then chill it for at least 4 hours. Serve in chilled crystal soup bowls and top each serving with a reserved peach slice.

Yield: 4 to 6 servings

Cold Strawberry Soup

This unusual summer soup is yet another example of Mother's ingenuity when it comes to creating dishes based on fresh seasonal ingredients. It originated a few years back after we'd been strawberry-picking on the North Fork of Long Island and, after making pint after pint of preserves plus two strawberry and rhubarb pies, she still had exquisite berries left over. Mother serves the soup as a first course in crystal bowls, each portion topped with a large, perfect strawberry.

3 cups fresh strawberries, hulled and washed
1½ cups water
1½ cups dry white wine
½ cup sugar
2 tablespoons fresh lemon juice
1½ tablespoons cornstarch mixed with 1½ tablespoons water
3 teaspoons grated lemon rind
¼ cup sour cream

Slice all but six strawberries and reserve the whole berries. In a stainless-steel or enameled saucepan, combine the sliced berries, water, and wine, bring to a simmer over moderate heat, and cook about 10 minutes. Add the sugar, lemon juice, and cornstarch mixture, bring to a boil, and stir till thickened. In batches, transfer the mixture to a blender, add the lemon rind and sour cream, and blend till smooth. Scrape into a bowl, let cool, taste for sugar, cover with plastic wrap, and chill thoroughly. Top each portion of soup with a whole strawberry.

Yield: 4 servings

4

Salads

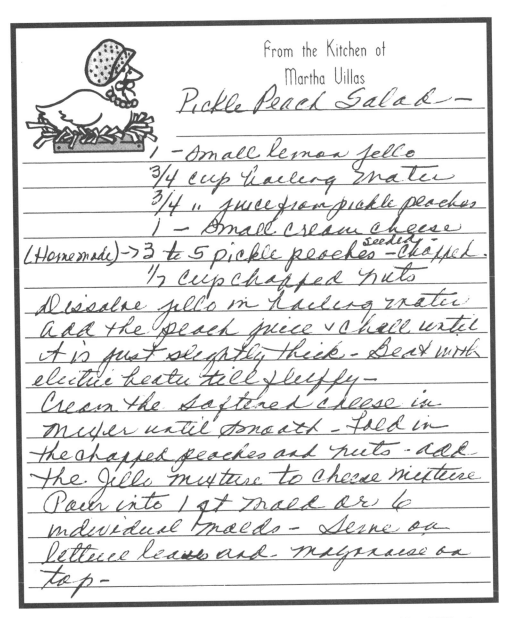

From the Kitchen of
Martha Villas

Pickle Peach Salad —

1 - small lemon jello
3/4 cup boiling water
3/4 " juice from pickle peaches
1 - Small cream cheese
(Homemade)→3 to 5 pickle peaches - seeded - chopped.
1/2 cup chopped nuts

Dissolve jello in boiling water
Add the peach juice & chill until
it is just slightly thick - Beat with
electric beater till fluffy -
Cream the softened cheese in
mixer until smooth - Fold in
the chopped peaches and nuts - add
the Jello mixture to cheese mixture
Pour into 1 qt mold or 6
individual molds - Serve on
lettuce leaves and - mayonaise on
top -

ABOVE: *Pickled Peach Salad remains one of Mother's most delectable creations and one of the few congealed salads I truly relish. People always beg for this recipe.*

RIGHT: *Mother and her oldest childhood friend, "Flossie" Anders, have been exchanging this type of simple recipe for decades.*

None of the men in our family (myself included) ever cared much for any salad except the tossed greens always served with steak, but I truthfully believe that Southern ladies could eat a salad for lunch every day of their lives. Composed seafood, meat, and poultry salads are religiously included on cafeteria, church, country club, and department store menus, and so wildly popular are congealed salads at ladies' bridge clubs, church bazaars, and various charity get-togethers that I've almost come to the conclusion that gelatin salads must now be considered distinctively Southern (you certainly don't find them very often elsewhere in the country). "Polly [or Nancy or Isabel] served the most delicious salad for lunch I ever put in my mouth," I've heard Mother exclaim no less than a hundred times, a sure sign that she had the recipe in her pocketbook and would reproduce it at the first opportunity. Traditionally, she (like her mother and grandmother and, now, my sister) will serve a composed salad with little more than hot rolls, perhaps a relish tray with homemade pickles, and iced tea, but when it comes to one of her or my sister's many congealed salads, these are used mainly to accompany a lunch of fried chicken, cold meat loaf, spiced beef, and the like. I do feel almost obliged to add that, for someone who can usually take or leave any congealed salad, Mother's pickled peach salad is an absolute wonder.

Pork and Apple Salad

2 c diced cooked pork
2 c diced unpeeled red apple
1 c c celery
¼ c relish
1 T lemon juice
¼ tsp onion juice
dash of salt
⅓ c mayonnaise
combine all ingredients & chill
serve on lettuce   4 servings

Florence Anderson

Cold Shrimp and Wild Rice Salad

This was originally my sister's creation, and today when we decide to include the elegant salad on a summer deck buffet along with cold roast pork, ham biscuits, a fruit cobbler or pound cake, and churned ice cream, we've learned to double or triple the recipe.

2⅓ cups water
1½ cups wild rice
½ pound small fresh shrimp
¼ pound fresh mushrooms, sliced
1 cup firmly packed shredded fresh spinach (tough stems removed)
2 green onions (green tops included), sliced
⅓ cup dry white wine
¼ cup vegetable oil
2 teaspoons sugar
1 teaspoon salt
Freshly ground black pepper to taste
Cherry tomatoes for garnish

In a saucepan, bring the water to a boil, add the rice, reduce the heat to low, cover, and cook till the rice has absorbed all the water, about 30 minutes. Transfer to a large bowl, cover with plastic wrap, and chill.

Meanwhile, place the shrimp in another saucepan and add enough salted water to cover. Bring to a boil, remove pan from the heat, let stand 1 minute, and drain. When the shrimp have cooled, peel, devein, and add to the rice.

Add the mushrooms, spinach, and green onions and toss. In a small bowl, combine the wine, oil, sugar, salt, and pepper, whisk till well blended, then pour over the rice and shrimp. Toss well, cover, and chill till ready to serve.

Serve the salad on salad plates garnished with cherry tomatoes.

Yield: 4 servings

Shrimp and Pea Salad with Pork Cracklin's

I claim credit for creating this rather elaborate salad one hot day at the South Carolina beach cottage when we were expecting old friends for lunch and it was much more desirable to use what I could find in the refrigerator than braving the scorching heat to shop. I remember that we served the salad with homemade dill bread and a chilled chablis, followed by leftover peach cobbler with churned ice cream. Modifying the menu, Mother has prepared the salad many times since when she and her lady friends make one of their coastal excursions to cook and play bridge.

2 cups diced streak-o'-lean cooking meat (lean salt pork)
2 pounds fresh medium-size shrimp
½ lemon
2½ cups cooked green peas
2 small dill pickles, diced
1 cup homemade (page 305) or Hellmann's mayonnaise
3 tablespoons fresh lemon juice
3 tablespoons heavy cream
1 teaspoon prepared horseradish
Salt and black pepper to taste
Curly endive (chicory) leaves
2 medium-size tomatoes, quartered, for garnish
3 hard-boiled eggs, peeled and quartered, for garnish

In a large, heavy skillet, render the diced cooking meat over moderate heat till crisp and golden brown, about 20 minutes, watching carefully and reducing the heat if the fat threatens to burn. Drain the cracklin's on paper towels and set aside.

Place the shrimp in a large saucepan with enough salted water to cover, squeeze the lemon into the water, then toss it in. Bring to a boil, remove from the heat, let sit 1 minute, then drain. When the shrimp are cool enough to handle, shell, devein, and place in a large mixing bowl. Add the peas and pickles, mix, and chill 1 hour, covered with plastic wrap.

In a small bowl, whisk together the mayonnaise, lemon juice, cream, horseradish, salt, and pepper. Add to the shrimp mixture and toss well.

Line a large salad bowl with the curly endive, mound the salad in the middle, sprinkle the top with cracklin's, and garnish with the tomatoes and eggs.

Yield: 6 servings

Spicy Crabmeat and Grape Salad

1 pound fresh lump crabmeat, picked over for shells
½ pound seedless green grapes
2 hard-boiled eggs, peeled and chopped
1 celery rib, chopped
2 green onions (part of the green tops included), chopped
¼ cup chopped fresh parsley
1 teaspoon salt
Black pepper to taste
2 tablespoons fresh lemon juice
½ teaspoon Worcestershire sauce
Dash of Tabasco sauce
¾ cup homemade (page 305) or Hellmann's mayonnaise
¼ cup sour cream
4 leaves romaine or leaf lettuce
8 fresh plum tomatoes for garnish

In a mixing bowl, combine the crabmeat, grapes, eggs, celery, onions, parsley, salt, and pepper and toss lightly. Add the lemon juice, Worcestershire, Tabasco, mayonnaise, and sour cream and mix just enough to bind the ingredients. Taste for seasoning.

To serve, place the lettuce leaves in the center of salad plates, pile salad on top of each leaf, and garnish each portion with two tomatoes.

Yield: 4 servings

Martha Pearl Says:

"Although I usually serve this as a luncheon salad, it's also nice stuffed into partly scooped-out avocado halves to accompany a main-course soup."

Grouper Salad

Mother has never been enthusiastic about fish salads, but when my sister Hootie came up with this delicious concoction after we'd all been fishing at

Wrightsville Beach, North Carolina, it was immediately incorporated into the repertory. The salad is just as good made with red snapper, Spanish mackerel, or bass.

2 pounds grouper fillet, cut into small chunks
Salt to taste
2 medium-size onions, finely diced
3 celery ribs, finely diced
3 tablespons finely diced pimiento
Freshly ground black pepper to taste
1 cup homemade (page 305) or Hellmann's mayonnaise
2 tablespoons fresh lemon juice
1 tablespoon prepared horseradish
Lemon wedges, seeded, for garnish
Sprigs of watercress for garnish

Place the grouper chunks in a saucepan with enough salted water to cover, bring to a simmer over moderate heat, and cook until just cooked through, about 10 minutes. Drain the fish, place in a large bowl, cover, and chill about 1 hour.

Flake the fish. Add the onions, celery, pimiento, pepper, and salt and mix gently. In a small bowl, combine the mayonnaise, lemon juice, and horseradish and add it to the fish mixture, mixing gently and adding a little more mayonnaise if desired. (Or substitute about 1 cup Curried Cucumber Mayonnaise, page 307.)

Serve the salad on salad plates garnished with lemon wedges and watercress.

Yield: 4 to 6 servings

Bridge Club Ground Chicken Salad

I don't know another human soul who grinds chicken for chicken salad, but to this day I've never seen Mother prepare her popular salad without hauling out the same heavy steel meat grinder that her mother and grandmother used, rinsing it, placing it in the oven momentarily to dry, and pushing the pieces of chicken slowly through the ominous thick blades. (She even *travels* with her grinder when she knows there's important grinding to be done!) "I don't know why you criticize this old custom," she harps in frustration. "Sure, it takes extra time and effort, but ground chicken absorbs other flavors more easily, the salad packs evenly into tomatoes and on sandwiches, and it doesn't fall all over the plate the way chunky chicken salad does."

One 3- to 3½-pound chicken, cut up
Small bunch celery leaves
Salt to taste
1 cup minced celery
1 tablespoon finely chopped pimientos
1 tablespoon minced fresh parsley
½ cup homemade (page 305) or Hellmann's mayonnaise
1 teaspoon fresh lemon juice
Freshly ground black pepper to taste

Place the chicken and celery leaves in a large pot with enough salted water to cover, bring to a boil, reduce the heat to moderate, cover, and simmer about 1 hour. With a slotted spoon, transfer the chicken to a plate and, when cool enough to handle, remove and discard the skin, clean the meat from the bones, and cut into chunks. Chill the chicken for 1 hour, covered.

Pass the chicken through the medium blade of a meat grinder into a large mixing bowl, then add the remaining ingredients, mix till well blended, and taste for seasoning.

Either serve the salad stuffed into quartered ripe tomatoes or use to make small sandwiches with trimmed white bread.

Yield: About 4 cups

Martha Pearl Says:

"Be sure to chill the chicken about an hour before grinding it. Unlike Jimmy, who likes to keep chicken salad in the refrigerator to nibble on, I like only fresh *salad and never make more than I plan to use."*

Turkey Salad with Celery Seed Dressing

For some reason, Mother has never been fond of turkey in any form or fashion—possibly because she finds the meat too bland. On the other hand, she's not about to discard even leftover turkey, not when it can be combined with numerous other tasty ingredients to make a colorful Oriental-style salad such as this. And here, by the way, is still another dish where Mother has no qualms whatever about using crispy iceberg lettuce. "I don't care what all those food snobs say about iceberg," she huffs. "It's the perfect lettuce for this and certain other dishes."

6 leaves escarole
3 cups very coarsely chopped iceberg lettuce
4 tomato slices
4 hard-boiled egg slices
2 cups cubed cooked turkey
8 fresh pea pods
2 cups bean sprouts
½ cup slivered green onions (white part only)
Six ¼-inch-thick slices cucumber, scored and halved
¼ cup thinly sliced water chestnuts
¼ cup sliced toasted (page 38) almonds
1 cup Celery Seed Dressing (page 304)

Line a large serving platter with the escarole leaves and fill with a bed of iceberg lettuce. Arrange the tomato slices at the two ends, and top each with an egg slice.

Spread the turkey across the center and place the pea pods in the outer quarters of the platter. Top the turkey with the sprouts, then the onions. Scatter the cucumber slices, water chestnuts, and almonds around the platter and drizzle the dressing over the entire salad.

Martha Pearl Says:

"Jimmy usually makes his poultry salads with tasteless white meat. I have to have more flavor, so I much prefer using the thighs and legs for my chicken or turkey salad."

Yield: 4 to 6 servings

Ham and Macaroni Salad

This type of simple, old-fashioned salad evolved in the South long before Americans ever heard the word "pasta." Today, it might be looked down upon by more "sophisticated" cooks, but to Southern ladies like my mother, it is still the perfect salad to serve at club meetings and on a large luncheon buffet. Personally, I love it.

3 cups cooked elbow macaroni
1 pound lean cooked ham, cut into 1-inch cubes
½ pound Swiss cheese, cubed
2 hard-boiled eggs, peeled and chopped
1 medium-size onion, chopped
2 celery ribs, chopped
½ cup chopped sweet pickle
1 cup Mustard Buttermilk Dressing (page 305)
Cherry tomatoes for garnish

In a large mixing bowl, combine the macaroni, ham, cheese, eggs, onion, celery, and pickle and toss to mix well. Add the dressing, stir till well blended, cover with plastic wrap, and chill till ready to use.

Serve the salad on salad plates garnished with cherry tomatoes.

Yield: 6 servings

Pork and Apple Salad

When Mother asked her childhood friend Florence Anders for this recipe after the tasty dish was served at a church luncheon, Flossie said she was "almost embarrassed to give it since it's so simple." Despite all the modesty, it is a delicious fall salad and a clever way to use up leftover pork roast.

2 cups diced cook pork
2 cups cored and diced unpeeled Red Delicious apples

1 cup diced celery
¼ cup pickle relish
1 tablespoon minced onion
1 tablespoon fresh lemon juice
¼ teaspoon salt
⅓ cup homemade (page 305) or Hellmann's mayonnaise
Mixed salad greens

In a large mixing bowl, combine all the ingredients except the salad greens and mix well. Cover the bowl with plastic wrap, chill about 1 hour, and serve the salad on beds of mixed greens.

Yield: 4 servings

Frozen Fruit Salad

Mother traces this salad back to her high school days in Charlotte when she and seven other girls met regularly at different homes to play bridge. So popular were Martha Pearl's frozen fruit salad and pimiento cheese sandwiches that whenever it was her turn to hostess the club, there was never any question as to what would be served. Charmingly enough, some half a century later, she often serves the exact same salad and sandwich to her more mature bridge-playing and hungry gals.

One 8-ounce package cream cheese, at room temperature
3 tablespoons homemade (page 305) or Hellmann's mayonnaise
Pinch of salt
One 9-ounce can crushed pineapple, drained
1 can mandarin oranges, drained
1 cup seedless green grapes
½ cup maraschino cherries
2 bananas, peeled and sliced into thin rounds
1 cup chopped toasted (page 38) almonds
1 cup heavy cream
Bibb lettuce leaves

With a heavy fork, mash the cheese in a large bowl till fluffy, then add the mayonnaise and salt and stir till well blended. Add the fruit and almonds and stir till well blended.

In another bowl, whip the cream till stiff peaks form, then fold into the fruit mixture. Transfer to a shallow 9 x 7 x 2-inch covered baking dish (or divide among eight individual molds), cover, and freeze till hard.

Serve the salad on top of lettuce leaves.

Yield: 8 to 10 servings

Martha Pearl Says:

"If you use individual molds for any salad, grease them lightly with mayonnaise so that the salad will unmold easier."

Pickled Peach Salad

Of all Mother's congealed salads, this one is by far my favorite—most likely because she uses nothing but the delectable pickled Elberta peaches she puts up every summer in both Charlotte and East Hampton. The salad is utterly celestial when consumed with a beautifully glazed baked ham or a chicken or ham casserole.

One 3-ounce package lemon-flavored Jell-O
¾ cup boiling water
¾ cup pickled peach juice (page 292)
One 3-ounce package cream cheese, at room temperature
3 to 4 pickled peaches, chopped
½ cup chopped pecans
Lettuce leaves

In a bowl, combine the Jell-O and boiling water and stir till dissolved. Add the peach juice, stir, and chill till the mixture begins to thicken. Beat with an electric mixer till light and fluffy.

In another bowl, cream the cheese with the mixer till smooth, then add the peaches and pecans and stir till well blended. Add the cheese mixture to the Jell-O mixture, stir till well blended, transfer to a 1-quart mold, and chill till firm.

Serve the salad on lettuce leaves.

Yield: 6 servings

Congealed Sunshine Salad

No Southern housewife worth her aspic is without her special version of Sunshine Salad, partly, I'm sure, because it is so easy to prepare. Mother says that the original (the one her mother and grandmother made regularly) always contained grated carrots, and most of the old Southern Junior League and church cookbooks I checked do indeed include this ingredient. Mother, however, has simply never been that crazy about carrots in salads (including my coleslaw!), so at some point she began substituting the grapes.

One 3-ounce package lemon-flavored Jell-O
1 cup boiling water
One 9-ounce can crushed pineapple, drained
½ cup coarsely chopped orange sections (all white pith and membrane removed)
½ cup chopped seedless grapes
½ cup chopped walnuts
Mayonnaise for garnish

In a large bowl, combine the Jell-O and boiling water and stir till the Jell-O has dissolved. Add the pineapple and orange sections, stir, let cool, and chill till slightly thickened. Fold in the grapes and walnuts, scrape the mixture into small greased molds or one large mold, and chill till firm.

Serve the salad topped with a little mayonnaise.

Yield: 4 to 6 servings

Nancy's Congealed Grapefruit Salad

Interestingly enough, Mother got this recipe from her friend Nancy Bates, who had been given a similar recipe by a relative who was a Presbyterian missionary in China for forty years. Nancy, who was paralyzed by a car accident when I was a child, has been a friend of the family for fifty years and has never allowed her infirmity to affect her incredible cooking ability. She and Mother are forever exchanging recipes, and it is Nancy (bless her) who sends regular shipments of real, old-fashioned country sausage to my home in East Hampton.

Two 6-ounce packages lime-flavored Jell-O
2 cups grapefruit juice
One 16-ounce carton sour cream
3 cups grapefruit sections, seeded
Boston lettuce leaves
Mayonnaise for garnish

Place the Jell-O in a large bowl. In a saucepan, heat the grapefruit juice to the boiling point, then add to the Jell-O and stir till dissolved completely. Place in the refrigerator and chill till slightly thick (about the consistency of egg whites), about 20 minutes. Fold in the sour cream, then gently fold in the grapefruit sections till well distributed. Turn the mixture into a 3 x 9 x 2-inch flat dish and return to the refrigerator to set completely.

   To serve, cut the salad into squares, place each square on a lettuce leaf, and top with dollops of mayonnaise.

Yield: 10 to 12 servings

Summer Potato Salad

When guests in East Hampton rave about this potato salad and ask the secret, Mother explains why Southerners use nothing but unpeeled Red Bliss new potatoes ("they're firm, not mealy, and full-flavored"), how nothing but home-made or Hellmann's mayonnaise will do, and how the potatoes must be mixed while still warm so that they absorb the mayonnaise properly. When I make the salad, I like to add chives plus a few fresh herbs, but, purist that she is, Mother says I destroy the flavor of the potatoes.

2 pounds new potatoes, scrubbed gently
2 medium-size onions, diced
2 celery ribs, diced
$\frac{1}{2}$ small green bell pepper, seeded and diced
$\frac{1}{2}$ cup diced sweet pickles
$\frac{1}{4}$ cup chopped fresh parsley
2 teaspoons salt
Freshly ground black pepper to taste
2 cups homemade (page 305) or Hellmann's mayonnaise

Cut the potatoes into $\frac{1}{2}$-inch dice and place in a pot with enough water to cover. Bring to a boil, reduce the heat to moderate, and cook just till the potatoes can be pierced with a knife, about 7 minutes.

Drain the potatoes well in a colander and transfer to a large mixing bowl. Add the onions, celery, bell pepper, pickles, parsley, salt, and pepper and toss gently. Add the mayonnaise, toss gently but thoroughly, cover with plastic wrap, and chill at least 1 hour before serving.

Yield: 6 to 8 servings

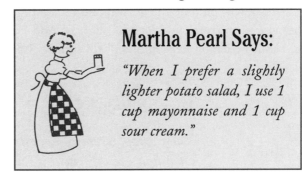

Martha Pearl Says:

"When I prefer a slightly lighter potato salad, I use 1 cup mayonnaise and 1 cup sour cream."

Molded Asparagus Salad

About once a year, Mother's old friend Doris Van Every invites her and a few other ladies down to a cottage at Myrtle Beach, South Carolina, where "all the girls do nothing but eat, drink, exchange recipes, and spend hours cooking together." After the "girls" had been crabbing late one afternoon, this salad materialized when Doris got up the next morning and simply announced "Today we're doing to make an asparagus salad to go with the deviled crab."

2 cups water
1 cup sugar
1 teaspoon salt
½ cup cider vinegar
3 envelopes unflavored gelatin
½ cup fresh lemon juice
2 cans whole asparagus spears, drained (liquid reserved) and cut into thirds
½ cup finely chopped celery
1 small onion, finely chopped
One 4-ounce jar pimientos, drained and chopped
Red-tipped leaf lettuce leaves
Mayonnaise for garnish

In a saucepan, combine 1 cup of the water, the sugar, salt, and vinegar and bring to a boil.

In a bowl, combine the gelatin and remaining water, stir to dissolve, add to the hot vinegar mixture, and let cool slightly. Add 1 cup of the reserved asparagus liquid and the lemon juice and chill till syrupy and thick. Add the asparagus spears,

Martha Pearl Says:

"Some people get in a huff when they see that canned asparagus are used in this recipe. Well, I've tried using the fresh more than once, and they just don't work since you need the canning liquid for correct texture."

the celery, onion, and pimiento and stir till well blended. Transfer the mixture to a 12 x 8 x 1½-inch baking dish or twelve individual molds, cover, and chill till firm. Serve the salad on the lettuce leaves topped with a dollop of mayonnaise.

Yield: 12 servings

Cardinal Salad

How typically Southern (and quaint) to name a colorful dish after some closely identifiable animate object—cardinal (beet) salad, grasshopper (mint) pie, bunny (carrot) bread, etc. My father loved this salad, and Mother is convinced that most men love the salad since it's not sweet (as if females have sweet tooths and males don't!). Whatever, since the salad is indeed tart, it goes well with virtually any meat or poultry casserole, as well as with rich game dishes.

One 3-ounce package lemon-flavored Jell-O
1 cup boiling water
One 16-ounce can beets, drained (liquid reserved) and chopped
3 tablespoons cider vinegar
¾ cup finely chopped celery
2 teaspoons grated onion
1 tablespoon prepared horseradish
1 teaspoon salt
Escarole leaves

In a bowl, combine the Jell-O and boiling water, stir till dissolved, add ¾ cup of the reserved beet juice, and chill slightly.

Add the beets, vinegar, celery, onion, horseradish, and salt and stir till well blended. Transfer the mixture to a large mold, cover with plastic wrap, and chill till firm.

Serve the salad on top of lettuce leaves.

Yield: 6 to 8 servings

Cold Shrimp & Rice Salad

1 6 oz. Wild Rice ⎫ Cook until
2⅓ cup water ⎬ water absorbed -
          ⎭ about 25 minutes

Cover cooked rice in bowl
& chill —

Add: 1 cup cooked & cleaned shrimp
      ¼ lb. sliced mushrooms.
      1 cup firmly packed fresh spinach
      2 green onions & TOPS - sliced

Mix: ⅓ cup white wine
      ¼ cup. veg. oil or olive oil
      2 teaspoons sugar
      3/4 teaspoons salt
      ¼ teaspoon pepper

Toss rice, shrimp & vegetables with
dressing. Chill until serving.
Garnish with cherry tomatoes.

Jimmy, great for luncheon salad
or cold supper in
summertime!!

Green Olive Tomato Aspic

One day Mother created this unusual tomato aspic using V-8 Juice for the simple reason that she was tired of overly sweet versions dependent on Jell-O and wanted a more savory aspic to serve with a chicken casserole. This is always a big hit on virtually any brunch or lunch buffet.

4 cups V-8 Juice
3 envelopes unflavored gelatin
1 tablespoon Worcestershire sauce
1 tablespoon cider vinegar
2 tablespoons fresh lemon juice
1 tablespoon grated onion
¼ teaspoon salt
Dash of Tabasco sauce
1 cup finely chopped celery
1 cup sliced stuffed green olives
8 romaine or leaf lettuce leaves
Mayonnaise for garnish

In a large bowl, combine ½ cup of the V-8 Juice and the gelatin and let soak to soften.

In a saucepan, heat the remaining V-8 Juice, add it to the gelatin, and stir till the gelatin has dissolved. Add the Worcestershire, vinegar, lemon juice, onion, salt, and Tabasco and stir well. Place the bowl in the refrigerator and chill till the mixture is slightly thickened.

Add the celery and olives and stir till well blended. Transfer the mixture to a shallow baking dish or eight individual molds, cover with plastic wrap, and chill till firm. Serve the aspic on lettuce leaves and top each portion with a dollop of mayonnaise.

Yield: 8 servings

Molded Avocado Salad

This is one of Mother's most popular salads when she and the members of her Charity League get together at the house to sew and create exquisite little gifts to be sold at their annual bazaar. I've never cared that much for any dish involving avocados, but to watch Mother shop for the delicate fruit and tend them so lovingly in the kitchen attests to her passion for them.

One 3-ounce package lemon-flavored Jell-O
¼ teaspoon salt
1⅔ cups boiling water
2 tablespoons fresh lemon juice
1 tablespoon prepared horseradish
1 teaspoon grated onion
2 medium-size ripe avocados, peeled, pitted, diced, and sprinkled with lemon
   juice
½ cup finely chopped celery
6 romaine lettuce leaves
1 cup Herb Mayonnaise (page 306)
¼ cup chopped pimientos

Martha Pearl Says:

"Nothing exasperates me more in the supermarket than to see either rock-hard avocados or overripe ones covered with big, black, soft spots. Perfect avocados are dark green and "give" just slightly when pressed. If forced to buy avocados that are not perfect, you should place them in a closed paper bag to ripen evenly. Never place an avocado in the refrigerator since the chill blackens them quickly, and once you've cut an avocado, be sure to sprinkle the exposed flesh with lemon juice to prevent discoloration."

In a large bowl, combine the Jell-O, salt, and boiling water and stir till the Jell-O has dissolved. Add the lemon juice, horseradish, and onion, stir, and chill till slightly thickened. Beat the mixture with an electric mixer till smooth and fold in the avocados and celery. Scrape into a large greased mold, cover with plastic wrap, and chill till firm.

Serve the salad on lettuce leaves topped with dollops of the herb mayonnaise and chopped pimientos.

Yield: 6 servings

Thanksgiving Cranberry Salad

Mother wouldn't dream of serving a Thanksgiving (or Christmas) luncheon without including this colorful salad that she first tasted decades ago at the Myers Park Country Club in Charlotte. Most congealed salads I can take or leave, but I must admit that I utterly relish this one with either baked ham or turkey—as my father did.

One 3-ounce package lemon-flavored Jell-O
1 cup boiling water
One 16-ounce can whole-cranberry sauce
2 cans mandarin oranges, drained
One 9-ounce can crushed pineapple, drained
1 cup chopped toasted (page 38) pecans or hazelnuts
Lettuce cups

In a saucepan, combine the Jell-O and boiling water and stir till dissolved. Add the cranberry sauce, oranges, pineapple, and nuts and stir till well blended. Transfer the mixture to a large mold, cover with plastic wrap, and chill till firm.

Serve the salad in lettuce cups.

Yield: 6 to 8 servings

5
Meats

Mother, myself, and Daddy (cocktails in hand) at the grill in Charlotte when I was in college and nothing was more popular than a good backyard barbecue.

SHORT RIBS OF BEEF

6 pieces of lean short ribs of beef
Cook with salt and pepper in simmering water for 3-4 hours
until tender. During the last hour of cooking add;
6 medium or 12 small whole onions
½ hour before ribs are done, add;
6 to 10 small to medium whole potatoes. After they are done;
Lift out ribs and arrange them in a flat baking dish; Put
potatoes and onions around the meat; Pour 2 small or one
large can of tomatoes with the juice over all; Add beef
stock if the juice is not about 3/4 up in the baking dish.
Salt and pepper well. Put in 375 oven and let bake about
45 minutes, basting from tine to time. When brown, serve
from baking dish with hot homemade biscuits.

Considering Mother's incurable tendency to neglect exact measurements and precise cooking instructions when writing out recipes, this one for her Daddy's baked short ribs of beef is a masterpiece!

As throughout most of the South, the pig rules supreme in Mother's kitchen, to the extent that there's virtually no part of the animal that she's not capable of utilizing in one way or another. For everyone in my family, making and acquiring good pork sausage has always been a religious experience equaled in importance only by our periodic trips to Glendale Springs in the mountains of North Carolina to acquire superlative country hams and our never-ending efforts to produce great Carolina pork barbecue. Nobody, not even Mother, could turn out the luscious spareribs I remember my granddaddy Paw Paw cooking on Saturday nights, and if today people rave about Mother's baked ham stuffed with collard greens, her unctuous ham hocks with turnip greens, and her savory pork pie with a biscuit crust, they're simply paying tribute to a proud tradition passed down to her by her parents and grandparents.

Since fine lamb and veal were rarely available in the South till a decade or so ago, neither has ever figured prominently on Mother's menus—with the certain exception of the glorious lamb stew my Greek paternal grandfather once taught her to make. Lesser cuts of beef, like brisket, short ribs, shoulder, and rump, however, account for numerous wonderful dishes on which I was weaned and which we still prepare with regularity for both family and friends; and perhaps none evokes more delectable memories or symbolizes the true flavor of the South like my granddaddy's short ribs of beef baked slowly with tomatoes, onions, and potatoes.

Paw Paw's Short Ribs of Beef

Mother remembers her father preparing these short ribs when she was a child, and she still believes the idea was to stretch a lean budget by serving one hearty dish that included both meat and vegetables. Whatever, to this day we love nothing more than these ribs served with a squash soufflé, hot buttermilk biscuits, and a modest red wine or beer, and no meal in Mother's home or mine is more popular with hungry guests. It infuriates us that so many markets carry ribs that are nothing less than anemic, so no matter when or where we shop, we're forever on the lookout for meaty ribs at least four inches wide and three inches thick to freeze. You almost can't overcook this beef, but do follow the timing once the vegetables are added.

6 meaty short ribs of beef
Salt and black pepper to taste
12 small onions, scored on the root ends
10 small red potatoes, peeled
One 16-ounce can whole tomatoes with juice
Beef stock (optional)

Place the short ribs in a large saucepan or pot with enough water to cover and season with salt and pepper. Bring to a boil, reduce the heat to low, cover, and simmer at least 3 hours, adding more water if necessary to cover. During the last hour of simmering, add the onions. During the last 30 minutes, add the potatoes.

Preheat the oven to 375°F.

Transfer the meat to a shallow baking dish with a slotted spoon, place the onions and potatoes around the meat, and add the tomatoes with their juice. If the juice does not fill the baking dish by three quarters, add a little of the cooking liquid or beef stock. Season with salt and pepper and bake till the top is slightly crusted, about 45 minutes. Serve directly from the baking dish.

Yield: 4 to 5 servings

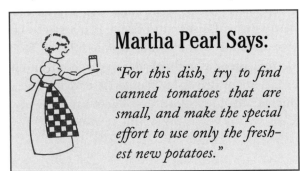

Martha Pearl Says:

"For this dish, try to find canned tomatoes that are small, and make the special effort to use only the freshest new potatoes."

Oven-Barbecued Brisket of Beef

With her innate prejudice for North Carolina pork barbecue, it took years for me to convince Mother that the huge briskets that Texans smoke in pits over mesquite were every bit as good as our pig shoulders barbecued over hickory. Once, however, she tasted the genuine items at Goode's and Otto's in Houston and was later served this oven-barbecued version by friends down in Brownsville, a new dimension was added to her repertory. No, it's by no stretch of the imagination real Texas barbecue, but, unless you care to dig a big pit and import a few hundred pounds of mesquite, it's mighty good eating—and guests love it.

1 tablespoon salt
1 tablespoon freshly ground black pepper
1 tablespoon dry mustard
1 tablespoon paprika
One 4-pound brisket of beef (thin cut)
½ cup (1 stick) butter
2 tablespoons vegetable oil
¼ cup Worcestershire sauce
1½ cups white vinegar
1 teaspoon sugar
Tabasco sauce to taste

Preheat the oven to 300°F.

In a small bowl, combine the salt, pepper, mustard, and paprika, mix well, and rub the mixture thoroughly and evenly into both sides of the meat.

In a large, heavy skillet, heat half the butter and the oil till very hot over high heat, add the meat, and sear quickly on both sides. Transfer the meat to a large roasting pan lined with enough aluminum foil to fold completely over the meat.

While the meat is searing, combine the remaining butter, the Worcestershire, vinegar, sugar, and plenty of Tabasco in a saucepan, bring to a boil, reduce the heat to moderate, and simmer 5 to 10 minutes, stirring. Pour the sauce over the meat, fold the foil snugly around the meat, place the pan in the oven, and cook 4 hours. Remove the pan from the oven, fold the foil back and tuck around the sides of the pan, return the pan to the oven, and cook the meat until fork tender, 1 hour longer, adding a little water if the sauce dries up and basting the meat from time to time with the liquid.

Serve the brisket in thick slices with plenty of coleslaw, sliced raw onions, cornbread, and ice-cold beer.

Yield: 6 servings

Chilled Spiced Beef

Although this unusual beef preparation seems to be of English origin (I've had the dish in various guises all over Britain), Mother got the recipe years ago from a friend in an old New Orleans family. The dish is time-consuming and slightly tricky to prepare, but never will you serve anything more elegant and delicious on a formal buffet.

One 4-pound brisket of beef (thin cut)
2 tablespoons finely chopped fresh parsley
1 tablespoon minced fresh sage
1 tablespoon minced fresh thyme
$\frac{1}{2}$ teaspoon ground cloves
$\frac{1}{2}$ teaspoon ground allspice
$\frac{1}{2}$ teaspoon ground nutmeg
Salt and cayenne pepper to taste

Rinse the brisket well under cold running water. Combine the herbs and spices in a small bowl, add salt and cayenne, mix well, and rub the mixture over all the surfaces of the meat. Roll up the meat lengthwise as tightly as possible, firmly bind with kitchen string, then wrap in cheesecloth and tie securely. Wrap in plastic wrap and place in the refrigerator for 6 hours.

Remove the plastic wrap, place the rolled beef in a kettle just large enough to hold the bundle, and cover with cold water. Bring the water to a boil, reduce the heat to low, cover, and simmer until the beef is fork tender, about 5 hours, adding more water if necessary to keep the beef covered.

Transfer the beef to a deep bowl, pour a little cooking broth on top, fit a plate atop the meat, then place 8 to 10 pounds of weight (large canned goods, bricks, etc.) on the plate to press the meat down. Place the bowl in the refrigerator and chill 12 hours.

To serve, remove the cheesecloth and string, cut the cold beef against the grain in thin slices, and serve with an assortment of mustards on the side.

Yield: 8 servings

Braised Beef Rump Roast

This is basically the way Mother taught me to cook a beef roast when I left home for college and the way I still do at least once a month—and in the same blue enameled roaster she gave me thirty-five years ago. (She has *three* such roasters, each a different size.) We both like to add a few quartered potatoes during the last 30 minutes of cooking, and we both love to serve this roast with string beans and a squash soufflé. Do make special note: If you must have your roast beef cooked rare, forget about this dish. Southerners like their prime ribs and strip steaks as rare as anybody else, but when it comes to cuts like bottom and top round, shoulder, and rump, we know that only long, slow cooking guarantees tenderness.

One 4-pound boneless beef rump rost, tied with twine
Salt and freshly ground black pepper to taste
1 large onion, chopped
1 celery rib, chopped
1 carrot, scraped and chopped
1 garlic clove, chopped
2 cups water
1 cup Horseradish Sauce (page 307)

Preheat the oven to 350°F.

Season the roast all over with salt and pepper and place on a rack in a large roasting pan. Sprinkle the onion, celery, carrot, and garlic around the sides, add the water, cover, and braise in the oven till the meat is well done and very tender, about 2½ hours, adding a little more water if necessary.

Martha Pearl Says:

"Today everybody talks about fatless sauces and gravies. Well, my gravies have never had much fat, the one for this roast being a perfect example—and with no loss of flavor. The trick is not to rush making the gravy."

Transfer the roast to a platter. To make gravy, remove the rack from the pan and strain the drippings through a medium sieve into a bowl. Discard the solids, pour off as much fat from the drippings as possible, and return the drippings to the pan. Place the pan over high heat and cook till the drippings begin to burn. Add about 2 cups of water and stir constantly with a large spoon, slowly scraping the bits and pieces of debris from the bottom and sides till the liquid is slightly reduced and thickened. Pour the gravy into a heated gravy boat.

Serve the meat in slices with gravy and horseradish sauce on the side.

Yield: 6 to 8 servings

Old-Fashioned Beef Stew

Simple as it looks, no recipe is more sacred and unalterable to Mother than this one for beef stew. For years, I tampered with the dish, adding wine, herbs, olives, anything to add even a hint of sophistication; and the more I tampered, the more outraged she became. "Son," she carped, "will you never, ever learn that nothing beats simplicity in cooking?" Well, eventually I did learn, and what I learned is that, even with a stew so plain and humble as this one, rarely can you improve the natural flavor of certain classic dishes.

¼ cup vegetable oil
One 2½-pound beef bottom round or rump roast, trimmed of fat and cut into
    1½-inch cubes
2 large onions, chopped
One 16-ounce can whole tomatoes with juice, chopped
Salt and black pepper to taste
6 medium-size potatoes
6 medium-size carrots

In a large pot, heat the oil over moderate heat, then add the beef and onions and brown lightly, stirring. Drain off any excess oil. Add the tomatoes and their juice and enough water to cover. Season with salt and pepper, bring to a boil, reduce the heat to low, cover, and simmer till the meat is very tender, about 1½ hours.

Peel the potatoes, cut into quarters, and add to the meat. Scrape the carrots, cut into thirds, and add to the meat. Return the stew to a simmer and cook till the potatoes and carrots are tender, 20 to 30 minutes.

Yield: 6 servings

Martha Pearl Says:

"The secret here is, of course, the quality of the ingredients— which is why I never order beef stew in restaurants. If you buy that packaged stew meat in supermarkets, you're only asking for trouble. Ditto poor-quality onions, potatoes, and carrots. I don't even trust tomatoes that we don't grow ourselves, which is why I tell people to use canned ones."

Missy's Perfect Meat Loaf

This simple meat loaf recipe, which can be traced back at least to my maternal great-grandmother, is as sacred to Mother as the one for beef stew. Although I pride myself on a much more elaborate loaf, Mother considers my recipe pretentious nonsense, a desecration of my Southern heritage. "Meat loaf is meat loaf and not something that resembles a French pâté," she's forever chiding. I've made Mother's meat loaf many times, and perhaps the problem is that, for some strange reason, it simply never tastes as wonderful as the one her grandchildren are always begging "Missy" to make. "Maybe you've just been living up North too long," she quips. In any case, she has convinced me that a free-form loaf baked on a rack (as opposed to one packed into a baking dish) is the only way to minimize the fat while retaining plenty of flavor.

1 pound ground beef sirloin
1 pound ground beef chuck
2 medium-size onions, finely chopped
¼ cup or more catsup
2 tablespoons Worcestershire sauce
3 slices white bread, moistened with water and squeezed dry
2 teaspoons salt
Freshly ground black pepper to taste
2 large eggs, beaten

Preheat the oven to 350°F.

In a large mixing bowl, combine all the ingredients and mix well with your hands. Form the mixture into an oval loaf, place the loaf on a rack over a shallow baking pan, and bake till nicely browned on top, about 1 hour.

(To make a simple mushroom sauce, bring 2 cups beef stock or broth to a boil in a saucepan, add 3 tablespoons tomato catsup, stir, and cook till slightly reduced. Add 1 cup finely chopped mushrooms, a pinch dried thyme, ½ teaspoon salt, and freshly ground pepper to taste. Reduce the heat to moderate and cook till the sauce is reduced to desired consistency, about 10 minutes.)

Yield: 8 servings

Martha Pearl Says:

"Jimmy won't listen to me, but one secret to my meat loaf is that I use moistened bread instead of bread crumbs to tighten the mixture. Also, I've never had much regard for catsup in or on anything, but I do think it helps produce a good meat loaf."

Sweet Maa's Stuffed Bell Peppers

Once was the time when every Southern cookbook included at least a couple of recipes for stuffed bell peppers, but when our Houston friend Betsy Parish was recently hit with the idea of serving the dish at a Sunday night supper, her only recourse was to call Mother and ask the directions. This particular recipe using ground beef can be traced to Mother's Georgia grandmother, but today she's just as likely to stuff the peppers with chopped ham, shrimp, pork, or whatever other meat, poultry, or shellfish might be on hand. Mother does prefer to serve the dish in the summertime when the peppers are large and fleshy.

6 medium-size green bell peppers
1 pound ground beef chuck
1 medium-size onion, finely chopped
One 16-ounce can whole tomatoes, drained and finely chopped
$\frac{1}{2}$ cup water
$\frac{1}{2}$ cup long-grain rice
$\frac{1}{2}$ teaspoon salt
Black pepper to taste
1 teaspoon Worcestershire sauce
5 ounces sharp cheddar cheese, shredded

Cut off the tops of the peppers, cut out the seeds and membranes, and place the peppers in a large pot. Add enough water to cover, bring to a boil, cook 5 minutes, and drain on paper towels.

In a large saucepan, combine the ground chuck and onion and cook over moderate heat till the meat is lightly browned, stirring. Drain off the fat. Stir in the tomatoes, water, rice, salt, pepper, and Worcestershire, bring to a simmer, cover, and cook till the rice is tender, about 20 minutes. Stir in 4 ounces of the cheese and mix till well blended.

Preheat the oven to 350°F.

Arrange the peppers cut side up in a large baking dish, stuff with equal amounts of the rice mixture, sprinkle the remaining cheese over the tops, and bake till the tops are golden and slightly crusty, 20 to 25 minutes.

Yield: 6 servings

Dixie Pork Chops with Apples and Raisins

Since they usually turn out "hard and dry as a rock," Mother, unlike many Southerners, truly loathes fried pork chops, insisting that they always be either slowly baked or braised with other ingredients for ultimate flavor and moistness. This is one of her oldest and most delicious versions.

3 slices bacon
6 large loin pork chops
Salt and black pepper to taste
3 apples, cored, peeled, and coarsely chopped
1/3 cup firmly packed light brown sugar
2 tablespoons all-purpose flour
1 cup water
1 tablespoon cider vinegar
1/4 teaspoon dried sage
1/2 cup seedless raisins

In a large, heavy skillet, fry the bacon till crisp, drain on paper towels, and crumble well.

In batches, brown the pork chops on both sides in the bacon fat, adding a little vegetable oil if necessary. Arrange the chops in a large baking dish, season with salt and pepper, divide the chopped apples equally over them, and sprinkle with the brown sugar.

Preheat the oven to 350°F.

Add the flour to the fat in the skillet and stir over moderate heat 1 minute. Add

Martha Pearl Says:

"No matter how I plan to cook them, I never buy thin pork chops since, even when braised, they're almost guaranteed to be dry and tough. My pork chops are always at least 1/2 inch thick."

the water, vinegar, and sage and cook till thickened, stirring. Add the raisins and crumbled bacon, pour the mixture around the chops, cover with aluminum foil, and bake 1 hour.

Yield: 6 servings

Barbecued Spareribs

M artha Pearl, honey," I can hear my Unca' Nalle begging in his thick South Carolina drawl, "when are you gonna fix us some spareribs and succotash and a big butterscotch pie?" For decades, members of the family and friends have raved about Mother's spareribs, and for decades she has raged about the difficulty of finding good meaty ribs outside the South. "The only thing worse in this world than scrawny spareribs are meaty spareribs that aren't cooked slowly and basted frequently," I've heard her lecture guests in East Hampton. Yes, Mother has her chronic sparerib worries, but when everything comes up to her standards, and she puts platters of ribs and succotash and corn pudding and cornbread on the table, the smiles are as big as the appetites.

4 to 5 pounds pork spareribs
Salt to taste
1 cup catsup
1 cup molasses
2 medium-size onions, finely chopped
Juice of 1 orange
3 tablespoons minced orange rind
2 tablespoons butter
2 tablespoons white vinegar
2 tablespoons vegetable oil
2 garlic cloves, minced
5 cloves
1 teaspoon Worcestershire sauce
1 teaspoon prepared mustard
$^1/_2$ teaspoon Tabasco sauce
Black pepper to taste

Preheat the oven to 325°F.

Sprinkle the short ribs lightly with salt, place them on a rack in a large roasting pan, cover the pan with aluminum foil, and bake the ribs 1 hour.

Meanwhile, make the sauce by combining the remaining ingredients plus salt to taste in a saucepan, bringing the mixture to a boil over moderate heat, and cooking 5 minutes, stirring. Remove from the heat till ready to use.

Increase the oven heat to 400°F. Brush the ribs with some of the sauce and continue baking till tender, about 45 minutes, turning the ribs about every 15 minutes and brushing and basting. To serve, pile the ribs on a large platter.

Yield: 4 to 6 servings

Carolina Chopped Pork Barbecue

They said it couldn't be done off native turf: home-cooked pork barbecue just like the succulent pig smoked in huge outdoor pits all over the state of North Carolina. Well, after a few embarrassing failures at my home in East Hampton, I finally managed to accomplish the impossible on a regular outdoor kettle grill and watched as Mother, my neighbor Craig Claiborne, and a dozen other Southern souls proclaimed the chopped barbecue authentic. Ever since, I produce this barbecue exactly one time each summer. The ritual takes all day, the entire house has to be sealed off from the smoke, but everybody has lots of fun and gobbles down barbecue and coleslaw and pickled peaches and hush puppies and cold beer and iced tea like there's no tomorrow. Be sure to use nothing but fresh pork shoulder and hickory chips, don't cheat on the timing, and follow the recipe to the letter.

For the barbecue

One small bag hickory chips (available at nurseries and hardware stores)
One 10-pound bag charcoal briquets
One 6- to 7-pound boneless fresh pork shoulder, securely tied with butcher's string

For the sauce

4 cups cider vinegar
¼ cup Worcestershire sauce

1 cup catsup
2 tablespoons prepared mustard
2 tablespoons firmly packed brown sugar
2 tablespoons salt
Black pepper to taste
1 tablespoon red pepper flakes

Soak 6 handfuls of hickory chips in water for 30 minutes.

Open one bottom and one top vent on a kettle grill. Place a small drip pan in the bottom of the grill, stack charcoal briquets evenly around the pan, and ignite. When the coals are gray on one side (after about 30 minutes), turn and sprinkle 2 handfuls of soaked chips evenly over the hot coals.

Situate the pork shoulder skin side up in the center of the grill directly over the drip pan (not over the hot coals), lower the lid, and cook 4 hours, replenishing the coals and chips as they burn up. Turn the pork, lower the lid, and cook 2 hours longer.

Meanwhile, prepare the sauce by combining all the ingredients in a large saucepan. Stir well, bring to a simmer over moderate heat, and cook 5 minutes. Remove from the heat and let stand 2 hours.

Transfer the pork to a plate, make deep gashes in the meat with a sharp knife, and baste liberally with the sauce. Replenish the coals and chips as needed, replace the pork skin side down on the grill, and cook 3 hours longer, basting with the sauce from time to time.

Transfer the pork to a chopping board and remove the string. Remove and discard most (but not all) of the skin and excess fat and chop the meat coarsely with

Martha Pearl Says:

"Yeah, I must say it does taste like our famous North Carolina barbecue, but when I know Jimmy's planning that smoky ordeal, I wear clothes I can throw away. Also, I don't think he's ever gotten the sauce just right, so I usually bring up bottles of sauce from Flip's Barbecue Restaurant down in Wilmington."

an impeccably clean hatchet, Chinese cleaver, or large, heavy chef's knife. Add just enough sauce to moisten the meat, toss till well blended, and either serve the barbecue immediately with the remaining sauce on the side or refrigerate and reheat in the top of a double boiler over simmering water when ready to serve. (The barbecue can be frozen up to 3 months.)

Yield: at least 8 servings

Barbecued Country-Style Pork Back Ribs

Nobody loved barbecued back ribs more than my grandfather Paw Paw, and I can remember clearly going with him on Saturday mornings down to Mr. Hord's butcher shop in Charlotte to pick up his custom order of ribs. Today, Mother selects her ribs from a long display at the local fresh market, has them cut in half, bakes or grills them exactly the way her father did, and usually serves them with turnip greens, baked sweet potatoes, and baked quartered apples.

6 lean country-style pork back ribs
Salt and black pepper to taste
1 cup All-Purpose Barbecue Sauce (page 309)

Place the back ribs in a large pot with enough water to cover and add salt and plenty of pepper. Bring to a boil, reduce the heat to low, cover, and simmer $2\frac{1}{2}$ hours.

Preheat the oven to 350°F.

With a slotted spoon, transfer the ribs to a large, shallow baking dish, pour the sauce over the ribs, and bake till slightly browned, about 15 minutes. Turn the ribs over and bake 15 minutes longer, basting several times with the sauce and adding more sauce if necessary.

Transfer the ribs to a platter and serve immediately.

Yield: 6 servings

Pork Pie with Biscuit Crust

No doubt the origins of Southern biscuit crusts on sweet and savory pies, cobblers, shortcakes, and the like can be traced back to the lard crusts on our English ancestors' numerous raised pies. One of Mother's reasons for making a meat pie such as this is the same as for her parents and grandparents: to use up leftovers while providing a good bread substitute. This same pie can just as easily be prepared with ham, poultry, veal, beef, and game, any of which would be enhanced by a Cardinal Salad (page 93) or good tomato aspic.

For the pie

3 slices bacon
2 medium-size onions, chopped
1 celery rib, chopped
1 medium-size green bell pepper, seeded and chopped
1 garlic clove, minced
2 pounds lean cooked pork, cut into cubes
2 cups beef stock or broth
2 tablespoons cornmeal
2 tablespoons tomato paste
1 tablespoon Worcestershire sauce
Tabasco sauce to taste
1 teaspoon salt
Black pepper to taste

For the biscuit crust

2 cups all-purpose flour
2 teaspoons baking powder
1 teaspoon salt
3 tablespoons vegetable shortening
¾ cup milk
1 large egg, beaten

In a large, heavy skillet, fry the bacon till almost crisp and drain on paper towels. Add the onions, celery, bell pepper, and garlic to the skillet and cook over moderate heat about 3 minutes, stirring. Crumble the bacon over the vegetables, then add the pork, stock, cornmeal, tomato paste, Worcestershire, Tabasco, salt, and pepper and stir till well blended. Simmer the mixture about 30 minutes, stirring, then transfer to a 2-quart baking dish or casserole.

Preheat the oven to 350°F.

To make the crust, combine the flour, baking powder, salt, and shortening in a mixing bowl and work the mixture with your fingers till mealy. Add the milk and egg and stir just till well blended.

Spoon the batter over the top of the pork mixture and bake till the crust is golden brown, 40 to 45 minutes.

Yield: 6 servings

Essie's Ham Hocks with Collard Greens

Essie was my Georgia great-grandmother Sweet Maa's black maid, and every year when the winter collards came in, it was always a real treat when Essie would saw off the hock from a ham and cook up the season's first collards. Mother says she can still see Sweet Maa sitting at the dinner table with a tall glass of warm "pot likker" from the collards and a big piece of cornbread, dropping morsels of bread in the liquid, taking them out with a spoon, and offering them to the grandchildren. Today, Mother would no more serve a mess of greens without a small bowl of "likker" for dunking than she'd serve biscuits without butter.

One 2- to 2½-pound uncooked ham hock
1 large onion, coarsely chopped
1 hot red pepper, seeded and chopped
1 teaspoon sugar
3 pounds collard greens (about 2 bunches), leaves stripped from stems and
    washed well

Place the ham hock in a large, heavy pot or casserole and add enough water to cover by 1 inch. Bring to a boil, reduce the heat to moderate, cover, and simmer till tender, 1 hour.

Add the onion, red pepper, sugar, and greens, return to a simmer, cover, and cook 1 hour longer.

Transfer the greens with a slotted spoon to a large platter and place the ham hock on top. Pour part of the cooking liquid ("pot likker") into a bowl and serve with plenty of cornbread for dunking.

Yield: 6 servings

Baked Ham Stuffed with Turnip Greens

In the South, nothing is more ceremonial than a majestic Smithfield ham stuffed and baked with greens and perhaps some type of fruit, but since Mother has (inexplicably) never liked the flavor of Smithfields, she sometimes prepares this rather elaborate regular ham and serves it in place of turkey for Thanksgiving. It's delicious, as are the North Carolina and Kentucky hams I've prepared in the same manner with dried apricots added to the stuffing.

4 slices bacon
½ cup finely chopped green onions (including 2 inches of the green tops)
¼ cup finely chopped celery
¼ cup chopped fresh parsley
2 cups chopped turnip greens (tough stems removed)
1 cup chopped spinach (tough stems removed)
1 teaspoon dry mustard
¼ teaspoon dried marjoram
1 teaspoon red pepper flakes
Black pepper to taste
One 12-pound smoked ham
2 cups bourbon
Sprigs of watercress

In a large skillet, fry the bacon until crisp, drain on paper towels, crumble, and pour all but 4 tablespoons of the fat from the skillet. Add the green onions and celery and cook over low heat 3 minutes, stirring. Add the crumbled bacon, parsley, greens, spinach, mustard, marjoram, red pepper, and pepper. Toss the mixture, cover, and cook till the greens are soft, about 20 minutes. Transfer the mixture to a large bowl and mix well.

Preheat the oven to 350°F.

Trim all but ¼ inch of fat from the ham. With a sharp paring knife, cut about 10 deep X-shaped incisions over the surface of the ham, spread the incisions apart, and, using your fingers, force the stuffing deeply into each pocket. Wrap the ham in a large piece of cheesecloth and tie the edges securely. Place the ham in a large oval roasting pan, pour on the bourbon, cover, and bake 2 hours, basting occasionally and adding a little water to the pan if necessary. Remove the ham from the oven, remove and discard the cheesecloth, return the ham to the oven, and continue baking till the top is nicely glazed, 30 to 45 minutes. Place the ham on a rack or large serving platter surrounded by watercress and carve thick slices.

Yield: at least 10 servings

Ham and Sweet Potato Hash

My granddaddy Paw Paw prided himself on this quintessential Southern hash, and since there was always a ham in the refrigerator (or, in his day, "icebox") and plenty of sweet potatoes stored in the basement during the winter, the dish was served frequently for supper with baked apples, turnip greens, cornbread, *and* biscuits. "Daddy would even fix the hash for breakfast," Mother remembers. Today we like to make this type of hash for a casual Sunday dinner, always accompanied by a green vegetable, perhaps some applesauce, and Mother's pickled peaches.

1 pound baked ham, cut into small cubes
1½ cups peeled and diced sweet potatoes, boiled in water to cover till slightly
    firm and drained
1 medium-size onion, minced
½ medium-size green bell pepper, seeded and chopped
½ teaspoon dried basil

Salt and black pepper to taste
¹/₂ cup heavy cream
¹/₄ cup (¹/₂ stick) butter
6 large eggs
Minced fresh parsley for garnish

In a large bowl, combine the ham, potatoes, onion, bell pepper, basil, salt, and pepper and toss to mix well. Add the cream and stir till well blended.

In a large, heavy skillet, melt half the butter over moderately high heat, add the ham mixture, and press down evenly with a spatula. Reduce the heat to moderate and cook the hash till the underside is browned and crusty, about 5 minutes. Loosen the hash with a spatula and invert onto a plate. Melt the remaining butter in the skillet, slide the hash into it to brown the other side, transfer to a large, heated platter, and cover with aluminum foil to keep hot.

In a poacher, poach the eggs 3 minutes according to manufacturer's directions, arrange the eggs on top of the hash, and sprinkle with minced parsley.

Yield: 6 servings

Martha Pearl Says:

"To poach the eggs without a poacher, bring the water in a small saucepan to a rolling boil and add ¹/₂ teaspoon white vinegar. Break one egg into a small saucer, swirl the water rapidly in the pan with a slotted spoon, slide the egg imme-diately into the swirl of water, and poach 3 minutes. Remove the egg with the slotted spoon, drain on paper towels, and repeat the procedure with the remaining eggs."

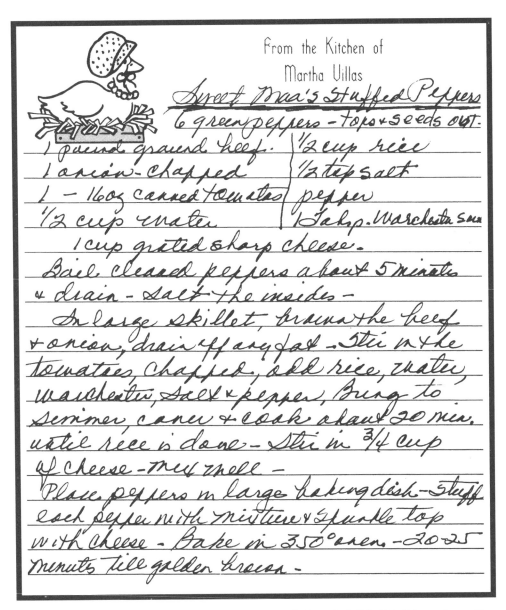

From the Kitchen of
Martha Villas

Sweet Maa's Stuffed Peppers

6 green peppers - tops & seeds out.

1 pound ground beef.	1/2 cup rice
1 onion - chopped	1/2 tsp salt
1 - 16oz canned tomatoes	pepper
1/2 cup water	1 Tahp. Warchester sau
1 cup grated sharp cheese.	

Boil cleaned peppers about 5 minutes
& drain - Salt the insides -
 In large skillet, brown the beef
& onion, drain off any fat - Stir in the
tomatoes, chopped, add rice, water,
warchester, salt & pepper, Bring to
simmer, cover & cook about 20 min.
until rice is done - Stir in 3/4 cup
of cheese - mix well -
Place peppers in large baking dish - Stuff
each pepper with mixture & Spunkle top
with cheese - Bake in 350° oven - 20-25
minutes till golden brown -

*Mother's grandmother, Sweet Maa, lived with the family her whole life. Of all her recipes, this
is perhaps Mother's favorite.*

Papa's Greek Lamb Stew

Ironically, Mother learned to make this stew from my Swedish grandmother, who learned to make it from my Greek grandfather. Like Mama Sigrid, Mother varies the other major ingredients besides the lamb—sometimes orzo, sometimes spinach or green beans, and, in authentic Greek tradition, macaroni. Both my grandfather and my daddy loved this stew, and it always impressed our Southern relatives and friends that Martha Pearl was just as adept at cooking "exotic foreign dishes" as plain old short ribs of beef.

½ cup olive oil (preferably Greek)
2 medium-size onions, chopped
2 garlic cloves, minced
2 pounds lean boneless lamb, cut into 1-inch cubes
Salt and black pepper to taste
2 bay leaves
1 stick cinnamon, broken in half
3 cloves
½ teaspoon dried rosemary
One 8-ounce can prepared tomato sauce
One 16-ounce can whole tomatoes with juice
1 cup dry white wine
1 pound macaroni
½ pound feta cheese

In a large, heavy skillet, heat 2 tablespoons of the oil, add the onions and garlic, and cook over low heat 2 minutes. Add 2 more tablespoons oil and increase the heat to moderate. Season the lamb cubes with salt and pepper, add to the skillet, and cook 3 minutes, turning. Add the bay leaves, cinnamon, cloves, rosemary, tomato sauce, tomatoes, and wine and stir well. Cover the skillet, reduce the heat to low, and simmer till the lamb is tender, about 1 hour, adding water to cover if necessary.

Boil the macaroni according to the package directions, drain in a colander, and arrange half on a heated platter. Crumble a little feta on top, add the remaining macaroni, and crumble on a little more cheese. In a small saucepan, heat the remaining oil, pour it over the macaroni, then arrange the lamb with its juices on top, crumbling on the remaining cheese or to taste.

Yield: 6 servings

6
Poultry and Game

Turkey time again, and I'd guess that this hefty gobbler (ordered at least 2 weeks in advance) weighed close to 25 pounds.

OPPOSITE: *Mother must have a dozen different fried chicken recipes, some highly detailed, others ridiculously abbreviated, but all basically the same.*

erhaps the reason Mother no longer prepares half the wild game dishes she did when we had relatives and friends and farmers who kept us in fairly steady supply of fresh bobwhite quails, squirrels, field rabbits, mallard ducks, and venison is because "so much of the domesticated and frozen game you find in the market today is bland as nine-week-old chickens." Once was the day when Paw Paw and Mother wouldn't have dreamed of making Brunswick stew with anything but the flavorful squirrels that my Uncle Robert would peg and drop off at the house, and just the idea of their roasting or grilling an under-aged haunch of venison or frying frozen, puny quails would have been inconceivable. "These young restaurant chefs think the game they serve now is really something special," Mother argues, "but I can tell you that you've got to do a lot of doctoring today to make the dishes taste good."

Ditto this country's mass-produced, scientifically fed chickens, not one of which has the delicious flavor and delicacy of the barnyard birds that our neighbor in Charlotte, Mr. Nunn, used to raise to a respectable age before subjecting their necks to the hatchet and plucking, drawing, and singeing them by hand. When Mother cooks her luscious chicken pie or Low Country hash, she still goes out of her way to find a flavorful old hen that she simmers for hours, and when we want to serve truly great fried chicken while she's visiting me on Long Island, nothing will do but to pay the price for a few fat free-range beauties at Iacono Farm in East Hampton. And suffice it that when Thanksgiving approaches, she reserves her twenty-pound fresh turkey literally weeks in advance.

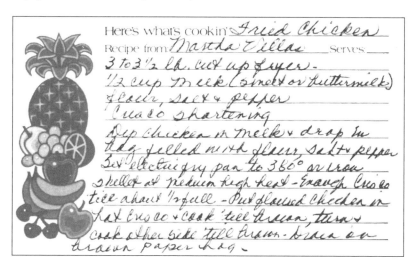

Here's what's cookin' *Fried Chicken*
Recipe from *Martha Villas*   Serves:_____
3 to 3½ lb. cut up fryer.
½ cup milk (sweet or buttermilk)
flour, salt & pepper
Crisco shortening
Dip chicken in milk & drop in
bag filled with flour, salt & pepper
Set electric fry pan to 360° or iron
skillet at medium high heat - Enough Crisco
till about ½ full - Put floured chicken in
hot Crisco & cook 'till brown, then &
cook other side 'till brown - Drain on
brown paper bag.

Perfect Southern Fried Chicken

What is there left to say about Mother's legendary fried chicken except that it has been consumed by various friends and relatives from coast to coast, featured in cookbooks and food magazines, and praised by the likes of Craig Claiborne, Pierre Franey, and Paul Bocuse. Succinctly, there is simply no other fried chicken like it.

Two 3-pound chicken fryers
2 cups all-purpose flour
Salt and black pepper to taste
1 cup milk
Crisco vegetable shortening
1 tablespoon bacon grease

Cut the chicken carefully and evenly into serving pieces, taking great care to keep the skin of each piece intact, and rinse under running water.

In a heavy brown paper bag, combine the flour and salt and pepper and shake till well blended. Pour the milk into a soup bowl.

Set an electric fry pan at 375°F. or place a large cast-iron skillet over moderate heat, fill half full of melted Crisco, and add the bacon grease. When a drop of water flipped into the fat sputters, dip some of the chicken pieces into the milk, then place in the bag. Shake vigorously to coat evenly, shake the excess flour back

Martha Pearl Says:

"I've never understood all the big to-do about my fried chicken. Yes, I do insist on cutting up my own chicken, not only because it's a disgrace the way butchers hack birds apart today but also because I like to cut the wish (pully) bone from the breast. And yes, I refuse to fry chicken in any shortening but Crisco, or drain it on anything but brown paper bags. Then, there's the exact cooking temperatures, and the careful timing and . . . the point is that you have to respect fried chicken."

into the bag, and arrange the pieces in the fat, making sure not to overcrowd the pan. Fry the chicken till golden brown and crisp, 15 to 20 minutes, turn with tongs, reduce heat to 350°F. and fry till golden brown, about 15 minutes longer. (Turn the chicken only once.) Drain on another paper bag and repeat the procedure with the remaining chicken, adding a little more shortening and bacon grease if necessary and maintaining the heat at moderate.

Transfer the chicken to a large platter and do not cover. Serve warm or at room temperature.

Yield: 8 servings

Paper-Bag Barbecued Chicken

This was my sister's answer to feeding hungry young people when her son and daughter were in college and would bring fraternity and sorority friends home for a weekend of boating and fishing. At first, Mother snickered at the paper-bag method of baking chicken practiced in coastal Carolina by certain natives, but once she realized that the chicken was indeed the moistest she'd ever tasted, she gave her stamp of approval. What I find impressive about this sort of interchange of recipes is the way, as time goes by, the Southern daughter began to master the cooking tradition passed on by the mother.

¼ cup catsup
¼ cup water
3 tablespoons cider vinegar
2 tablespoons Worcestershire sauce
3 tablespoons firmly packed light brown sugar
1 teaspoon dry mustard
1 teaspoon chili powder
½ teaspoon cayenne pepper
1 teaspoon salt
1 teaspoon black pepper
3 tablespoons butter
3 tablespoons minced onion
One 3- to 3½-pound chicken, cut up into serving pieces

Preheat the oven to 400°F.

In a saucepan, combine all the ingredients except the chicken, bring to a boil, reduce the heat to moderate, and simmer about 15 minutes, stirring once or twice. Remove the pan from the heat.

Grease the inside of a medium-size heavy paper bag with no open folds or creases. Dip each piece of chicken in the sauce and place in the bag. Spoon the remaining sauce over the chicken, fold, and secure the top of the bag with a metal skewer, place the bag in a large roasting pan, and bake 1½ hours, never opening the bag.

With tongs, transfer the chicken to a platter and pour on the sauce from the bag.

Yield: 4 servings

Chicken and Spinach Rollups

Except when it is fried according to her sacred method, chicken has always bored Mother unless it is "perked up" in one way or another. Perhaps none of her dishes demonstrates that conviction more than this rather elaborate creation involving all sorts of ingredients and seasonings.

Half of a 10-ounce package frozen chopped spinach, thawed and drained
½ cup storebought herb-seasoned bread stuffing
1 small onion, finely chopped
2 large eggs, beaten
3 tablespoons butter, melted
2 tablespoons grated Parmesan cheese
1 teaspoon benne (sesame) seeds
¼ teaspoon garlic powder
¼ teaspoon dried thyme
¼ teaspoon black pepper
3 whole large chicken breasts, split, boned, and skinned
One 1½-ounce jar sliced dried beef
6 slices bacon, fried till partly done but still pliable
Half of a 10¾-ounce can condensed cream of celery soup
One 8-ounce container sour cream

In a mixing bowl, combine the spinach, stuffing, onion, eggs, butter, cheese, benne seeds, garlic powder, thyme, and pepper and mix till blended thoroughly. Using your hands, form the mixture into six separate balls and set aside.

Preheat the oven to 350°F.

Place each chicken breast half on a large piece of waxed paper and, using a meat mallet or rolling pin, flatten each ¼ inch thick. Place 1 slice of dried beef on each breast, place 1 spinach ball on top of the beef, roll up each breast, and secure well with toothpicks. Wrap 1 slice of bacon securely around each rollup and place the rollups in a medium-size greased baking dish. In a bowl, combine the soup and sour cream, mix well, and spoon the mixture over the rollups. Cover the dish with aluminum foil and bake 30 minutes. Remove the foil and bake 30 minutes longer, basting occasionally.

Yield: 6 servings

Brunswick Stew

D ebate still rages around the South over whether this stew originated in Brunswick County, North Carolina, Brunswick County, Virginia, or Brunswick, Georgia, as well as whether it should be made with squirrel or chicken. All I know is that my granddaddy Paw Paw's family was making Brunswick stew with squirrel down in Georgia before the turn of the century, that any barbecue house in North Carolina worth its hot vinegar sauce keeps a big pot of the stew simmering at all times, and that I've never even seen, much less tasted Brunswick stew in the genteel state of Virginia. Although Mother has always been around to supervise and criticize, I've always been the Brunswick stew maker in the family, the most passionate consumers having been my daddy and Unca' Nalle Belliveau from South Carolina. Since dressed squirrel hasn't been exactly readily available in the last fifty or so years, I use hen in my stew, as do most Southerners these days. For years, I also included beef according to the age-old Georgia tradition, but when Mother finally convinced me that my Brunswick stew was not unlike her vegetable soup, I discontinued it—much to the better. We usually serve the stew as a main course with nothing more than a congealed salad and cornbread, and since it freezes beautifully, I often double this recipe.

½ cup vegetable oil
One 4-pound chicken (preferably a hen), quartered
1 cup chopped onions
1 cup chopped celery (leaves included)
1 medium-size ham hock, trimmed
3 large ripe tomatoes, chopped
1 small hot red pepper, seeded and minced
Salt and black pepper to taste
2½ quarts water
1½ cups fresh or frozen corn kernels
1½ cups fresh or frozen sliced okra
1½ cups fresh or frozen lima beans
1½ cups mashed cooked potatoes

In a large, heavy skillet, beat half the oil over moderate heat, then add the chicken, brown on all sides and transfer to a large plate. In a large casserole, heat the remaining oil over moderate heat, add the onions and celery, and cook 2 minutes, stirring. Add the chicken, ham hock, tomatoes, red pepper, salt, pepper, and water, bring to a boil, reduce the heat to low, cover, and simmer 1 hour. Remove the chicken with a slotted spoon and simmer the mixture 1 hour longer. When the chicken has cooled, skin, bone, and shred the meat and set aside.

Bring the mixture in the casserole to a boil, add the corn, okra, and lima beans, and cook over moderate heat for 30 minutes. Remove the ham hock with a slotted spoon and, when cool enough to handle, bone, shred the meat, and return the meat to the casserole along with the reserved chicken. Add the mashed potatoes, stir well, and continue cooking till nicely thickened, about 15 minutes.

Serve the stew in wide soup bowls as a main course or in small bowls as a side dish to pork barbecue.

Yield: 6 to 8 servings as main a course; 10 servings as a side dish

Chicken Creole

Since my family always traveled a good deal to New Orleans and Louisiana Cajun country, the cooking from those remarkable areas has had a considerable influence on Mother's kitchen. This is her interpretation of a simple but delicious Creole classic.

$^2\!/_3$ cup all-purpose flour
Salt and black pepper to taste
1 tablespoon chili powder
2 whole chicken breasts, split in half
$^1\!/_2$ cup vegetable oil
1 large onion, finely chopped
$^1\!/_2$ large green bell pepper, seeded and cut into thin strips
1 garlic clove, minced
$^2\!/_3$ cup long-grain rice
One 12-ounce can crushed tomatoes

In a heavy brown paper bag, combine the flour, salt, pepper, and chili powder and shake till well blended. Add the chicken pieces, shake till well dredged, and place on a plate.

Preheat the oven to 350°F.

In a large, heavy skillet, heat the oil over moderate heat, add the chicken, brown on both sides, and transfer the pieces back to the plate. Add the onion, bell pepper, garlic, and rice to the skillet, stir well, and cook, stirring, till slightly browned, about 4 minutes. Add the tomatoes and their juice, season with salt and pepper, and stir well.

Arrange the chicken in a casserole or baking dish, spoon the rice and tomato mixture on top, cover tightly with aluminum foil, and bake 1 hour.

Yield: 4 servings

Chicken and Rice with Tomatoes

Of the multiple ways Mother has come up with to utilize leftover chicken, this is probably her favorite. Typically, she would serve the dish with spiced baked apple slices and angel biscuits.

3 tablespoons vegetable oil
1 large onion, sliced
1½ large green bell peppers, seeded and cut into thin strips
2 cups fresh chicken stock (page 55)
¼ cup cornstarch
3 tablespoons soy sauce
1 small can water chestnuts, drained and sliced
2 cups bite-size pieces cooked chicken
3 medium-size ripe tomatoes, cut into small wedges
Salt and black pepper to taste
3 cups hot cooked long-grain rice

In a large saucepan, heat the oil, then add the onion and bell peppers and cook over moderate heat 3 minutes, stirring. In a bowl, combine the stock and cornstarch, stir till well blended, add to the onions and peppers, and cook till the mixture thickens, stirring. Add the soy sauce, water chestnuts, and chicken, stir gently, and heat well. Just before serving, add the tomatoes and salt and pepper, stir gently till well heated, and serve over hot rice.

Yield: 4 to 6 servings

Missy's Sacred Home-Style Chicken Pie

This is the exact same chicken pie that my grandmother made for Mother and her brother and sister when they were children and the one that my sister and I grew up preparing. So beloved is the dish that when twenty-five relatives got together some years ago to celebrate my Unca' Nalle's birthday, nothing would do but for "Missy" to bake two gigantic chicken pies as the main dish on a ceremonial buffet that would have made any Southerner proud.

One 3½-pound chicken, cut up
1 medium-size onion, quartered
2 celery ribs (leaves included), each broken into 3 pieces
Salt and black pepper to taste
Double recipe Basic Pie Shell (page 234)
2 medium-size carrots, scraped, cut into thin rounds, and blanched 5 minutes in
    boiling water
1 cup fresh or frozen green peas
2 tablespoons butter, melted

Place the chicken pieces in a large pot and add the onion, celery, salt, and pepper. Add enough water to cover, bring to a boil, reduce the heat to low, cover, and simmer 30 minutes. With a slotted spoon, transfer the chicken to a cutting board and, when cool enough to handle, bone, cut the meat into bite-size pieces, and set aside. Strain the stock and set aside.

On a lightly floured surface, roll out half the pastry about ⅛ inch thick and line the bottom and sides of an 8 x 10-inch casserole or baking dish with it. Roll out the remaining pastry about ⅛ inch thick and cut half of it into 1-inch-wide strips, reserving the other half for the top of the pie.

Preheat the oven to 350°F.

Arrange half the chicken pieces over the bottom of the casserole, arrange half the carrots and peas over the chicken, and top with the pastry strips. Arrange the remaining chicken, carrots, and peas on top of the strips, season with salt and pepper, and pour enough reserved stock to almost cover the top layer. Fit the remaining pastry over the top of the pie, pressing down the edges and trimming off the excess. Brush the top with the melted butter and bake till the top is golden brown, 30 to 40 minutes.

Yield: 6 servings

Low Country Chicken Hash

Following an age-old custom in the stately homes of Charleston and Savannah, Mother likes to feature this chicken hash served in her elegant silver chafing dish at small wedding receptions, at one of her ladies auxiliary meetings, and on

Sunday brunch buffets. She is adamant about using only a well-aged, flavorful hen for this dish and will go from market to market till she finds just the right bird. "There's no way you can make a great hash with plain supermarket chicken," she insists. "Not only is the meat bland by comparison, but nothing equals the stock you get by slowly simmering a tough old hen."

One 4- to 5-pound hen, cut up
4 medium-size carrots, scraped and sliced
1 bay leaf
2 teaspoons salt
Black pepper to taste
6 tablespoons (¾ stick) butter
6 tablespoons all-purpose flour
1 cup half-and-half
½ pound fresh mushrooms, sliced
¼ teaspoon paprika
¼ cup Madeira
8 to 10 pieces toast

Wash the chicken pieces thoroughly, place in a large pot with enough water to cover, and add the carrots, bay leaf, salt, and pepper. Bring to a boil, reduce the heat to low, cover, and simmer till the chicken is tender, 3 to 4 hours, adding more water if necessary. Transfer the chicken to a work surface, strain the stock and discard the solids, and reserve 3 cups of the stock.

Clean the chicken meat from the bones and cut into bite-size pieces. In the top of a double boiler, melt the butter, add the flour, and stir till smooth. Gradually add the reserved chicken stock and stir till thickened. Add the half-and-half, mushrooms, paprika, and Madeira, stir, and taste for seasoning. Fold the chicken pieces into the cream sauce, heat thoroughly, and transfer to a heated chafing dish.

Serve the hash on top of toast.

Yield: 8 to 10 servings

Country Club Chicken Livers

Mother can't remember exactly where she got this recipe, but since one of her favorite lunches with her old friend Margaret at the Myers Park Country Club in Charlotte was always chicken livers on toast and an avocado salad, she figures that at some point she must have had words with the chef. "Of course, I have to be careful when I'm thinking about serving the dish at bridge club or a Charity League get-together since there are some Southern ladies who simply will not touch chicken livers. Ridiculous but true."

¼ cup (½ stick) butter
1 pound chicken livers, trimmed well and cut into bite-size pieces
1 medium-size onion, finely chopped
½ pound fresh mushrooms, sliced
1 teaspoon all-purpose flour
Salt and black pepper to taste
2 large ripe tomatoes, peeled and chopped
⅔ cup dry white wine
½ teaspoon Worcestershire sauce
2 teaspoons chopped fresh parsley
Toast points

In a medium-size skillet, melt the butter, then add the chicken livers and cook over moderate heat, stirring, till slightly browned, about 5 minutes, and drain on paper towels. Add the onion and mushrooms to the drippings and stir till the onion is golden. Add the flour, salt, and pepper and stir till well blended. Add the tomatoes and their juice, the wine, Worcestershire, and parsley and bring to a boil. Reduce the heat to low and simmer about 10 minutes, stirring. Add the chicken livers, stir, simmer about 5 minutes, and serve over toast points.

Yield: 4 servings

Roast Turkey with Cornbread Dressing and Giblet Gravy

The preparation of holiday turkey, dressing, and gravy has always been a religious experience in Mother's kitchen, so much so that when even her celebrated cooking buddy Craig Claiborne once bothered her in East Hampton while she was making her sacred gravy, she simply turned to him and, to the amazement of all, pronounced "Craig, honey, if you don't get out of my kitchen this instant, there's not going to be any Thanksgiving dinner." When it comes to this ritual meal, nobody interferes with her work, questions, or criticizes the way she's been cooking turkey and dressing for well over half a century. There are no shortcuts, but once you've followed her directions and technique to the letter, you'll understand why Mother's turkey dinner is legend in and out of the South.

For the gravy

Giblets from a 15- to 17-pound turkey
1/4 cup all-purpose flour
Salt and black pepper to taste

For the turkey

One 15- to 17-pound turkey
Salt and black pepper to taste
4 slices bacon

For the dressing

2 cups chopped onion
2 cups chopped celery
1/2 cup (1 stick) butter
4 cups finely crumbled toasted bread
4 cups finely crumbled cornbread (page 222)
1 tablespoon salt
2 teaspoons black pepper
1 tablespoon dried sage
2 teaspoons poultry seasoning
Turkey giblet broth
4 large eggs, beaten

Place the turkey giblets in a large saucepan with at least 3½ cups of water, bring to a boil, reduce the heat to low, cover, and simmer 45 minutes.

To cook the turkey, preheat the oven to 300°F. Season the turkey inside and out with salt and pepper and position breast side up on a rack in a large roasting pan. Drape the bacon slices over the breast and legs, pour about 1 cup of water into the pan, cover, and cook 2¾ hours, basting from time to time. Remove the cover and roast till the turkey is golden, 15 to 20 minutes longer. Transfer to a large platter and cover loosely with a piece of aluminum foil till ready to carve.

While the turkey is cooking, transfer the cooked giblets to a chopping board, chop coarsely, and chill till ready to make the gravy, reserving the broth in the pan. Start the dressing by combining the onions, celery, and butter in a large saucepan, adding enough water to cover, and simmering the mixture till the vegetables are very tender, about 1 hour.

About 20 minutes before the turkey finishes roasting, combine the toasted bread and cornbread in a large bowl and mix. Add the onions and celery plus their cooking liquid, the salt, pepper, sage, and poultry seasoning, and mix thoroughly. Using a bulb baster, add just enough turkey giblet broth to make a very moist mixture, then stir in the eggs and scrape the dressing into a large greased baking pan or dish.

When the turkey is finished roasting, increase the oven to 400°F and bake the dressing till nicely browned, 30 to 40 minutes.

To make the gravy, drain off and reserve all but a small amount of drippings from the pan the turkey was roasted in, then place the pan over moderately high heat and let the drippings brown till nearly burned, scraping the pan occasionally.

Martha Pearl Says:

"Years ago, when I watched my turkeys being killed and dressed right on a farm outside Charlotte, I would never have dreamed of using a frozen bird. But today I really prefer the frozen since I just don't trust those "fresh" turkeys lying around in meat counters. Nor do I ever stuff my dressing inside the turkey. Not only is it wet and gummy but it can be unsafe if not handled right."

Start adding about ¹/₂ cup of the reserved drippings, letting them brown and again stirring and scraping. Repeat till all the drippings are used and the liquid in the pan is very dark. Add enough water to the cooking liquid from the giblets to equal 5 cups and add about half this mixture to the liquid in the pan, stirring and scraping. Add the flour to the remaining liquid, mix gradually, and add to the liquid in the pan, stirring well till the gravy is thickened. Strain the gravy through a medium-size sieve into a large saucepan and stir in the chopped giblets. Season with salt and pepper, heat till very hot, and pour the gravy into a sauceboat.

To serve, carve the turkey, cut the dressing into squares and place on a platter, and pass the gravy to be spooned over the turkey and dressing.

Yield: 8 to 10 servings

Turkey Hash Cakes

This is one of numerous ways that Mother has been using up leftover holiday turkey for as long as I can remember. I personally think the cakes take on a whole new dimension when about 2 teaspoons of curry powder are added to the mixture, but, with her lack of enthusiasm for any curried dish, Mother disagrees.

2 medium-size potatoes, peeled, boiled in water to cover till very tender, drained, and chopped
¹/₂ cup (1 stick) butter, cut into pieces
3 cups chopped cooked turkey
¹/₂ cup chopped onions
¹/₂ cup seeded and chopped green bell peppers
¹/₄ cup chopped celery
3 large eggs, 2 of them beaten together
¹/₂ cup heavy cream
1¹/₂ teaspoons salt
Black pepper to taste
³/₄ cup all-purpose flour
2 cups pulverized plain bread crumbs
4 to 5 tablespoons vegetable oil

Place the potatoes in a large mixing bowl and mash with a heavy fork. Add half the butter and mash till it is completely absorbed.

In a blender, grind the turkey, onions, bell peppers, and celery to a medium texture and transfer to a large bowl. Add the whole egg to the mixture and stir till well blended. Add the mashed potatoes, cream, salt, and pepper and beat till smooth. Cover the bowl and chill about 30 minutes to firm up the texture and allow the flavors to blend. Shape the hash into oval cakes, dust each evenly in the flour, dip into the beaten eggs, roll in the bread crumbs, and chill 30 minutes.

Melt the remaining butter with the oil in a large, heavy skillet over moderate heat and cook the cakes on both sides till golden brown.

Yield: 4 to 6 servings

Smothered Quail with Grapes

Mother still remembers the bags of fresh quail that friends would bring to my grandmother and granddaddy during hunting season, and it was always a special occasion when Maw Maw would place a big platter of fried quail surrounded by wild rice and chutney on the table. Once she herself began serious cooking, however, it didn't take Mother long to realize how much moister the small birds were if baked or braised instead of fried, the result being this classic dish that she likes to serve with wild rice and pickled peaches at "fancy" dinners. The frozen quail now widely available in markets are just fine, but do remember that you need two birds per person.

¾ cup (1½ sticks) butter
12 quail, dressed and oven-ready
12 slices bacon
5 tablespoons all-purpose flour
2 cups fresh chicken stock (page 55)
1 cup dry sherry
1 teaspoon Worcestershire sauce
Salt and black pepper to taste
1 cup halved seedless green grapes
12 slices toast

In a large, heavy skillet, melt the butter, then add the quail and brown lightly over moderate heat on all sides, taking care not to overcrowd the pan. Transfer the quail to a platter and, when cool enough to handle, wrap each securely with a slice of bacon. Arrange the quail evenly in a large baking dish.

Preheat the oven to 350°F.

Add the flour to the skillet and stir over moderate heat till smooth. Gradually add the stock and sherry and stir till slightly thickened. Add the Worcestershire, salt, and pepper and stir. Pour the sauce over the quail, cover the dish with aluminum foil, and bake 30 minutes, basting occasionally. Add the grapes and bake 10 minutes longer.

Serve the quail on toast topped with grapes and a little sauce.

Yield: 6 servings

Roasted Stuffed Wild Duck

Duck hunting has always been a favorite Southern sport, and although my family has never shot birds of any variety, Mother never refused the braces of dressed mallards and teals offered us by friends. Today you really have to search far and wide to find wild ducks in this country (unlike in Great Britain and France), but anybody who's ever tasted roasted mallard never forgets the unique experience. Unfortunately, it's really not worth fooling with mallards and teals that don't weigh at least two pounds, so if you're not successful with friendly hunters or butchers, remember that this stuffing works just as well with a 4½- to 5-pound domesticated bird.

Three 2-pound mallards or teals, dressed
Salt and black pepper to taste
2 medium-size onions, chopped
2 celery ribs, chopped
1 large orange, peeled, seeded, and chopped
3 tablespoons bourbon
¼ cup (½ stick) butter
¼ cup bacon grease
Pickled peaches (page 292) for garnish

Preheat the oven to 400°F.

Rinse the ducks thoroughly, dry with paper towels, and season inside and out with salt and pepper. In a bowl, combine the onions, celery, orange, and bourbon, toss well, and fill the cavity of each bird with the mixture. Close the openings and secure the neck skin to the back with skewers and place the ducks on their sides on a rack in a shallow roasting pan. In a small saucepan, melt the butter and bacon grease together, brush each duck with some of the mixture, and roast 15 minutes. Turn the ducks on their other sides, brush with more fat, and roast 15 minutes longer. Reduce the oven to 375°F, turn the ducks breast side up, brush again, and roast till the juices run clear, about 40 minutes longer, basting from time to time.

Transfer the ducks to a work surface, remove the skewers, discard the stuffing, and split each bird in half lengthwise with a cleaver or heavy sharp knife.

Arrange the ducks on a heated platter and garnish the edges with pickled peaches.

Yield: 4 to 6 servings

Fried Rabbit with Cream Gravy

Of all Mother's memories of childhood, none is warmer than that of a certain Mrs. Norwood, who would come by the house once a week in a small truck loaded with fresh butter, eggs, chickens, vegetables, berries, and, best of all, fat rabbits. "I can see Mama now," she remembers, "checking those rabbits and watching like a hawk as Mrs. Norwood weighed them on the hanging scale. Then, that day we'd feast on fried rabbit with wonderful smooth cream gravy that we'd sop up with biscuits. It was always such a treat for us children."

1¼ cups all-purpose flour
½ cup cornmeal
Salt and black pepper to taste
1 cup lard or vegetable shortening
Two 3-pound rabbits, dressed and cut into serving pieces
1 cup buttermilk
1 cup fresh chicken stock (page 55)
1½ cups milk

In a brown paper bag, combine 1 cup of the flour, the cornmeal, salt, and pepper and shake vigorously. Heat the lard in a very large cast-iron skillet till moderately hot, or to 325°F in an electric skillet. Dip the rabbit pieces in batches into the buttermilk, dredge by shaking in the paper bag, and brown evenly on all sides in the fat. Make sure not to crowd the pieces in the skillet. Reduce the heat slightly and continue to cook, turning frequently with tongs, till the rabbit is tender, about 45 minutes. Drain the rabbit on another brown paper bag.

Pour off all but about 3 teaspoons of the fat from the skillet, add the remaining ¼ cup flour, and stir over moderate heat till smooth, scraping up drippings from the bottom. Add the stock and milk, season with salt and pepper, and stir constantly till the gravy is thickened.

Serve the rabbit on a platter and pass the gravy separately.

Yield: 6 to 8 servings

Carolina Rabbit Stew

In addition to the various foods that grandmother Maw Maw would purchase each week off Mrs. Norwood's truck, Mother tells us how her daddy knew an old black farmer who would occasionally stop by the house with a big washtub of dressed rabbits covered with ice. Never one to turn down fresh rabbit, Paw Paw asked the man one day how he made rabbit stew, only to learn that you toss the cut-up rabbit into a pot with water, a chunk of cooking meat, a few chopped vegetables, and salt and pepper and simmer it till tender. Needless to say, as the years passed, Mother learned to refine the stew considerably.

8 slices bacon, finely chopped
One 5-pound rabbit, dressed and cut into serving pieces
Salt and black pepper to taste
½ cup all-purpose flour
2 medium-size onions, finely chopped
1 garlic clove, finely chopped
1 cup dry red wine
1 cup fresh chicken stock (page 55)
2 tablespoons brandy

1 teaspoon currant jelly
1 bay leaf
¼ teaspoon dried rosemary
¼ teaspoon dried thyme

In a large, heavy casserole, fry the bacon till crisp, drain on paper towels, crumble, and set the casserole aside.

Wash the rabbit, pat dry, salt and pepper it, and dust lightly in the flour. Over moderate heat, brown the rabbit on all sides in the casserole, transfer the pieces to a plate, and pour off all but 2 tablespoons of the fat. Reduce the heat slightly, add the onions and garlic, and cook 2 minutes, stirring. Add the wine and stock, stir in the brandy, jelly, and herbs, then return the rabbit to the casserole. Add the crumbled bacon, cover, and simmer over low heat till the rabbit is fork-tender, about 1½ hours.

Yield: 4 to 6 servings

7
Seafood

The Pawleys Island Inn
Restaurant and Bar

CRAB CAKES

1 Lb. Fresh Cooked Lump Crabmeat
1 C. Homemade or Good Quality Mayonaisse
1 1/2 Tbs. Extra-Fine Cracker Meal
Large Pinch Cayenne Pepper
1/8 Tsp. Ground Celery Seed
1/8 Tsp. Colemans Dry Mustard
1/4 Tsp. Lemon Juice
1 Egg White
1 1/4 C. Fresh Bread Crumbs (made from five (5) slices fresh white bread
        with crusts removed)

Mix all ingredients (except crabmeat) in a small mixing bowl taking care to
avoid lumps. Carefully pick crabmeat free of shells without breaking up the
nice large pieces. Gently fold crabmeat into mayonnaise mixture. Divide
and form the mixture into six (6) equal patties rolling carefully in the fresh
bread crumbs. Refrigerate one (1) hour before cooking. Just before cooking
re-roll in the fresh bread crumbs.

Heat a ten (10) inch skillet or saute pan with six (6) tbs. of clarified butter.
When hot add crabcakes and saute gently for two (2) minutes. Carefully
turn and continue sauteeing for two (2) additional minutes. Remove with
spatula and place crab cakes on absorbent paper towels for a few seconds
to drain. Place on a warm serving platter, serve with plenty of lemon wedges
melted butter and tartar sauce.

Variation: Replace the crabmeat with cooked an
adding a few drops each of tabasco and worches
receipe into wonderfully spicey Pawleys Island C

(803) 237-9033
Post Office Box 567 • Pawleys Island, S

About 15 years ago, when Mother, Daddy, and I were once again eating our way through the South Carolina Low Country, Mother proclaimed Louis Osteen's crab cakes at The Pawleys Island Inn the best she'd ever tasted and talked and talked him into sending the recipe. She simply stuck it into her recipe book.

My sister, Hootie, at home in Charlotte not long before her marriage—no doubt testing the fine points of one of her many seafood concoctions learned from Mother at an early age.

Unlike many landbound Southerners, much of my family's life has been spent either living or vacationing regularly along the coasts of North Carolina, South Carolina, and Georgia, the result of which has been a preponderance of fish and shellfish dishes first in my Georgia grandmother's and grandfather's kitchen repertory and next in my mother's and sister's. As children, Hootie and I (like our mother before us) were taught how to surf-fish for blues, spots, and flounder, string-fish for blue crabs, and troll for Spanish mackerel and the large gray shrimp found in Carolina waters; and after Hootie got married and moved to Wilmington, not a summer passed that Mother, Daddy, and I didn't head eastward in June to deep-sea fish, go crabbing, participate in the local oyster roasts, and, of course, roam from one seafood restaurant and shack to the next (usually collecting new recipes). Today, our passion for great seafood remains undiminished, and when Mother and Hootie aren't scouting with me the docks and restaurants of Montauk in summer, we're casting for blues in October somewhere along the Carolina coasts.

One important thing to remember is that we, like most Southerners, had just as soon not eat seafood unless it is impeccably fresh, simply prepared, and served with little more than coleslaw and piping-hot hush puppies. The idea of Mother purchasing a whole flounder or a pound of crabmeat without sniffing it carefully for freshness, for instance, is about as silly as her destroying the natural sweet subtlety of oysters or Spanish mackerel by serving either with some alien sauce. Southerners might not be the most creative seafood cooks, but from the finest homes of Louisiana to the fried-seafood houses of Myrtle Beach, South Carolina, they know plenty about quality and flavor.

The Pines Crab Imperial

When I was a starving student at the University of North Carolina at Chapel Hill and Mother and Daddy would come up to visit, it was a real treat when they would take me to a restaurant called The Pines for this rich, inimitable crab imperial consumed with no more than a tossed salad and homemade yeast rolls. After I had raved and raved over the dish, Mother finally asked the owners for the formula, which appears here exactly as it was given and transferred to her disorganized but sacred recipe book. Nothing makes a more elegant luncheon dish, and we serve it often during the early summertime around the pool in East Hampton.

1 pound fresh lump crabmeat, picked over for shells
1 cup homemade (page 305) or Hellmann's mayonnaise
1 tablespoon fresh lemon juice
1 teaspoon Worcestershire sauce
Salt and freshly ground black pepper to taste
Fine dry bread crumbs
¼ cup (½ stick) butter, melted
Lemon wedges, seeded

Preheat the oven to 375°F.

"Put the crabmeat in a large bowl and add the mayonnaise, lemon juice, Worcestershire, salt, and pepper. Mix everything gently with your hands, lifting the crabmeat up and down in the air the way a child lifts soapsuds to play with them (this motion separates the mixture in such a way that the crabmeat has the airy quality of a soufflé). Divide equal handfuls of the mixture among four oven-proof seafood shells and sprinkle the top of each with a few bread crumbs. Now drizzle some of the butter over the tops and place the shells on a heavy baking sheet. Bake them up 15 to 20 minutes, till just lightly browned and crusty on top but not at all burned. Serve with lemon wedges for people to squeeze on top."

Yield: 4 servings

Deviled Crab

Here, in her exact words, are Mother's reminiscences about this old family recipe: "When we went to the beach as young children, Mama and Daddy would take Jane and I and Nalle to the little inlets near the cottage and we would 'crab' by tying a piece of chicken or meat on a string, throwing it out in the water, and when a crab would grab it, pulling it in very gently, scraping it up with a net, and dropping it into a bucket of water. Mama cooked them, but it was our job to pick out the meat. We didn't like this part, but how we loved these delicious deviled crabs she fixed."

3 tablespoons butter
2 tablespoons all-purpose flour

1 cup half-and-half
1 small red bell pepper, seeded and finely chopped
2 green onions (part of tops included), finely chopped
1 pound fresh lump crabmeat, picked over for shells
2 hard-boiled eggs, minced
½ teaspoon dry mustard
2 teaspoons Worcestershire sauce
2 teaspoons fresh lemon juice
¼ teaspoon Tabasco sauce
¼ teaspoon cayenne pepper
1 teaspoon salt
1 cup fine dry bread crumbs
3 tablespoons butter, melted

Preheat the oven to 375°F.

In a saucepan, melt the butter, then add the flour and stir over moderate heat for 2 minutes. Gradually add the half-and-half, stirring till smooth. Add the bell pepper and onions, stir about 3 minutes longer, and remove the pan from the heat.

Add the crabmeat, eggs, mustard, Worcestershire, lemon juice, Tabasco, cayenne, and salt and stir gently but thoroughly to blend well. Spoon equal parts of the mixture into four greased ovenproof seafood shells or ramekins, sprinkle the top of each with ¼ cup of the bread crumbs, drizzle melted butter on top, and bake till bubbly and golden, about 15 minutes.

Yield: 4 servings

Pawleys Island Crab Cakes

Some years ago, when my parents and I were dining at the Pawleys Island Restaurant on Pawleys Island, South Carolina, Mother was so taken with Louis Osteen's crab cakes that she not only asked for the recipe but virtually demanded that the chef take her back to the kitchen to show her exactly how he fixed them. As he worked, Louis (who now owns Louis's Charleston Grill down in Charleston) explained that "procuring the blue crab locally varies from the efficient and easy trap method, to the common method using nut, string, and chicken necks, to the most basic and skillful method of 'bogging' whereby you simply wade through the marsh creeks and scoop up the crustaceans." Having "crabbed" in the Low Country throughout much of her youth, Mother listened patiently before relating plenty of anecdotes about the second method.

1 cup homemade (page 305) or Hellmann's mayonnaise
1½ tablespoons extra-fine cracker crumbs
Large pinch cayenne pepper
⅛ teaspoon ground celery seeds
⅛ teaspoon dry mustard
¼ teaspoon fresh lemon juice
1 large egg white
1 pound fresh lump crabmeat, picked over for shells
1¼ cups fine dry bread crumbs
6 tablespoons (¾ stick) butter
Lemon wedges for garnish

In a large mixing bowl, combine the mayonnaise, cracker crumbs, cayenne, celery seeds, mustard, lemon juice, and egg white and mix till thoroughly blended. Gently fold the crabmeat into the mayonnaise mixture, taking care not to break up lumps. Divide the mixture into six equal portions, form each portion into a patty, and gently roll the patties in half the bread crumbs. Refrigerate the patties for 1 hour, then roll lightly in the remaining bread crumbs once more before cooking.

In a 10-inch heavy skillet, melt the butter, then add the crab cakes and cook 2 minutes on each side over moderately low heat, taking care not to burn. Drain the cakes momentarily on paper towels, transfer to a heated platter, and serve immediately with lemon wedges.

Yield: 6 servings as an appetizer, 3 servings as a main course

Hot Seafood Shroup

My sister got this recipe from a boat captain's wife she befriended for years in Wilmington, North Carolina, and when there's a large group to be fed, both Mother and Hootie often turn to the tasty seafood concoction that people always gobble up quickly.

10 slices white bread
1 pound fresh shrimp, shelled and deveined
$\frac{1}{2}$ pound fresh crabmeat, picked over for shells
$\frac{1}{2}$ cup homemade (page 305) or Hellmann's mayonnaise
1 medium-size onion, diced
1 medium-size green bell pepper, seeded and diced
2 celery ribs, diced
Black pepper to taste
3 cups milk
4 large eggs
Two 10$\frac{3}{4}$-ounce cans condensed cream of mushroom soup
$\frac{3}{4}$ cup grated sharp cheddar cheese
Paprika to taste

Cut 5 slices of the bread into dice and spread over the bottom of a large baking dish. Scatter the shrimp and crabmeat on top. In a bowl, combine the mayonnaise, onion, bell pepper, celery, and pepper and mix till well blended, then spread the mixture over the seafood. Trim and discard the crusts from the remaining bread, cut the bread into dice, and spread over the mayonnaise mixture. In a bowl, beat together the milk and eggs, pour over the bread, cover the dish with plastic wrap, and refrigerate overnight.

Preheat the oven to 325°F.

Spoon the soup evenly over the mixture and bake 1 hour. Remove the dish from the oven, sprinkle the cheese and paprika on top, and bake 15 minutes longer. Serve the shroup directly from the baking dish.

Yield: 8 to 10 servings

Low Country Boil

Throughout the coastal South, a "boil" refers to any number of ingredients that are quickly boiled in highly seasoned broth and consumed country-style on big wooden tables by lots of people. Mother and I have attended crab boils on Maryland's Chesapeake Bay, crawfish boils in western Louisiana, a snapper boil outside Vero Beach, Florida, and, mostly, Carolina Low Country boils featuring both seafood and other ingredients. To be sure, this is messy business, but, my, is it good eating, especially outside on a summer day.

⅓ cup Old Bay seasoning (available in most supermarkets)
3 pounds small new potatoes, skins on and lightly scrubbed
1 pound smoked sausage (such as kielbasa), cut into 1-inch slices
5 ears fresh corn, shucked and broken in half
3 pounds fresh large shrimp
Cocktail Sauce (page 308)

Fill a stockpot or large, deep baking pan half full of water, add the Old Bay seasoning, and bring to a boil. Add the potatoes and sausage and cook 15 minutes, maintaining the boil. Add the corn and shrimp, return the liquid to a boil, and cook 5 minutes. With a slotted spoon, transfer the potatoes, sausage, corn, and shrimp to a large serving platter and serve the boil with plenty of napkins and cocktail sauce on the side.

Yield: 10 servings

Shrimp Bog

One of the most gracious ladies we ever encountered on our many visits to Savannah was the mother of the well-known New York publicist Bobby Zarem. A true Southern grande dame in the old tradition, Mrs. Zarem knew as much about Low Country cooking as her gifted black cook, and one morning we sat fascinated as she explained how "bog" ("wetland") was a local culinary term referring to any dish that includes "wet, soggy rice." Unlike in a pilau, the rice in a bog should be very moist.

½ pound sliced bacon, finely diced
1½ cups long-grain white rice
2 medium-size onions, finely chopped
2¼ cups fresh chicken stock (page 55)
3 medium-size ripe tomatoes, peeled and finely chopped

2 teaspoons fresh lemon juice
1½ teaspoons Worcestershire sauce
1 teaspoon salt
¾ teaspoon ground nutmeg
¼ teaspoon black pepper
¼ teaspoon cayenne pepper
2 pounds fresh medium-size shrimp, shelled and deveined
¼ cup minced fresh parsley

Preheat the oven to 350°F.

In a large, heavy skillet, fry the bacon till crisp over moderate heat, then drain on paper towels, crumble, and reserve 3 tablespoons of the grease.

In a fine sieve, rinse the rice well under cold running water and drain.

In a large ovenproof casserole, heat the reserved bacon grease, then add the onions and cook 3 minutes over moderate heat, stirring. Add the rice and stir well. Add the stock, tomatoes, lemon juice, Worcestershire, salt, nutmeg, and black and cayenne peppers, bring to a boil, cover, and bake 20 minutes. Stir in the crumbled bacon and the shrimp and continue baking, uncovered, 15 minutes. Remove the casserole from the oven and let stand 10 minutes. Stir the bog with a fork, taste for seasoning, and sprinkle the parsley on top.

Yield: 6 servings

Shrimp Pie

Once, when I was on assignment to do a food article on the Carolina and Georgia Low Country and was joined in Charleston by Mother and Daddy, members of the Junior League prepared for us an incredible buffet of local specialities at someone's beach cottage that included this delectable shrimp pie. Needless to say, Mother had already learned how to make the pie before I even had a chance to ask the hostess for the recipe, and it's been a luncheon staple in her kitchen and mine ever since.

2½ cups fresh bread crumbs (about 5 slices dry white bread)
1 cup milk
6 tablespoons (¾ stick) butter, melted
1 small onion, minced
½ medium-size green bell pepper, seeded and minced
1 tablespoon Dijon mustard
1 tablespoon Worcestershire sauce
1 tablespoon dry sherry
Tabasco sauce to taste
Salt and black pepper to taste
1½ pounds fresh medium-size shrimp, shelled and deveined

Preheat the oven to 350°F.

In a large bowl, combine 2 cups of the bread crumbs with the milk and let soak.

In a small skillet, melt 2 tablespoons of the butter, then add the onion and bell pepper and cook over low heat 2 minutes, stirring. Add the vegetables to the soaked bread and stir. In a small saucepan, over moderate heat melt 2 more tablespoons of the butter with the bread mixture and stir. Add the mustard, Worcestershire, sherry, Tabasco, salt, and pepper and stir to blend thoroughly. Melt the remaining butter. Fold the shrimp into the mixture and transfer the mixture to a buttered casserole or baking dish. Distribute the remaining bread crumbs over the mixture, drizzle the melted butter on top, and bake till the top is golden, 25 to 30 minutes.

Yield: 4 to 6 servings

Baked Oyster and Mushroom Ramekins

1½ cups homemade (page 305) or Hellmann's mayonnaise
2 tablespoons Dijon mustard
1 small hot red pepper, seeded and minced
2 teaspoons fresh lemon juice
Salt and black pepper to taste
6 strips bacon
⅓ pound fresh mushrooms, finely chopped
16 fresh large oysters, shucked and drained
¾ cup grated Parmesan cheese

In a bowl, combine the mayonnaise, mustard, red pepper, lemon juice, salt, and pepper, and set aside.

In a large skillet, fry the bacon till crisp, drain on paper towels, and crumble. Pour off all but 2 tablespoons of the bacon grease from the skillet, add the mushrooms, and cook over low heat 2 minutes, stirring.

Preheat the oven to 375°F.

Butter the bottom and sides of four individual ramekins and place 4 oysters in each. Add equal amounts of mushrooms to each ramekin, then spoon on equal amounts of the mayonnaise mixture. Sprinkle crumbled bacon over each, sprinkle with the cheese, and bake till slightly puffy and the cheese begins to brown, 12 to 15 minutes.

Yield: 4 servings

Aunt Toots's Oyster and Almond Pie

Mother got this recipe from the wonderful aunt who nursed her first cousin whose own mother had died giving birth and who Mother always considered to be her brother since he was raised by my grandmother. I only faintly remember the old lady, but I recall clearly the lavish Southern feasts that Aunt Toots prepared on Sunday afternoons that went on for hours. Unca' Nalle himself passed on a couple of years ago, but I can still hear him asking his "sister," "Martha Pearl, when are you gonna fix me Aunt Toots' oyster pie and your buttermilk pie?"

$^{1}/_{2}$ cup slivered almonds
2 cups crushed soda crackers
$^{1}/_{4}$ teaspoon ground nutmeg
Salt and cayenne pepper to taste
1 quart freshly shucked oysters, liquor reserved
$^{1}/_{2}$ cup dry sherry
1 teaspoon Worcestershire sauce
$^{1}/_{4}$ cup ($^{1}/_{2}$ stick) butter, cut into small pieces
1 cup half-and-half

Preheat the oven to 300°F.

To toast the almonds, spread them evenly on a baking sheet and bake, stirring several times, till slightly browned, 10 to 15 minutes. Set aside.

In a bowl, combine the crackers, nutmeg, salt, and cayenne. In another bowl, mix together the reserved oyster liquor, sherry, and Worcestershire. In a 2-quart baking dish, arrange alternate layers of seasoned crackers and oysters, drizzling the oyster liquor mixture over each layer, dotting each layer with pieces of butter, and finishing with a layer of crackers dotted with butter. Pour the half-and-half around the sides and bake 20 minutes. Scatter the reserved almonds over the top, baste with a little of the cooking liquid, and bake till the top is nicely browned but the pie is still moist, about 10 minutes longer.

Yield: 6 servings

Martha Pearl Says:

"You must watch the timing of this dish very carefully. Even though it bakes at a slow 300°F, oven temperatures can vary dramatically, so keep a sharp eye to make sure the pie remains moist and the oysters don't overcook."

Tommy's Clam Fritters

Of all the recipes that Mother and our friend Tom Bernstein have exchanged in East Hampton, none has elicited such praise as the one for these clam fritters that he served as a first course one evening after they and two others had completed one of their bridge marathons. Mother also sometimes serves the fritters with cocktails.

½ cup all-purpose flour
1 teaspoon baking powder

Salt to taste
Cayenne pepper to taste
1 tablespoon finely chopped fresh dill or 1 teaspoon dried
1 cup canned baby clams, drained
2 large eggs, separated
Vegetable oil for frying
Tartar Sauce (page 308)

In a bowl, sift together the flour, baking powder, salt, and cayenne and stir in the dill. Add the clams and egg yolks and mix till well blended. In another bowl, beat the egg whites with an electric mixer till stiff but not dry peaks form and fold them into the clam mixture.

In a large skillet or electric fry pan, heat 1 inch of vegetable oil to 325°F or till a small piece of bread tossed in browns quickly. Drop the clam batter by tablespoons into the oil and cook till the fritters are browned, about 1 minute. With a slotted spoon, turn the fritters over and cook till the other sides are browned, 1 minute longer. Drain on paper towels and serve immediately with tartar sauce on the side.

Yield: 4 servings as a first course or with cocktails

Salmon Mousse with Dill Dressing

Mother has belonged to a lot of social clubs over the years, but surely none has been more gastronomically oriented than the group of 15 to 20 church members who meet periodically for a late breakfast in different homes on Sunday mornings. Typical of what she might serve at the "breakfast club" is this delicate salmon mousse, a dish that can be prepared well in advance and that also makes a very nice light summer lunch.

1 envelope unflavored gelatin
$\frac{1}{4}$ cup cold water
$\frac{1}{2}$ cup boiling water
$\frac{1}{2}$ cup homemade (page 305) or Hellmann's mayonnaise
1 tablespoon fresh lemon juice
1 tablespoon grated onion
$\frac{1}{4}$ teaspoon paprika
1 teaspoon salt
2 cups finely flaked poached salmon (or two 14$\frac{3}{4}$-ounce cans red salmon, drained and picked over for bones and skin)
$\frac{1}{2}$ cup heavy cream, whipped to firm peaks
1$\frac{1}{2}$ cups Dill Dressing (page 303)
Sprigs of watercress

In a bowl, dissolve the gelatin in the cold water, add the boiling water, stir till well dissolved, and set aside.

In a mixing bowl, combine the mayonnaise, lemon juice, onion, paprika, and salt, mix till well blended, and chill about 15 minutes. Add the gelatin and stir, then add the salmon and stir till blended. Fold in the whipped cream, scrape the mixture into a 2-quart fish mold, cover, and chill till firm.

To remove the mousse from the mold, dip the bottom of the mold in hot water for several seconds, then turn out the mousse onto a platter. Slice or spoon the mousse onto small serving plates, serve with the dill dressing on the side, and garnish the plates with watercress.

Yield: 6 to 8 servings

Dilled Salmon Croquettes

Salmon croquettes were a staple in our home when I was growing up, and I still love them as much as when Mother would serve them with Greek beans and garlic mashed potatoes on cold winter nights. Today she fixes them in any season, and while she believes firmly that canned pink salmon (the red is too expensive) has just the right texture for croquettes, I must say that some of the most flavorful were made with leftover fresh salmon that had either been poached or grilled. For an unorthodox but interesting variation, you might also add about ¼ cup freshly grated Parmesan to the mixture.

Two 14¾-ounce cans pink salmon, drained and picked over for skin and bones
Juice of 1 lemon
1 tablespoon dry mustard
¼ cup chopped fresh parsley
1 tablespoon chopped fresh chives
1 tablespoon chopped fresh dill
½ cup homemade (page 305) or Hellmann's mayonnaise
1 to 1½ cups fresh bread crumbs
¼ cup fresh chicken stock (if needed; page 55)
1 to 1½ cups Tartar Sauce (page 308)
Paprika
Fine dry bread crumbs for dredging
6 tablespoons (¾ stick) butter

In a large mixing bowl, combine the salmon, lemon juice, mustard, parsley, chives, dill, and mayonnaise and toss till the salmon is fully flaked and the mixture well blended. Add enough of the bread crumbs to tighten the mixture, then add enough chicken stock to produce a firm but moist consistency.

Using your hands, form the mixture into 8 to 10 oval croquettes and brush each on both sides with a little of the tartar sauce. Sprinkle each with paprika and roll lightly in the bread crumbs.

In a large, heavy skillet, melt the butter, then add the croquettes and cook over moderate heat till golden brown, 4 to 5 minutes on each side. Drain on paper towels. Keep the croquettes warm till ready to serve, and serve with a bowl of tartar sauce on the side, coleslaw, and hush puppies.

Yield: 4 to 5 servings

Aunt Saats' Oyster and Almond Pie

1 qt fresh oysters (save juice)
2 cups saltines, crushed
a little salt & cayenne pepper
dash nutmeg
½ cup dry sherry
1 teasp worchestu sauce
½ stick butter
1 cup ½ & ½ cream
½ " slivered toasted almonds

Combine saltines, nutmeg, salt and cayenne.
In 2 quart baking dish, put alternate layers of saltines and oysters. Drizzle oyster juice, sherry & worchestu over each layer. Dot each layer also with butter. Pour the ½ & ½ cream over top & around sides. Sprinkle almonds over top. baste with a small amount of oyster juice. Bake in 300° oven 10 - 15 minutes or until top is slightly browned but pie is not dry.
Serves 6 —

Broiled Spanish Mackerel

When my sister and her family had a cottage at Carolina Beach, North Carolina, some of our most exciting times were spent in my brother-in-law's large boat trolling for Spanish mackerel. We caught bluefish, pompano, flounder, mullet, and sea bass, but nothing thrilled Mother more than when the pull on her line was especially powerful and she could scream "It's a Spanish, a big Spanish." Back home, of course, it was she who always cleaned the fish, and since there is no sweeter, more flavorful fish in the ocean than Spanish mackerel, she would never hear of preparing it any other way than in this simple manner. Unfortunately, very little Spanish mackerel (like Louisiana redfish) ever makes its way outside the Southern market, but flounder and bass are excellent substitutes.

1½ cups fine dry bread crumbs
1 teaspoon salt
Freshly ground black pepper to taste
Four ½-pound Spanish mackerel fillets
½ lemon
¼ cup (½ stick) butter, cut into small pieces
Paprika to taste
Chopped fresh parsley for garnish

Preheat the oven broiler.

In a baking dish, combine the bread crumbs, salt, and pepper. Dredge the fish fillets lightly on both sides in the seasoned bread crumbs and arrange skin side down on a large broiling pan. Squeeze the lemon over each fillet, dot each with equal amounts of the butter, sprinkle lightly with paprika, and broil about 5 inches from the heat till golden but still moist, about 8 minutes. Sprinkle the fillets with parsley and serve immediately.

Yield: 4 servings

Fillet of Flounder with Shrimp-Tomato Sauce

E ast Coast Southerners love flounder almost as much as inhabitants of the Gulf states relish pompano and redfish, and while Mother and I both agree that there's no finer fish than a whole large flounder or Spanish mackerel (preferably one that we snag ourselves) simply broiled with butter and lemon, this is one of the many ways she prepares small to medium fillets when the tomatoes are ripe and the herb garden is at its summer peak.

½ cup (1 stick) butter
1 medium-size onion, diced
1 garlic clove, minced
½ pound fresh shrimp, shelled, deveined, and diced
2 large ripe tomatoes, peeled, seeded, and chopped
1 tablespoon finely chopped fresh basil
2 tablespoons finely chopped fresh parsley
Salt and black pepper to taste
1 large egg
½ cup milk
4 medium-size flounder fillets
¼ cup all-purpose flour
Sprigs of fresh parsley for garnish

In a heavy saucepan, melt half the butter, then add the onion and garlic and cook over low heat 2 minutes, stirring. Increase the heat to moderate, add the diced shrimp, tomatoes, basil, chopped parsley, salt, and pepper, stir well, and cook 10 minutes, stirring occasionally. Keep the sauce warm.

In a bowl, beat the egg with the milk, then dip the fish fillets into the mixture and dredge in the flour, tapping off any excess.

In a large skillet, melt the remaining butter, then add the fillets two at a time and cook on both sides over moderate heat till golden but still moist. Transfer the fish to a heated serving platter, spoon on the shrimp-tomato sauce, and garnish with parsley sprigs.

Yield: 4 servings

Greek-Style Baked Catfish with Vegetables

Remembering how I used to catch ugly old catfish from the Catawba River outside Charlotte, then watch my maternal grandfather clean and throw them on a grill, I snicker today when I see the farmed varieties displayed so elegantly in trendy Northern markets and fetching top dollar in restaurants around the country. Most Southerners have always preferred their catfish fried, but since both my father and his Greek father demanded a little more sophistication, Mother used to satisfy them by cooking first red mullet, then those sweet catfish in this manner.

3 tablespoons olive oil
1 medium-size onion, finely chopped
½ small green bell pepper, seeded and finely chopped
1 garlic clove, minced
1 small ripe tomato, chopped
2 tablespoons fresh lemon juice
Salt and black pepper to taste
Four 8-ounce catfish fillets
¼ pound feta cheese
2 tablespoons chopped fresh parsley

In a skillet, heat the olive oil, then add the onion, bell pepper, and garlic and cook over moderate heat about 5 minutes, stirring. Add the tomato, lemon juice, salt, and pepper, stir well, cook 5 minutes, and remove from the heat.

Preheat the oven to 350°F.

Arrange the catfish fillets in a baking dish, spoon the vegetable mixture over the top, crumble the feta over the vegetables, and bake till the fish flakes easily, 15 to 20 minutes. With a spatula, gently transfer the fish and vegetables to a heated platter and sprinkle the top with the parsley.

Yield: 4 servings

8
Casseroles

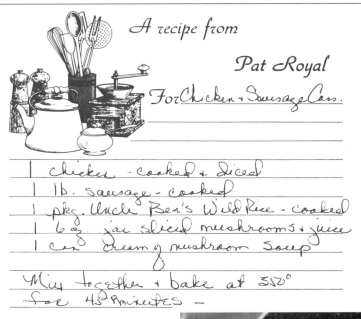

A recipe from

Pat Royal

For Chicken & Sausage Cass.

1 chicken - cooked & diced
1 lb. sausage - cooked
1 pkg. Uncle Ben's Wild Rice - cooked
1 6 oz. jar sliced mushrooms + juice
1 can cream of mushroom soup

Mix together + bake at 350°
for 45 minutes -

Today, my sister's casserole recipes are considerably more complex than this simple one she sent to Mother shortly after she was married. Like Mother, however, Hootie would never waste time explaining exactly how to deal with the chicken.

I'm looking on as Mother handpicks the fresh Silver Queen corn to be included in the sausage and vegetable casserole that one of our house guests in East Hampton has begged her to prepare for a Sunday evening supper.

Although casseroles of every food imaginable exist in cuisines all over the world, nowhere is this simple approach to cooking more popular than in the American South. The result, no doubt, of deprivation in Reconstruction days when entire families had to be fed on a minimum of available ingredients, the main-course casserole remains a major component of Southern cookery—as well as the butt of countless jokes by more sophisticated cooks gagged by haunting memories of tuna fish and cornflake casseroles and leaden macaroni and cheese in school cafeterias and at church benefits. Nothing is worse than a careless, insipid casserole thrown together primarily to utilize inferior ingredients; and nothing is better or more satisfying than the deftly conceived, sumptuous casseroles that Mother proudly served her large family while I was growing up and that she and my sister still prepare lovingly for all sorts of social, religious, and charity occasions.

More pretentious cooks today, of course, seem to relish ridiculing and condemning Southerners' liberal use of canned soups in making certain casseroles. At one time, I did too, until I began trying to reproduce some of Mother's creations and realized that my more refined substitutes for the liquid base simply never yielded the same tasty results. "Sometimes I do make my own cooking sauce," Mother informs, "but there are some clasic Southern casseroles that are just not right without the canned soup base—and I don't care what other people say. It's not a question of economy or laziness; it's a question of texture and flavor. Period."

Chicken and Broccoli Party Casserole

Half of Mother's recipes seem to have evolved over the years from her various bridge luncheons where she and other club members are forever preparing different dishes. After her friend Isabel introduced this casserole, everyone loved it so much that it was decided to serve it at a kitchen shower for the bride of one member's son; and some years later, it was this same casserole that my sister decided to include on a wedding brunch for her daughter. When I once criticized the canned soup in the recipe, Mother snapped "All real Southern cooks use canned soup in certain casseroles. Why don't you taste it before ridiculing?" I did; it was delicious. Later, I tried using chicken stock thickened with half-and-half, but, alas, what resulted was an altogether different (and inferior) dish. So much for "gourmet cooking."

1 large head broccoli, cut into florets
One 3-pound chicken, boiled in water to cover till cooked through, boned, and
    meat cut into 1-inch pieces
Fresh ground black pepper to taste
Two 10¾-ounce cans condensed cream of chicken soup
½ cup homemade (page 305) or Hellmann's mayonnaise
Juice of ½ lemon
1 cup grated extra-sharp cheddar cheese
1 cup storebought herb-seasoned bread stuffing
¼ cup (½ stick) butter, melted

Place the broccoli florets in a saucepan with ½ inch of water and bring to a boil.
Reduce the heat to low, cover, steam the florets 3 minutes, and drain.

Preheat the oven to 350°F.

Arrange the florets across the bottom of a flat, rectangular 2-quart casserole,
arrange the chicken pieces evenly over the top, and sprinkle with the pepper. In a
large bowl, combine the soup, mayonnaise, and lemon juice, stir well, and pour
over the chicken and broccoli. Sprinkle the cheese and herb stuffing evenly over
the top, drizzle with the melted butter, and bake till brown and bubbly, 25 to 30
minutes, making sure not to overcook. Serve hot.

Yield: 6 to 8 servings

Poppy Seed Chicken

Over the years, reciprocal cooking interests have been shared by each and every
member of our large extended family, as children and grandchildren have
grown up and married other Southerners, and all seem to have contributed something to Mother's kitchen repertory. She was first exposed to this simple casserole
when she once drove up to Raleigh to baby-sit a few days with her two great-
grandchildren and found the refrigerator full of prepared dishes so that she
wouldn't have to cook. She later got the recipe from her granddaughter-in-law,
Alice Royal, and has since shared it with other family members and friends.

6 chicken breast halves
One 10¾-ounce can condensed cream of chicken soup
1 cup sour cream
2 tablespoons fresh lemon juice
2 tablespoons poppy seeds, plus extra for topping
Salt and black pepper to taste
¼ pound (1 stack) Ritz crackers, crushed
½ cup (1 stick) margarine or butter, melted

Place the chicken breasts in a pot with enough water to cover, bring to a boil, reduce the heat to low, and cook till tender, about 20 minutes. With a slotted spoon, transfer the chicken to a plate and, when cool enough to handle, bone and skin the chicken, cut into bite-size pieces, and place in a mixing bowl.

Preheat the oven to 325°F.

Add the soup, sour cream, lemon juice, and poppy seeds to the chicken and mix till well blended. Transfer the mixture to a medium-size baking dish and spread the crackers over the top. Drizzle the margarine over the crackers, sprinkle poppy seeds liberally on top, and bake till bubbly and slightly browned on top, about 30 minutes.

Yield: 6 to 8 servings

Martha Pearl Says:

"This is one of a number of simple dishes I like to make for sick people, shut-ins, and bereaved friends. What I do is prepare the unbaked casserole in disposable aluminum pans and include instructions for cooking. That way, all that has to be done is to pop the casserole into the oven with no worry about having to return the container."

Chicken Tetrazzini

Named for the famous coloratura soprano Luisa Tetrazzini, who toured America in the early years of the century and had a prodigious appetite, this casserole is found in virtually every Southern cookbook published since the early fifties. There are some who say that it was created for the soprano in San Francisco, but given its overwhelming popularity in the South (plus Madame Tetrazzini's abundant praise for this style of food during her triumphant stay in Charleston, South Carolina), I'm convinced that its origins are in Dixie.

2 tablespoons butter
2 tablespoons all-purpose flour
1½ cups fresh chicken stock (page 55)
Salt and freshly ground black pepper to taste
1 cup milk
2 tablespoons dry sherry
3 cups bite-size pieces cooked chicken
8 ounces thin spaghetti, boiled according to package directions and drained
½ pound fresh mushrooms, sliced
½ cup toasted slivered almonds (page 38)
½ cup grated Parmesan cheese
Paprika to taste

In a saucepan, melt the butter, then add the flour and stir 1 minute over moderate heat. Add the stock, salt, and pepper and stir till thickened. Remove the pan from the heat, add the milk and sherry, and stir till well blended.

Martha Pearl Says:

"There are what I call two Chicken Tetrazzini schools: one in which the main ingredients are layered separately in the casserole, the other in which everything is mixed together. My daughter, who loves the dish, never layers her ingredients, but if I want my casserole to look particularly attractive on a formal buffet, I will make the extra effort. Either way, people in the South just love the dish."

Preheat the oven to 350°F.

In a large mixing bowl, combine the chicken, spaghetti, mushrooms, and almonds, pour on the sauce, and stir till well blended. Transfer the mixture to a large greased baking dish, sprinkle the cheese on top, sprinkle with paprika, and bake till nicely browned, 20 to 30 minutes.

Yield: 8 servings

Hot Chicken Salad

In many ways, this is the quintessential Southern casserole and one that Mother has been serving with congealed salads, hot rolls, and iced tea to bridge clubs since she was a young girl. It's also another dish that I once virtually destroyed by trying to substitute a fresh cream sauce for the canned soup. My sister, Hootie, thinks nothing of featuring the simple casserole at her fanciest Saturday lunches for her lady friends, and, personally, I love the dish.

2 cups diced cooked chicken
3 hard-boiled eggs, peeled and coarsely chopped
1 medium-size onion, finely chopped
2 celery ribs, finely chopped
$\frac{1}{2}$ cup toasted (page 38) sliced almonds
$\frac{1}{2}$ cup homemade (page 305) or Hellmann's mayonnaise
1 tablespoon fresh lemon juice
Salt and black pepper to taste
One 10$\frac{3}{4}$-ounce can condensed cream of chicken soup
2 cups crushed soda crackers
2 tablespoons butter, melted

Preheat the oven to 400°F.

In a large mixing bowl, combine the chicken, eggs, onion, celery, and almonds and toss till well blended. Add the mayonnaise, lemon juice, salt, pepper, and soup and mix thoroughly. Transfer to a casserole or baking dish, sprinkle on the crackers, drizzle over the butter, and bake till lightly browned, about 20 minutes.

Yield: 4 to 6 servings

Turkey Dressing Bake

For years, we used to attend the annual fund-raising bazaar at St. Martin's Episcopal Church in Charlotte, the highlight of which was always a huge luncheon buffet featuring numerous Southern dishes prepared by the church's old black cook. Nothing was more highly praised than Annie's turkey dressing bake, the recipe for which she once proudly agreed to share with Mother.

1¾ cups storebought herb-seasoned bread stuffing
1 small onion, finely chopped
1 celery rib, finely chopped
¼ teaspoon poultry seasoning
2 cups diced cooked turkey
¼ cup (½ stick) butter
¼ cup all-purpose flour
¼ teaspoon salt
¼ teaspoon black pepper
2 cups fresh chicken stock (page 55)
3 large eggs
Half of a 10¾-ounce can condensed cream of mushroom soup
¼ cup milk
½ cup sour cream
¼ cup chopped pimiento

In a bowl, combine the bread stuffing, onion, celery, and poultry seasoning, then sprinkle over the bottom of a medium-size baking dish. Place the diced turkey over the top.

Preheat the oven to 325°F.

In a saucepan, melt the butter over moderate heat, then add the flour, salt, and pepper and stir for 1 minute. Add the stock, stir until thickened, and remove from the heat. In a small bowl, beat the eggs and add a small amount of the hot stock, stirring constantly, then add the eggs to the stock, stirring constantly till well blended and smooth. Pour the sauce over the turkey and dressing and bake till custardy, about 45 minutes.

In another saucepan, combine the soup, milk, sour cream, and pimiento and stir over moderate heat till well blended and hot.

To serve, cut the turkey dressing into squares and top each portion with the pimiento sauce.

Yield: 6 servings

Turkey and Ham Supreme

Always in the extravagant old days (and quite often today), Mother thought nothing of cooking both a large ham *and* turkey for our holiday table since "we had so many people and some much preferred one meat over the other." Part of the leftovers, of course, went into her "supreme," a sumptuous casserole that my sister and I anticipated with almost more excitement than the original festive dinner. This is the ideal dish for cooks who like to experiment with different ingredients.

2 tablespoons butter
1 small onion, finely chopped
3 tablespoons all-purpose flour
$\frac{1}{2}$ teaspoon salt
$\frac{1}{4}$ teaspoon black pepper
$1\frac{1}{4}$ cups milk
$\frac{1}{4}$ pound fresh mushrooms, thinly sliced
One 5-ounce can water chestnuts, drained and sliced
2 cups diced cooked turkey
1 cup diced cooked ham
2 tablespoons dry sherry
$\frac{1}{2}$ cup shredded Swiss cheese
1 cup soft bread crumbs
3 tablespoons butter, melted

In a large skillet, melt the butter, then add the onion and cook over low heat, stirring, till glossy. Add the flour, salt, and pepper and stir about 1 minute. Gradually stir in the milk and cook until smooth and thickened, stirring constantly. Add the mushrooms, water chestnuts, turkey, ham, and sherry and stir well.

Preheat the oven to 400°F.

Scrape the mixture into a shallow, lightly greased 2-quart casserole and sprinkle the cheese on top. Sprinkle the bread crumbs over the cheese, drizzle the melted butter over the top, and bake till lightly browned, about 35 minutes.

Yield: 6 servings

Margaret's Ham and Cheese Soufflé

Mother got this recipe decades ago from her oldest childhood friend, Margaret Farr, who used to serve the soufflé at large parties with scooped-out orange halves stuffed with congealed fruit salad, hot rolls, blackberry cobbler, and pitchers of minted iced tea. What the casserole lacks in sophistication it makes up for in soul-warming flavor, and I've noticed that whenever Mother includes it on one of her sprawling buffets, there's never a morsel left. Perhaps best of all, the dish can be made in advance and frozen for later use.

16 slices day-old white bread, crusts removed and cut into small cubes
1½ pounds cooked ham, cut into small cubes
1 pound New York State sharp cheddar cheese, grated
1½ cups grated Swiss cheese
1 teaspoon minced onion
6 large eggs
3 cups milk
½ teaspoon dry mustard
Salt and black pepper to taste
3 cups crushed soda crackers
½ cup (1 stick) butter, melted

Grease a 9 x 13 x 2-inch glass baking dish. Spread half the bread cubes evenly over the bottom, top with the cubed ham and two cheeses, and cover with the remaining bread cubes. In a large bowl, combine the onion, eggs, milk, mustard, salt, and pepper till well blended and pour slowly over the casserole till all the milk and egg mixture is absorbed. Cover with plastic wrap and refrigerate overnight.

When ready to bake, preheat the oven to 375°F and combine the crushed crackers and butter in a bowl. Spread the cracker mixture over the top and bake the casserole till golden, about 40 minutes.

Yield: 10 to 12 servings

Greco

When I was young, it became almost customary for our next-door neighbor, a widow who loved to cook, to show up about once a month with a big vessel of Captain's Chicken, Greco, and any other composed dish she might have taken mind to bake up in quantity. Exactly why she made such generous gestures, and where she got the name "Greco" for this typical Southern casserole, we never figured out; but when Mother has to produce a quick supper and doesn't feel like going to lots of trouble, this is still one of her favorite staples.

3 tablespoons vegetable oil
1 medium-size onion, chopped
1 medium-size green bell pepper, seeded and chopped
½ pound ground beef round
½ pound ground veal
½ pound fresh mushrooms, chopped
3 cups shell macaroni, boiled till tender and drained
Two 8-ounce cans tomato sauce
1 large (about 15 ounces) can cream-style corn
Salt and black pepper to taste
1 cup grated Parmesan cheese

In a large, heavy skillet, heat the oil, then add the onion and bell pepper and cook over moderate heat till glossy, stirring. Add the beef and veal, mix well, separating the meat with a fork, and cook till the meat is browned, stirring. Add the mushrooms, macaroni, tomato sauce, corn, salt, and pepper and stir till well blended. Transfer the mixture to a greased casserole or baking dish, cover with plastic wrap, and refrigerate about 1 hour.

When ready to bake, preheat the oven to 325°F, sprinkle the cheese over the top of the casserole, and bake till browned and firm, about 1 hour.

Yield: 6 servings

Sunday Sausage and Vegetable Casserole

In my mother's gracious, old-fashioned Southern world, people still attend church each and every Sunday, followed often by a simple lunch at someone's home. For such an occasion, no dish makes more sense than an imaginative casserole like this that can be made in advance and stuck in the oven while everyone's having a glass of sherry. We think the dish also makes an awfully nice casual Sunday supper.

1 pound Fresh Country Sausage (page 10) or commerical bulk pork sausage
4 medium-size potatoes, peeled and boiled in water to cover till tender
1 cup lima beans, boiled in water to cover till tender
1 cup fresh corn, cut and scraped from cobs
Salt and black pepper to taste
¾ cup half-and-half
½ cup fine dry bread crumbs
3 tablespoons butter, melted

In a skillet, crumble the sausage, fry over moderate heat till browned, and drain on paper towels.

Preheat the oven to 350°F.

Cut the potatoes into thin slices. In a greased 2-quart casserole or baking dish, arrange alternate layers of potatoes, sausage, lima beans, and corn and add salt and pepper. Pour on the half-and-half, sprinkle the bread crumbs over the top, drizzle with the melted butter, and bake till golden brown, about 30 minutes.

Yield: 6 servings

Shrimp and Mushroom Casserole

3 tablespoons butter
1 large onion, chopped
$\frac{1}{2}$ pound fresh mushrooms, sliced
2 pounds fresh shrimp, shelled and deveined
2 medium-size ripe tomatoes, peeled and diced
$1\frac{1}{2}$ teaspoons salt
$\frac{1}{4}$ teaspoon black pepper
$\frac{1}{8}$ teaspoon paprika
1 teaspoon Worcestershire sauce
$\frac{1}{3}$ cup dry sherry
$\frac{1}{2}$ cup half-and-half
2 tablespoons all-purpose flour
4 cups cooked rice
$\frac{1}{2}$ cup soft bread crumbs
2 tablespoons butter, melted

In a large, heavy skillet, melt the butter, then add the onion, mushrooms, and shrimp and cook over moderate heat, stirring, till the shrimp are just pink, about 3 minutes. Add the tomatoes, salt, pepper, and paprika, reduce the heat to low, cover, and cook 5 minutes. Stir in the Worcestershire and sherry.

Preheat the oven broiler.

In a small bowl, combine the half-and-half and flour and stir to make a smooth paste. Add to the shrimp mixture and bring to a boil, stirring constantly. Reduce the heat to low and cook 1 minute. Add the cooked rice and toss to mix well. Transfer the mixture to a 2-quart casserole or baking dish, sprinkle with the bread crumbs, drizzle the melted butter over the top, and broil till lightly browned.

Yield: 6 servings

Oyster and Spinach Casserole

2 tablespoons butter
1 medium-size onion, chopped
2 tablespoons all-purpose flour
1 quart freshly shucked oysters, drained and liquor reserved
1 cup milk
Salt and black pepper to taste
¼ teaspoon ground nutmeg
Two 10-ounce packages frozen chopped spinach, thawed, cooked according to
    package directions, and drained
¾ cup soft bread crumbs
2 tablespoons butter, melted

In a large skillet, melt the butter, then add the onion and cook over moderate heat 2 minutes, stirring. Sprinkle with the flour, stir, and cook 1 minute longer. Add ¾ cup of the reserved oyster liquor and the milk, stirring constantly till the sauce begins to thicken. Add the salt, pepper, and nutmeg and stir.

    Preheat the oven to 375°F.

    Spread the spinach over the bottom of a greased casserole or baking dish, layer the oysters over the spinach, and pour the milk mixture over the top. Sprinkle with the bread crumbs, drizzle the melted butter over the top, and bake till lightly browned, about 20 minutes.

Yield: 6 servings

Martha Pearl Says:

"This was originally my daughter's recipe, and when she first made the casserole the way they do down in Wilmington, it didn't take two bites for me to realize that the oysters had been brutally overcooked. The problem, of course, was that the oysters had first been simmered in the sauce, then baked, meaning they had toughened from overcooking. Remember that in any dish involving fresh oysters (soups, stews, casseroles, etc.), the oysters should not be added till the last possible minute."

Crabmeat and Corn Casserole

Generally, Mother uses only fresh lump back-fin crabmeat in her crab dishes since claw meat has to be picked for so many bits of shell. In a complex casserole such as this, however, it's almost a sin to waste expensive, delicate back-fin when sweet claw meat works just as well. Also, claw meat seems to have a better, more sturdy texture for dishes like this—so long, that is, as it's picked over carefully.

$\frac{1}{2}$ pound fresh crabmeat, picked over for shells
2 cups fresh or frozen corn kernels
3 hard-boiled eggs, peeled and chopped
3 tablespoons chopped fresh parsley
$\frac{1}{4}$ cup ($\frac{1}{2}$ stick) butter
1 pound fresh mushrooms, sliced
1 small onion, minced
2 tablespoons all-purpose flour
1 cup milk
2 teaspoons fresh lemon juice
1 teaspoon Worcestershire sauce
1 teaspoon dry mustard
Salt and black pepper to taste
$\frac{1}{2}$ cup soft bread crumbs
$\frac{1}{4}$ cup grated sharp cheddar cheese
1 tablespoon butter, melted

In a 1$\frac{1}{2}$-quart casserole, combine the crabmeat, corn, eggs, and parsley and toss well.

Preheat the oven to 350°F.

In a skillet, melt the butter, then add the mushrooms and onion and cook over moderate heat about 3 minutes, stirring. Add the flour, stir, and cook 1 minute. Gradually add the milk, stirring, then the lemon juice, Worcestershire, mustard, salt, and pepper and stir to blend well.

Combine the bread crumbs and cheese and sprinkle over the top of the casserole. Drizzle the melted butter over the top and bake till lightly browned, about 30 minutes.

Yield: 6 servings

Myrtle Beach Crab Casserole

Not long ago, Mother and my sister decided to drive from Charlotte down to Myrtle Beach, South Carolina, "just for a quiet weekend and to eat some really fresh seafood." While they were there, Mother called, exclaiming about an unusual crab casserole prepared with hush puppy crumbs that they'd been served in a restaurant. The manager promised to mail her the recipe (ha!), but when, of course, the recipe never arrived, she simply applied her wits and reproduced the following.

1 pound fresh lump crabmeat, picked over for shells
½ cup hush puppy (page 223) crumbs
2 large eggs, beaten
1 tablespoon minced fresh chives
¼ cup dry sherry
Salt and black pepper to taste

In a mixing bowl, combine all the ingredients and mix very gently, taking care not to break up the crabmeat. Divide the mixture among four individual small greased ramekins, cover with plastic wrap, and chill about 30 minutes.

When ready to bake, preheat the oven to 350°F and bake the ramekins till the mixture is set and tops are golden, 15 to 20 minutes.

Yield: 4 servings

Mixed Vegetable Casserole

Whether Mother contributes this casserole to a Dutch lunch for one of her clubs or to a church covered-dish supper, it's a dish that people relish as much today as they did forty years ago. When our summer vegetable garden is at its peak, she might well substitute anything that strikes her fancy, so feel free to experiment with it.

3 cups fresh or frozen shelled green peas
1 cup finely chopped celery
1 cup shredded carrots
1 cup finely chopped onions
2 large eggs, beaten
2½ cups milk
3 tablespoons all-purpose flour
1 teaspoon salt
½ teaspoon black pepper
1½ cups fine dry bread crumbs
2 cups shredded sharp cheddar cheese
5 tablespoons butter, melted

In a bowl, combine the peas, celery, carrots, and onions and set aside.

In a saucepan, combine the eggs, milk, flour, salt, and pepper, slowly heat to moderate, stirring, and cook till the sauce is thickened, stirring constantly.

Preheat the oven to 375°F.

Arrange half the vegetable mixture in a 2½-quart casserole and top with ½ cup of the bread crumbs, 1 cup of the cheese, and half the sauce. Repeat with the remaining vegetables, ½ cup of the bread crumbs, and the remaining cheese and sauce. Sprinkle the remaining bread crumbs over the top, drizzle with the melted butter, and bake till golden brown, 30 to 40 minutes.

Yield: 8 servings

Macaroni and Cheese

Purist that she is about certain dishes, Mother has an intense dislike for macaroni and cheese prepared with any sort of overly rich, highly seasoned sauce, insisting that "only with a simple custard can you really taste the macaroni and cheese." This is the way members of the family have made the casserole for generations, to be served not only with meat loaf and various roasted meats and game but also as a meat substitute at one of Mother's all-vegetable dinners.

½ pound elbow macaroni
Salt
½ pound New York State sharp cheddar cheese, very thinly sliced
2 large eggs, beaten
Milk

Cook the macaroni in salted water according to the package directions and drain in a colander.

Preheat the oven to 350°F.

Arrange half the macaroni in a medium-size casserole. Place half the cheese over the top and arrange the remaining macaroni over the cheese. In a bowl, combine the eggs and ½ cup of milk, stir well, and pour over the casserole. Top with the remaining cheese slices and add just enough milk to cover all the macaroni but not the top layer of cheese. Bake until the custard is firm and the top browned, 20 to 30 minutes.

Yield: 6 servings

Hot Fruit Casserole

Mother got this recipe many years ago when a member of her book club brought the dish to a big Christmas party. She still likes to serve it with ham biscuits and a good cheese at small luncheons, but the casserole also makes an unusual addition to elaborate holiday buffets. Do note that the dish must be prepared a day in advance so that the flavors blend nicely.

One 16-ounce can sliced pineapple
One 16-ounce can peach halves
One 16-ounce can pear halves
One 16-ounce can apricot halves
One 14-ounce jar spiced apple rings
2 tablespoons all-purpose flour
½ cup firmly packed light brown sugar
¾ cup (1½ sticks) butter
1 cup dry sherry

Drain all the fruits and cut the pineapple slices in half. In a large 18 x 28-inch baking dish, arrange the fruits in alternating layers, using the apple rings for the top.

Combine the flour, sugar, butter, and sherry in the top of a double boiler over simmering water and cook, stirring, till mixture is thickened and smooth, about 10 minutes. Pour the mixture over the fruit, cover with plastic wrap, and let stand in the refrigerator overnight.

Preheat the oven to 350°F.

Place the casserole in the oven and bake till bubbly hot and slightly glazed on top, 20 to 30 minutes.

Yield: 12 to 14 servings

Martha Pearl Says:

"Some people substitute 1 teaspoon of curry powder for the sherry, but I've never cared much for the taste of curry."

9
Vegetables

At least three times a week while visiting me on Long Island during the summer, Mother drives five miles to this particular roadside vegetable stand in Sagaponack "for Silver Queen corn, eggplant, and potatoes that are almost as good as what we have in the South." Here, the family's two children have run down from the house to greet the familiar face, but normally Mother just leaves the cash for her bounty in a large Mason jar left on the table.

Visions of squash soufflé, but I can tell by the look on Mother's face that the yellow crooknecks displayed in this particular Southern market are just too large and seedy for her taste.

Nowhere over the decades in this country have vegetables been utilized with such originality as in Southern home kitchens, and nowhere (not even in California) do they continue to figure so prominently in regional cookery as in the South. When I was young, it was never unusual to see as many as five different vegetable preparations on my grandparents', parents', and aunts' and uncles' dinner tables, and today it would be rare for Mother to serve any major meal that didn't include at least one hot starchy vegetable, a green one, plus something like sweet-and-sour coleslaw or sliced tomatoes.

Contrary to cooking practices elsewhere during these trendy times, we Southerners still insist that our vegetables (all except fresh corn and green peas, of course) not only be cooked till thoroughly done but that their flavor be heightened by the addition of numerous other ingredients. Never, for example, would Mother serve a mess of turnip greens, butterbeans, black-eyed peas, or snap beans that hadn't simmered at least an hour with a piece of salt pork or a ham hock, and anybody who's asked the secret of her addictive baked squash soufflé learns quickly that it's not just the perfect blend of the right ingredients but also the initial slow simmering of the squash and onions. Southerners are often accused of destroying some of the integrity of vegetables by overcooking them, but I can promise you that what we might lose in texture and nutrients, we gain in sublime flavor.

Such is Mother's passion for fresh vegetables that, especially during the bountiful summer, it's never unusual when we dine with family and close friends for her to serve a meal composed of nothing but five or six vegetable dishes and a pan of cornbread. "Some of these young restaurant chefs today with their vegetarian menus act as if they've just discovered the carrot and potato," she snickers. "Mercy, we Southerners have been eating like that for centuries!"

Summer Squash Soufflé

Ooh, just look at this beautiful squash," Mother will exclaim while fondling particularly firm and fleshy yellow crooknecks at a roadside stand. "We'll just have to do a soufflé, that's all there is to it." In the South, of course, a "soufflé" can be any baked dish that contains eggs, the most popular in our family being this wonder that Mother usually serves with short ribs of beef, meat loaf, roasts, and baked ham stuffed with turnip greens. "You've ruined the texture of this soufflé by using that silly food processor," she once ranted when I decided to puree the cooked vegetables in a Cuisinart. She was right, alas, so ever since I've followed her decades-old method to the letter and mashed them by hand. When shopping, look for bright yellow, firm, medium-size crookneck squash with no dark spots, and do not substitute zucchini in this particular recipe since the flavor and texture are altogether different. Also, be careful about the timing of this soufflé, checking after 25 to 30 minutes to make sure it isn't too dry.

6 medium-size yellow squash (about 2 pounds), scrubbed and cut into 1-inch
    rounds
2 large onions, coarsely chopped
$\frac{1}{4}$ cup ($\frac{1}{2}$ stick) butter, softened
1 jumbo egg, beaten
$\frac{1}{8}$ teaspoon finely minced garlic
Pinch of ground nutmeg
$\frac{1}{2}$ teaspoon salt
Black pepper to taste
$\frac{1}{4}$ cup plain bread crumbs
$\frac{3}{4}$ cup grated Parmesan cheese

In a large saucepan combine the squash and onions, add enough salted water to cover, and bring to a boil. Reduce the heat to low, cover, and simmer till the squash is tender, 20 to 30 minutes. Drain in a colander and mash well with a heavy fork or potato masher to extract any excess liquid.

Preheat the oven to 350°F.

Place the vegetables in a mixing bowl, add all remaining ingredients except about 3 tablespoons of the grated Parmesan, and mix thoroughly with a heavy spoon. Transfer the mixture to a well-buttered medium-size gratin or baking dish, sprinkle the top with the remaining Parmesan, and bake till the top is golden, about 30 minutes.

Yield: 4 servings

Flossie's Butternut Squash Orange Bake

O f all the recipes that Mother has exchanged with one of her oldest childhood friends, Florence Anders, she considers this one of Flossie's best and most original. Both ladies like to serve the bake with roasted meats and poultry.

1 large butternut squash (about 3 pounds)
$\frac{1}{4}$ cup ($\frac{1}{2}$ stick) butter
$\frac{1}{2}$ cup fresh orange juice
$\frac{1}{4}$ cup firmly packed light brown sugar
$\frac{1}{2}$ teaspoon salt
$\frac{1}{4}$ teaspoon ground cinnamon
$\frac{1}{8}$ teaspoon ground ginger
$\frac{1}{8}$ teaspoon ground cloves
Orange marmalade

Peel the squash and cut into chunks. Place the chunks in a large saucepan with enough salted water to cover, bring to a boil, reduce the heat to moderate, cover, and cook till fork tender, about 20 minutes.

Preheat the oven to 350°F.

Drain, the squash, place in a large bowl, and mash well with a potato masher till smooth. Add the butter and mix well. Add the orange juice, sugar, salt, cinnamon, ginger, and cloves and mix well. Scrape the mixture into a medium-size buttered casserole, spread a thin layer of orange marmalade over the top, and bake 30 minutes.

Yield: 6 servings

Okra and Tomatoes

I f I had to pick one summer dish that my mother couldn't live without, it would have to be the fresh okra and tomatoes she seems forever to be cooking for any and every occasion. Not just any okra and tomatoes, mind you. If our own vegetables haven't made, or if our okra is too large and the tomatoes too ripe, out she goes on her eternal quest through the farm stands for tiny okra that is firm but tender and for plump tomatoes just at the stage of ripeness where they can be cooked without falling apart. Place a platter of fried chicken, ears of fresh corn on the cob, a bowl of okra and tomatoes, and hot biscuits in front of my mother and you'll see a truly happy lady.

4 slices bacon
2 small onions, chopped
1½ pounds small fresh okra, washed, stemmed, and cut into ¾-inch rounds
4 ripe but firm large tomatoes, peeled and chopped
2 teaspoons salt
Black pepper to taste
1 small hot red pepper, seeded and chopped (optional)

In a skillet, fry the bacon over moderate heat till crisp, drain on paper towels, crumble, and set aside. Add the onions to the skillet, reduce the heat to low, and cook 10 minutes, stirring a couple of times. Add the okra, tomatoes, salt, pepper, and hot pepper, stir well, and simmer till the okra and tomatoes are just soft, about 20 minutes. Transfer to a bowl and sprinkle the top with the crumbled bacon.

Yield: 6 servings

Martha Pearl Says:

"If my okra and tomatoes end up too soupy, I thicken them up slightly with a few dry bread crumbs or crushed croutons."

Broccoli Casserole

Although my daddy disliked broccoli almost as much as George Bush, when he was served this casserole for lunch at the home of one of his health club chums, he loved the dish so much that he got the recipe and insisted that Mother reproduce it. In turn, she liked the dish so much that she insisted I try it. Naturally, I balked (as she had) over using canned soup as a base and so applied my ingenuity by creating and substituting a mushroom cream sauce. Don't ask me why but it was awful. Rarely do we use canned soups in cooking (unlike most Southerners), but here's one example when the results are indeed delicious. Therefore, I make no apologies.

1 large head fresh broccoli, stems removed
One 10¾-ounce can condensed cream of mushroom soup
1 cup homemade (page 305) or Hellmann's mayonnaise
½ cup (1 stick) butter, softened
2 large eggs, beaten
1 small onion, finely chopped
1 teaspoon salt
Black pepper to taste
1½ cups grated extra-sharp cheddar cheese
2 cups finely crushed Ritz crackers

Place the broccoli in a large saucepan with 1 inch of water, bring to the boil, cover, and steam the broccoli 5 minutes. Drain and chop coarsely.

Preheat the oven to 350°F.

In a large mixing bowl, combine the broccoli, soup, mayonnaise, butter, eggs, onion, salt, and pepper and mix thoroughly. Add 1 cup of the cheese, mix well, and scrape the mixture into a medium-size buttered casserole or baking dish. Sprinkled the remaining cheese and the crackers on top, bake till a straw inserted into the middle comes out clean, 30 to 40 minutes, and let stand 20 minutes before serving.

Yield: 8 servings

Southern Turnip and Mustard Greens

What Scarlett O'Hara thrust defiantly in the air when she proclaimed ". . . I'll never go hungry again" was a whole turnip green, a scene that implies to any good Southerner that maybe Mammy just didn't know how to cook greens correctly. One of the many Northern culinary practices that irritates Mother is the way turnip roots are usually sold minus their leaves, for she loves nothing more than to put the greens on to boil, peel the root bulbs, lay them on top of the greens, and steam them during the last 30 minutes of cooking. As for the cooking meat, she goes out of her way to find meaty streak-'o-lean, insisting that it imparts much more flavor than plain old salt pork.

3 pounds mixed fresh turnip and mustard greens
1 lean chunk streak-o'-lean (lean salt pork), sliced part way through
2 teaspoons salt
1 teaspoon sugar
Finely chopped onions
Cider vinegar

Remove and discard all stems from the greens, rinse them, then soak in water 15 minutes to remove any traces of grit. Rinse the greens again, place in a large pot, and add enough water to half cover. Add the meat, salt, and sugar and bring to a boil. Reduce the heat to low, cover, and simmer the greens 1½ hours. Drain well in a colander, remove and discard the meat, and serve hot with the onions and vinegar to be spooned over each serving.

Yield: 6 to 8 servings

Martha Pearl Says:

"The best seasons for turnip and mustard greens are early spring and late fall. Summer greens, which tend to be bitter, should always be parboiled about 10 minutes, drained, then cooked in fresh water with the meat, salt, and at least 2 teaspoons of sugar."

Orange Beets

No, no, no, honey, don't you dare cut off those tops!" Mother roared recently as a young girl at the farmers' market in Amangansett, Long Island, was about to take a knife to a big bunch of beets. "We eat those leaves—cooked just like turnip greens with a little streak-o'-lean." Although I often suspect that Mother buys fresh beets primarily for the tops, the various ways she prepares the bulbs (steamed, braised, in soups, salad, casseroles, etc.) do seem endless.

16 to 20 small beets
2 tablespoons cornstarch
1¼ cups firmly packed light brown sugar
One 6-ounce can frozen concentrated orange juice, thawed
¾ cup cider vinegar
1 tablespoon butter

Remove the beet tops and reserve for cooking like turnip greens. Scrub the bulbs thoroughly and place in a kettle or large saucepan with enough water to cover. Bring to a boil, reduce the heat to moderate, cover, and cook till tender, about 30 minutes. Transfer the beets to a colander, reserving the cooking liquid, and, when cool enough to handle, peel and set aside.

In a large saucepan, combine the cornstarch, brown sugar, concentrate, vinegar, and 1 cup of the re-served beet liquid and cook over moderate heat till thick and clear, 8 to 10 minutes, stirring constantly. Stir in the butter, add the beets, and heat thoroughly, stirring.

Yield: 4 to 6 servings

Martha Pearl Says:

"To keep beets from 'bleeding' while boiling, never cut off the root stems till the beets are cooked. Also, unless the beets are very small, slice them in half once they are boiled."

Gingered Carrots

Mother takes her carrots very seriously, going out of her way to find bunches with the leafy tops left on. "It means they're fresh and more moist," she insists. To counteract blandness, she prepares carrots with everything from brown sugar to fresh herbs to bourbon, and this version with ground ginger she likes to serve with scalloped oysters, salmon croquettes, fried rabbit, or ham and sweet potato hash.

2 pounds carrots, scraped and cut into ½-inch rounds
2 tablespoons butter
1 tablespoon sugar
2 teaspoons cornstarch
½ teaspoon salt
½ teaspoon ground ginger
Black pepper to taste
½ cup orange juice
Chopped fresh parsley for garnish

Place the carrots in a saucepan with enough water to cover, bring to a boil, reduce the heat slightly, and cook till the carrots are just tender, about 8 minutes. Drain the carrots in a colander.

In a saucepan, melt the butter, then add the sugar, cornstarch, salt, ginger, and pepper and stir well. Add the orange juice, stirring, bring to a boil, and cook till thickened, about 1 minute, stirring constantly. Add the carrots and stir till well coated with the glaze. Transfer to a heated serving dish and sprinkle parsley on top.

Yield: 6 to 8 servings

Corn Pudding

When Mother was young, her family virtually lived for June and July, when Silver Queen corn was in abundance, and once they'd had their fill of corn on the cob and corn stewed in a skillet with bacon grease, they'd make huge pots of this corn pudding and invite lots of company over for a barbecue. Today when she visits East Hampton, one of our daily summer rituals is going from one roadside farm stand to the next searching for the freshest Long Island corn just picked from the vast fields, and we have one close friend who literally flies up from Houston every August on the promise that she can eat Mother's corn pudding each and every day. Mother's stubborn insistence that white corn is sweeter and lighter than yellow or speckled drives me crazy.

3 large eggs
3 cups fresh corn kernels
2 teaspoons minced onion
3 tablespoons all-purpose flour
½ teaspoon salt
2 tablespoons sugar
Cayenne pepper to taste
Ground nutmeg to taste
¼ cup (½ stick) butter, melted and cooled
1½ cups half-and-half

Preheat the oven to 350°F. In a large mixing bowl, beat the eggs with an electric mixer until frothy, then stir in the corn and onion. In a small bowl, combine the flour, salt, sugar, cayenne, and nutmeg and add to the corn mixture, stirring. Add the butter and half-and-half and stir well.

Pour the mixture into a well-greased 1½-quart baking dish, place the dish in a large roasting pan, place the pan in the oven, and pour enough boiling water into the pan to come one quarter of the way up the sides of the baking dish. Bake the pudding 15 minutes, stir gently to distribute the corn as evenly as possible, and bake till the top is golden brown and a knife inserted into the center comes out clean, about 30 minutes longer.

Yield: 6 servings

Martha Pearl Says:

"When I prepare my corn pudding, I first cut the kernels from the ears, then scrape the cobs carefully with a knife to gather as much milk as possible. Also, lots of people don't use flour, but if you don't, the result can be a watery pudding."

Bourbon Spoonbread

As a child, Mother remembers her mother always preparing spoonbread as a main course for supper (the evening meal) with leftovers from dinner (the midday meal). Today, she likes to serve it when I do pork barbecue, as well as with fried fish and oyster pie. We've also been known to include a big dish of spoonbread on breakfast and brunch buffets.

2 cups milk
1 cup white cornmeal
½ cup (1 stick) butter, softened
½ teaspoon salt
1 tablespoon sugar
1 teaspoon baking powder
4 large eggs, separated
4½ teaspoons bourbon

Preheat the oven to 350°F.

In a saucepan, scald the milk, heating till bubbles form around the edges of the pan, then stir in the cornmeal, beat thoroughly with a spoon, and cook over low heat till thick. Remove from the heat, add the butter in pieces, the salt, sugar, and baking powder and beat well till the butter has melted. Set aside to cool.

In a small bowl, beat the egg yolks and stir them into the cooled cornmeal mixture. In another bowl, beat the egg whites with an electric mixer till stiff peaks form, fold them into the mixture, add the bourbon, and mix lightly. Pour the mixture into a medium-size buttered casserole or baking dish and bake till a straw inserted into the middle comes out clean, about 40 minutes.

Yield: 6 servings

Martha Pearl Says:

"Jimmy's always jumping on me about buying nothing but white cornmeal, but I'm absolutely convinced that you get lighter, more delicate results in cooking with white instead of yellow—especially in spoonbread."

Succotash

No doubt this old Southern dish (American Indian in origin) evolved as a means to use up leftover limas and corn, and one of my earliest memories is eating big bowls of succotash at outdoor coastal "pig pickin's" where meat was simply pulled from a whole barbecued hog. Mother, of course, wouldn't dream of making succotash with anything but fresh vegetables, but I must say I've had pretty good results out of season with the frozen items. Traditionally, the dish is served with barbecued pork or chicken, but we also serve it with fried chicken and almost any baked or broiled meats.

2 cups fresh or frozen lima beans
5 slices bacon
2 medium-size onions, finely chopped
2 cups fresh or frozen corn kernels
2 cups peeled and chopped fresh tomatoes
Salt and black pepper to taste
Tabasco sauce to taste

Place the beans in a saucepan and add enough salted water to cover. Bring to a boil, reduce the heat to moderate, cover, cook 15 minutes, and drain.

Meanwhile, fry the bacon in a large skillet over moderate heat till crisp, drain on paper towels, and crumble. Drain off all but 3 tablespoons of the fat, add the onions to the skillet, reduce the heat slightly, and cook, stirring, till softened, 3 minutes. Add the corn and tomatoes and continue cooking 5 minutes, stirring. Add the salt, pepper, Tabasco and cook the mixture, stirring, till it has thickened but is not dry. Transfer the succotash to an earthenware tureen or deep serving dish, sprinkle the crumbled bacon on top, and toss lightly.

Yield: 8 servings

Southern Green Beans and New Potatoes

Mother remembers her Uncle Henry always having the tiniest new red potatoes from a first-dug summer crop to cook with Kentucky Wonder string beans, and to this day she'll ride from one farm stand to the next on the eastern end of Long Island while visiting to search for minuscule fresh potatoes just out of the ground to add to her beans. "Honey, your Yankee potatoes are almost sweet," she's been led to exclaim more than once to rather startled farmers.

2 pounds fresh green beans (*not* thin French-style)
One 1-inch-thick chunk streak-o'-lean (lean salt pork) cooking meat
½ teaspoon salt
Black pepper to taste
1 dozen tiny new red potatoes

Remove the ends and, if necessary, strings from the beans. Snap the beans into 1½-inch pieces, rinse well in a colander, and transfer to a large pot. Add the cooking meat, salt, and pepper and add enough water to cover by 1 inch. Bring to a boil, reduce the heat to low, cover, and simmer the beans slowly for 1 hour.

Rinse the potatoes lightly to remove any grit and cut away a strip of skin around the center of each with a vegetable peeler. Add the potatoes to the beans, stir with a spoon, and simmer until tender, about 30 minutes, adding more water if necessary. Drain and serve in a large bowl.

Yield: 6 to 8 servings

Martha Pearl Says:

"I don't mince words when it comes to undercooked, under-seasoned string beans: I won't eat them—not in homes, not in restaurants, nowhere. Yes, I love the way the French cook their tiny green beans, but I've yet to see those exact beans in our markets—contrary to what those food people tell you. We Southerners must have beans that are tender and flavorful, and the only way to cook them is long and slowly and with plenty of seasoning meat. Period."

Papa's Greek Beans

Obviously influenced by my Greek paternal grandfather, Mother has been preparing these beans since I was a child, and nothing goes better with virtually any lamb dish. While she never uses herbs in her Greek beans, I always add a little fresh thyme or oregano or both.

2 pounds fresh green beans
One 28-ounce can whole tomatoes with juice
2 medium-size onions, finely chopped
3 garlic cloves, minced
¼ cup olive oil (preferably Greek)
Salt and black pepper to taste

String the beans if necessary, snap off the ends, break into 2-inch pieces, and place in a large pot. If whole, cut the tomatoes into quarters and add to the beans along with the juice from the can. Add the onions, garlic, olive oil, salt, and pepper, bring to a boil, reduce the heat to low, cover, and simmer 1½ hours, stirring occasionally. Transfer to a large serving bowl and serve with a slotted spoon.

Yield: 6 to 8 servings

Martha Pearl Says:

"Normally, I never touch canned vegetables, but when the only fresh green beans I can find are old and shriveled, I've found that high-quality Blue Lake canned beans are acceptable for this particular recipe."

Hoppin' John

The origins of the name of this old Southern dish have never been determined, but it's for certain that black-eyed peas and rice cooked in this manner was a staple of African slaves on the Low Country plantations of South Carolina and Georgia. Throughout the South, the dish served on New Year's day is supposed to bring good luck, a tradition Mother still observes each and every year when she invites neighbors over for country-style back ribs, collard greens, cornbread, and, of course, big bowls of hoppin' john.

3 slices bacon
1 large onion, finely chopped
1 garlic clove, minced
1 pound shelled fresh or frozen black-eyed peas
One 14-ounce can stewed tomatoes
1½ cups cooked long-grain rice
Salt and black pepper to taste
Big dash of Tabasco sauce

In a skillet, fry the bacon till crisp over moderate heat, drain on paper towels, crumble, and set aside. Add the onion and garlic to the skillet, reduce the heat to low, and cook about 3 minutes, stirring. Return the heat to moderate, add the peas, tomatoes, rice, salt, pepper, and Tabasco, stir well, and cook till the tomatoes are soft and the mixture is very hot, about 10 minutes.

To serve, transfer the mixture to a bowl and sprinkle the crumbled bacon on top.

Yield: 6 servings

Martha Pearl Says:

"I'd give anything if fresh black-eyed peas were available year-round for this dish, but since they're never around in January, and since I don't like the texture of dried peas, I use frozen ones with good results."

Yankee Baked Beans

Despite the fact that baked beans have been popular in the South for at least two hundred years, Mother continues to classify them "a Yankee dish," suitable only with meat loaf or baked ham. She likes to tell about how in the old days, her mother would split hot dogs, stuff them with cheese, wrap them with bacon, bake them, and serve them on top of baked beans as a wholesome lunch; and today she still insists that for baked beans to be really good, they have to be "dressed up" with lots of other ingredients.

1 pound dried navy or Great Northern beans, picked over and rinsed
8 ounces streak-o'-lean (lean salt pork), half cut into ½-inch dice, half cut into thin strips
1 medium-size onion, cut into medium dice
4 cups water
4 garlic cloves, finely chopped
2 medium-size tomatoes, peeled, seeded, and cut into medium dice
1 teaspoon salt
2 teaspoons black pepper
¼ cup prepared mustard
⅓ cup molasses
2 bay leaves
2 tablespoons cider vinegar

Place the beans in a pot, add enough water to cover, and let soak overnight.

Drain the beans. Sprinkle the diced cooking meat and onion over the bottom of an earthenware bean pot or crock and add the beans. In a saucepan, bring the water to a boil, add the garlic, tomatoes, salt, pepper, mustard, molasses, bay leaves, and vinegar, reduce the heat to moderate, simmer 1 minute, and pour over the beans.

Preheat the oven to 250°F.

Martha Pearl Says:

"Even Northerners know that good baked beans have to bake long and slow, so be patient."

Arrange the strips of cooking meat over the beans, cover the pot, and bake 4 hours, adding more boiling water halfway through the cooking if necessary to keep the beans covered. Uncover and bake 1 hour longer.

Yield: 6 to 8 servings

Dirty Rice

So named because of its dark color, "dirty rice" is almost as popular in the Carolinas as down in Cajun Louisiana. "In South Carolina," my granddaddy Paw Paw used to complain, "they give you dirty rice even with a bowl of ice cream," a sentiment echoed by my Unca' Nalle from Columbia who, Mother swears, could have eaten rice every day of his life. As far as I'm concerned, dirty rice is one of the world's great rice dishes and one of the best ways I know to utilize all the chicken giblets that collect in the freezer. We serve it with everything from roasts to elaborate casseroles to Brunwsick stew.

¼ cup vegetable oil
1 medium-size onion, finely chopped
2 celery ribs, finely chopped
1 medium-size green bell pepper, seeded and finely chopped
1 garlic clove, minced
¼ cup (½ stick) butter
1 pound chicken livers, trimmed and finely diced
½ pound chicken gizzards, trimmed and finely diced
½ teaspoon dried thyme
½ teaspoon dried oregano
Salt and black pepper to taste
2½ cups fresh chicken stock (page 55)
1 cup long-grain rice

In a large cast-iron skillet, heat the oil, then add the onion, celery, bell pepper, and garlic and cook over moderate heat 3 minutes, stirring. Add the butter, livers, gizzards, thyme, oregano, salt, and pepper, stir well, and cook till the meats are cooked through, 10 minutes, stirring. Add the stock, increase the heat to moderate, stir well, and let cook 7 to 8 minutes, stirring. Add the rice, stir, reduce the heat to low, cover, and cook till the rice has absorbed the liquid and is tender, 15 to 20 minutes.

Yield: 8 servings

Garlic Mashed Potatoes

When, as a child, Mother and her sister Jane (my Aunt Dee) were taken every summer back to Monticello, Georgia to "visit family," these were the potatoes served regularly at "Cuddin'" Berta's big white house and the ones my grandmother would reproduce back in Charlotte. Since Mother has always had a near-phobia about dirty potato skins and will go to extraordinary lengths to scrub away every trace of grit, I finally asked her one day why she simply didn't peel the potatoes before boiling them. "Because the skins add flavor to the flesh—everybody knows that!" she informed.

3 pounds (about 6) medium-size red potatoes, scrubbed thoroughly
2 tablespoons butter
3 green onions (just the white parts), minced
2 garlic cloves, minced
6 tablespoons (¾ stick) butter, at room temperature
Salt and black pepper to taste
⅓ cup milk

Place the potatoes in a large saucepan with enough water to cover, bring to a boil, reduce the heat to moderate, and cook till the potatoes are very tender, 30 to 40 minutes. Transfer to a colander and let cool slightly.

Meanwhile, melt the 2 tablespoons butter in a small skillet, then add the onions and garlic, cook over low heat till the onions just begin to brown, and set aside.

Peel the potatoes, cut into chunks, place in a large mixing bowl, and mash with a potato masher or large spoon. Add the softened butter, salt, and pepper and beat the potatoes with an electric mixer till very smooth. Add the milk, green onions

and garlic, and con-
tinue beating till the
potatoes are light and
fluffy. Serve immedi-
ately or place the bowl
in a container of hot
water to keep warm.

Yield: 6 servings

Martha Pearl Says:

"To dry out any excess water after boiling the potatoes, I always put them in a dry pot over low heat for a few minutes. This helps make them real fluffy when beaten."

Sweet Potato and Pecan Pudding

To this day Mother will wait each year till the more mature sweet potatoes come in just before the first frost before fixing them every way imaginable: candied, fried in bacon grease, mashed with raisins and stuffed into scooped-out orange halves, turned into pies, breads, and biscuits, and, of course, used to make this delectable pudding to serve with roast turkey or game.

6 medium-size sweet potatoes
2 large eggs, beaten
1 teaspoon pure vanilla extract
½ cup half-and-half
⅛ teaspoon ground cinnamon
1 cup firmly packed light brown sugar
⅓ cup all-purpose flour
6 tablespoons (¾ stick) butter
1 cup chopped pecans

Place the potatoes in a large pot with enough salted water to cover, bring to a boil, reduce the heat to medium, cover, and cook till very tender, about 30 minutes. Drain the potatoes and, when cool enough to handle, peel, place in a large mixing bowl, and mash with a potato masher or heavy fork.
  Preheat the oven to 350°F.
  Add the eggs, vanilla, half-and-half, and cinnamon to the mashed potatoes,

mix till well blended, and transfer the mixture to a large buttered baking dish or casserole.

In a bowl, combine the sugar and flour, cut in the butter with a pastry cutter or fork, add the pecans, and stir till well blended. Distribute the pecan mixture evenly over top of the potatoes and bake till golden brown, about 30 minutes.

Yield: 6 to 8 servings

Martha Pearl Says:

"I never buy a sweet potato that has a single dark spot—a sure sign that it's already over the hill. Nor do I ever settle for fat, creviced potatoes since I'm convinced that the long, slim, even ones are easier to handle and more attractive when baked or braised whole."

Cornwallis Yams

I don't know if these yams are still served at the historic Colonial Inn in Hillsborough, North Carolina, but when I was at the University in nearby Chapel Hill some thirty years ago and my parents and I once drove over for dinner, it didn't take Mother long to sweet-talk the manager into parting with the recipe for this remarkable dish.

3 medium-size yams or sweet potatoes
¾ cup milk
½ cup sugar
¼ cup canned crushed pineapple
¼ cup (½ stick) butter
2 large eggs, beaten
¼ teaspoon salt
¼ teaspoon ground cinnamon
¼ cup unsweetened shredded coconut

Wash the yams and place in a large saucepan with enough water to cover. Bring to a boil, reduce the heat to moderate, cover, and simmer till tender, about 30 minutes. Drain and place in a large bowl.

Preheat the oven to 350°F.

When cool enough to handle, peel the yams, return to the mixing bowl, and mash with a heavy fork. Add the remaining ingredients except the coconut and mix well. Pour the mixture into a greased medium-size baking dish and bake 45 minutes. When ready to serve, sprinkle the top with the coconut.

Yield: 6 servings

Spiced Baked Apple Slices

This is one of the many ways my grandmother Maw Maw utilized the bushel baskets of apples she stored in the fall when Mother was growing up. "Lord, we children loved Mama's baked apples," she recalls wistfully, "and today when I'm expecting the grandchildren and great-grandchildren, I always triple this recipe." I must admit I could eat a pound of these apples in a single sitting—especially when served with Mother's poppy seed chicken or rich rabbit stew.

4 Granny Smith apples, cored, peeled, and cut into quarters
½ cup sugar
1½ teaspoons ground cinnamon
1 teaspoon ground nutmeg
2 tablespoons butter, cut into pieces
¼ cup warm water

Preheat the oven to 350°F.

Arrange the apple quarters in a medium-size baking dish, sprinkle with half the sugar, sprinkle with the cinnamon and nutmeg, and sprinkle with the remaining sugar. Dot evenly with the butter, pour the water around the sides, and bake till the apples are tender, about 1 hour, basting several times and covering with aluminum foil if the apples get too brown.

Yield: 4 to 6 servings

Calabash Coleslaw

Although the only topic in the Carolinas that makes for more heated argument than barbecue and country ham is that of coleslaw, Mother and I both stopped discoursing on the subject years ago when we finally hit upon this ideal formula inspired by a glorious slaw served at an otherwise unglorious coastal fried-fish dive at Calabash, North Carolina. This is the slaw we serve with pork barbecue, on hot dogs, and at any big outdoor event where lots of people have to be fed.

4 to 5 cups shredded cabbage (1 small head)
1 small carrot, scraped and shredded
2 green onions (green tops included), minced
2 teaspoons celery seeds
Salt and black pepper to taste
3 tablespoons homemade (page 305) or Hellmann's mayonnaise
2 tablespoons cider vinegar
1 tablespoon sugar

In a large bowl, combine the cabbage, carrot, onions, celery seeds, salt, and pepper and toss well. In a small bowl, combine the mayonnaise, vinegar, and sugar, mix till well blended, and pour over the cabbage mixture. Mix till well blended, cover the bowl with plastic wrap, and refrigerate till ready to use.

Yield: 6 servings

Martha Pearl Says:

"Most people shred their cabbage for slaw on a grater, but I prefer to chop mine with a knife so I can control the size of the pieces. Nothing is worse or more unattractive than coleslaw with big long strands of cabbage."

10
Breads

Basic white bread - (Union County

3 Tbsp. sugar -   2 pkg yeast
1 teasp salt   2½ cup warm water   James Villas
3 Tbsp butter   5 - 6 cups bread flour -

Dissolve yeast, salt butter & sugar in warm
water - Add 4½ cups flour - Blend
Knead 7 to 10 minutes, until dough is
smooth & elastic. Dough will be slightly
sticky to touch -
Place in greased bowl - turning to
grease top -
Cover, let rise in warm place until
doubled in bulk about 1 hour -
Punch down - Let rest for 15 minutes
Divide dough in ½ - Shape each ½
into loaf - Place each loaf in greased
9 X 5 X 3 inch bread pan - Cover, let
rise until doubled, about 1 hour -
Bake at 400° for 30 minutes or until
done - Remove from pans & cool on
wire racks -
Note - For wheat bread: substitute
4½ cups whole wheat or graham
flour & 1½ cups white bread flour
Proceed by the recipe above

M̲ention bread anywhere in the South but New Orleans and the conversation will revolve not around the traditional daily loaf associated with so many other regions and cultures but around biscuits, cornbread, dinner rolls, muffins, and hush puppies. Mother does regularly make a standard white loaf intended for sandwiches and canapés, as well as various delectable vegetable and fruit breads to be included on more elaborate breakfast and brunch buffets, but to suggest that these play the same leading role on our table as biscuits and cornbread would be nothing less than absurd.

In more indulgent times when I was a child, it was of course standard procedure for Mother and Maw Maw to serve *both* biscuits and skillet cornbread at any major supper—and especially at one where only cornbread could be used to sop up the pot likker from turnip greens. Today, we serve either one or the other, my preference being buttermilk biscuits since I love them even better toasted the following morning(s) for breakfast. Unlike some Southerners, Mother does not make (or like) what is known as beaten biscuits, which are unleavened, pounded endlessly with a mallet, hard, and, to our taste, nothing compared with her soft, puffy, baking-powder wonders. Nor does she believe in making biscuits with self-rising flour—including the superior

Corn Bread

1 c plain cornmeal
2 t. baking powder
1½ " salt
2 eggs beaten
½ c oil
-t (8¼ oz) can cream Style Corn
mix — greased 8 in sq pan
375 - 35 men

This is the maddening way Mother typically jots down a recipe that she expects others to follow. "Anybody knows how to bake cornbread once they're given the ingredients," she huffs.

White Lily brand—since the texture is never perfect. Mother is forever open to new ideas about hush puppies, dinner and party rolls, muffins, and even cornbread, but when it comes to tampering with her age-old recipe and technique for making buttermilk biscuits, I always suggest that people keep their suggestions to themselves.

Union County White Bread

Monroe is a rural town in Union County, North Carolina, and ever since one of the local housewives sent this recipe to the *Charlotte Observer* some decades ago, Mother has baked the extremely light bread regularly for both sandwiches and breakfast toast.

2 envelopes active dry yeast
2½ cups warm water
3 tablespoons butter, melted
3 tablespoons sugar
2 teaspoons salt
5 to 6 cups bread flour

In a large mixing bowl, combine the yeast and water, stir, and let proof 5 minutes. Add the butter, sugar, and salt and blend well. Gradually add the flour and mix with a wooden spoon till the dough is sticky. Transfer to a floured surface and knead till the dough is smooth and elastic, 8 to 10 minutes. Gather the dough into a ball, place in a greased bowl, turning to coat all sides, cover with a clean towel, and let rise in a warm area till doubled in bulk, about 1 hour.

Punch down the dough, let rest 15 minutes, divide in half, and shape each half into a loaf. Place each half in a greased 9 x 5 x 3-inch bread pan, cover the pans with towels, and let rise till doubled in bulk, about 1 hour.

Preheat the oven to 400°F.

Bake the loaves till they sound hollow when thumped and are golden, about 30 minutes. Transfer to a wire rack and let cool completely before slicing.

Yield: 2 loaves

Bunny Bread

No source is beneath Mother when it comes to new recipes, and that includes cooking segments on TV. She has no idea what program she was watching at Eastertime some years ago when this unusual bread was featured, but since she was expected to prepare an Easter meal for her four great-grandchildren, she thought they'd get a big kick out of "Bunny Bread" and quickly copied down the recipe. "The children never forgot it and still ask me to make it when they come to visit," she reports.

4 large eggs
2 cups sugar
1¼ cups vegetable oil
1 teaspoon pure almond extract
3 cups all-purpose flour
2 teaspoons baking powder
1½ teaspoons baking soda
½ teaspoon salt
2 teaspoons ground ginger
2 cups shredded carrots
1 cup toasted (page 38) sliced almonds

Preheat the oven to 350°F.

In a mixing bowl, beat the eggs with an electric mixer, gradually add the sugar, and beat till well blended. Gradually add the oil while beating, then the almond extract. In another bowl, combine the flour, baking powder, baking soda, salt, and ginger, then gradually add to the egg mixture and beat till well blended. Stir in the carrots and almonds till well blended.

Grease and flour two medium-size loaf pans, divide the mixture between them, and bake till golden, 45 to 55 minutes. Turn out on a rack and cool before slicing.

Yield: 2 loaves

Orange Cranberry Bread

As if both Mother's and my freezers were not overloaded enough with nuts, peaches, corn, and other seasonal items we like to use year round, nothing will do when she visits East Hampton in the summer but for her to bring along a few bags of frozen fresh cranberries she bought the previous winter for the sole purpose of making this bread. It drives me crazy every time a big bag falls out of the freezer door, but then I change my tune when she serves the delicious bread with afternoon tea or toasts it for breakfast. Do be warned that fresh cranberries (even frozen) virtually do not exist in markets except during the cold months, meaning that you must clutter your freezer if you have any intention of cooking with them out of season.

¼ cup (½ stick) butter, melted
2 cups sugar
4 large eggs
Grated rind of 2 oranges
3 cups all-purpose flour
2 teaspoons baking powder
2 teaspoons baking soda
2 teaspoons ground cinnamon
1 teaspoon salt
1 cup fresh orange juice
2 cups fresh cranberries, picked over
1 cup chopped pecans
1 cup seedless golden raisins

Preheat the oven to 350°F.

In a large mixing bowl, cream the butter, sugar, eggs, and orange rind with an electric mixer. In another bowl, combine the flour, baking powder, baking soda, cinnamon, and salt. Alternately, add the dry ingredients and orange juice to the butter mixture and stir till well blended. Add the cranberries, pecans, and raisins and stir till well blended.

Grease and flour two medium-size loaf pans, pour the batter into the pans, and bake till slightly crusty, about 30 minutes. Turn out the loaves onto a wire rack and let cool completely before slicing.

Yield: 2 loaves

Peach Bread

This distinctive bread began to evolve one morning when, after putting up peach preserves and pickled peaches, Mother decided to modify and expand her banana bread recipe while substituting leftover peaches for the bananas. The first try was not totally successful, but eventually she created an altogether different bread that couldn't be any more original and Southern. We serve it as a dessert with ice cream, as well as toasted for breakfast.

3 cups crushed fresh peaches
6 tablespoons sugar
2 cups all-purpose flour
1 teaspoon baking soda
¼ teaspoon salt
1 teaspoon ground cinnamon
½ cup vegetable shortening
1½ cups sugar
2 large eggs
1 teaspoon pure vanilla extract
1 cup coarsely chopped pecans

In a bowl, combine the peaches and sugar, mix well, and set aside. In another small bowl, combine the flour, baking soda, salt, and cinnamon, mix well, and set aside.

Preheat the oven to 325°F.

In a large mixing bowl, cream the shortening and sugar together with an electric mixer, then add the eggs and vanilla and beat till well blended. Alternately, add the peach mixture and flour mixture to the egg mixture and beat till well blended and smooth. Fold in the pecans, scrape the batter into a floured and greased medium-size loaf pan, and bake till golden, about 55 minutes. Turn out on a rack and let cool before slicing.

Yield: 1 loaf

Lemon Tea Bread

Mother learned to make this delicate tea bread from my Swedish great-aunt Jenny when she and Uncle August once visited us in Charlotte. Whenever we had Swedish relatives in the house, of course, there was never a time when a pot of either tea or coffee was not brewing and a selection of pastries, breads, and cookies was not in full supply for the ritual morning and afternoon breaks. Today, Mother makes the tea bread only when she knows in advance that, in fine Southern tradition, friends will come "visiting" and tea or coffee is the most appropriate beverage to serve.

½ cup (1 stick) butter, at room temperature
1 cup sugar
2 large eggs
1½ cups all-purpose flour
1½ teaspoons baking powder
¼ teaspoon salt
½ cup milk
Grated rind of 1 lemon
1 cup confectioners' sugar
2 tablespoons fresh lemon juice
½ teaspoon pure vanilla extract

Preheat the oven to 350°F.

In a large mixing bowl, cream the butter and sugar together with an electric mixer, then add the eggs and beat till well blended. In another bowl, combine the flour, baking powder, and salt. Add the flour mixture alternately with the milk to the creamed mixture and mix till well blended. Stir in the lemon rind.

Scrape the batter into a 9 x 5 x 3-inch loaf pan and bake till a straw inserted into the center comes out clean, about 50 minutes. Transfer the bread to a wire rack and let cool completely before slicing.

In a bowl, combine the confectioners' sugar, lemon juice, and vanilla, stir till smooth, and pour the glaze over the cake.

Yield: 1 loaf

Southern Buttermilk Biscuits

If there's any preparation that might qualify officially as Mother's signature dish, it's not so much the fried chicken, short ribs of beef, peach cobbler, or fruitcake as the inimitable buttermilk biscuits that people have come to expect automatically when they dine in her home or mine. Why, for the hundredth time, discourse on why my biscuits never, ever turn out exactly like hers; how no Southern meal in our homes could ever be complete without these wonders; and why, for me, dinner biscuits are even better when split, buttered, and toasted under the broiler for breakfast? For us, biscuits are a way of life, and, believe me, to watch my mother fix a batch is a moving and unique experience. Do note that Mother *never* makes biscuits with any flour but Red Band or White Lily, both of which she brings in large quanitites when she visits me in East Hampton. Distributed only in the South, these superior flours are milled only from soft red winter wheat and are less dense and lower in gluten than flours milled from hard summer wheat. (The White Lily Foods Company will ship five-pound bags anywhere in the country. The address is P.O. Box 871, Knoxville, Tennessee 37901.) To clear up any confusion about whether Southerners consider the word "biscuit" to be both singular and plural, all I can relate is that in our family, everyone but Mother has always said "Please pass the biscuit*s*" when referring to a full platter.

2 cups all-purpose flour
4 teaspoons baking powder
$\frac{1}{2}$ teaspoon baking soda
$\frac{1}{2}$ teaspoon salt
$\frac{1}{4}$ cup Crisco vegetable shortening
1 cup buttermilk

Preheat the oven to 450°F.

Sift together the flour, baking powder, baking soda, and salt in a large mixing bowl. Add the shortening and cut it in with a pastry cutter or two knives till the mixture is well blended and mealy. Add the buttermilk and mix with a large spoon till the dough is soft, adding a little more buttermilk if necessary.

Turn the dough out onto a lightly floured surface and, using a light touch, turn the edges of the dough toward the middle, pressing with your hands. Press the dough out to a $\frac{1}{4}$-inch thickness, cut straight down into even rounds with a bis-

cuit cutter or small juice glass, and place the rounds ½ inch apart on a large baking
sheet. Gather up the scraps of dough and repeat the procedure. Bake the biscuits
just till lightly browned on top, about 12 minutes.

Yield: About 16 biscuits

Martha Pearl Says:

*"I have only three words of advice on making biscuit: 1)
Handle the dough just as little as possible, and never knead
it; 2) When cutting biscuit, be sure to cut straight down,
never twisting the cutter; 3) After the biscuit have baked
about 10 minutes, watch, watch, watch them to make absolutely sure they don't overbake."*

Mrs. Castanas's Angel Biscuits

The wife of the Greek owner of the Epicurean restaurant in Charlotte has been making this type of biscuit for over thirty years, and for over thirty years Mother has
been nagging Mrs. Castanas for the exact recipe. ("Now, Mrs. Villas, don't ask me
for the biscuit recipe," she still greets playfully everytime she sees Mother at the restaurant.) Since, unlike regular biscuits, these contain yeast, Mother began years ago trying to duplicate what she is convinced is simply a variation of Southern angel
biscuits. I'm sure that Mrs. Castanas would contradict every point in Mother's
interpretation, but, at least to my taste, the mystery has been solved.

1 package active dry yeast
¼ cup warm water
2½ cups all-purpose flour
2 tablespoons sugar
1½ teaspoons baking powder
½ teaspoon baking soda

¹/₂ teaspoon salt
¹/₂ cup vegetable shortening
1 cup buttermilk

In a small bowl, combine the yeast and warm water, stir, and set aside.

In a large mixing bowl, combine the flour, sugar, baking powder, baking soda, and salt and stir. Add the shortening and cut it in with a pastry cutter or two knives till the mixture is well blended and mealy. Add the yeast mixture and buttermilk and stir with a fork till well blended. Gather the dough into a ball, roll it out on a floured surface to ¹/₂-inch thickness, and cut into 2-inch biscuits. Place the biscuits close together on a baking sheet, cover with a clean towel, and let rise about 1 hour in a warm area.

Preheat the oven to 400°F.

Bake the biscuits till golden brown, 10 to 15 minutes.

Yield: About 2¹/₂ dozen biscuits

Sweet Potato Biscuits

Not all Southerners like sweet potato biscuits, which have an altogether different flavor and texture than regular biscuits. My Georgia granddaddy used to make them to eat with his short ribs of beef, and while they've never been one of Mother's favorites ("Just a little too heavy for my taste"), I love them from time to time—with any type of stew, with broiled fish, and toasted for breakfast.

5 medium-size sweet potatoes
²/₃ cup vegetable shortening
2¹/₂ cups all-purpose flour
3 teaspoons baking powder
¹/₂ teaspoon salt
Milk as needed

Place the potatoes in a large saucepan and add enough water to cover. Bring to a boil, reduce to moderately low heat, cover, and cook till the potatoes are very tender, about 30 minutes. When cool enough to handle, peel the potatoes, place them in a large mixing bowl, and mash with a potato masher or heavy fork. Immediately add the shortening, continue to mash till well blended, and let cool.

Preheat the oven to 425°F.

Add the flour, baking powder, and salt to the potato mixture and mix with a wooden spoon till well blended, adding a little milk if necessary to make a smooth dough. On a lightly floured surface, roll out the dough ½ inch thick, cut out biscuits with a biscuit cutter or small juice glass, and place on a baking sheet. Gather up the scraps of dough, reroll, and cut out more biscuits. Bake the biscuits till golden, about 12 minutes.

Yield: About 20 biscuits

Pocketbook Rolls

When a member of Mother's Charity League showed up for a workshop one morning with a batch of hot freshly baked yeast rolls to be served with coffee, it didn't take long for the other ladies to learn that Frances had simply gotten up very early, rolled out her rolls, let them rise, and popped them into the oven shortly before leaving. Ever since she got the recipe, Mother has never been without a batch of these buttery rolls in the freezer. Typically, she doubles the recipe, stores about half the baked rolls in the freezer, and heats them as needed. "They're great for emergencies," she says.

1 package active dry yeast
½ cup warm water
¼ cup vegetable shortening, at room temperature
¼ cup (½ stick) butter, at room temperature
¼ cup sugar
½ cup boiling water
1 large egg, beaten
3 cups all-purpose flour
1½ teaspoons salt
½ cup (1 stick) butter, melted

In a small bowl, combine the yeast and warm water, stir, and set aside.

In a large mixing bowl, cream the shortening, ¼ cup butter, and sugar together with an electric mixer, then gradually beat in the boiling water. Add the yeast mixture and stir till well blended. Add the egg and stir till well blended. Sift in the flour, add the salt, and mix well. Cover the bowl tightly with plastic wrap and chill in the refrigerator till ready to use. (The mixture will keep up to 1 week in the refrigerator.)

Three hours before ready to use, roll out the dough on a floured surface to ½-inch thickness and cut into rounds with a 2- to 2½-inch biscuit cutter. Fold each round in half and place on a large greased baking sheet. Brush each roll with the melted butter, cover with a tea towel, and let rise in a warm place about 2½ hours.

Preheat the oven to 400°F.

Bake the rolls till golden brown, 5 to 7 minutes. (If you're planning to freeze part of the rolls, remove those from the oven after 5 minutes, let cool, and store wrapped tightly in aluminum foil.)

Yield: About 2 dozen rolls

Potato Yeast Rolls

Today in Mother's kitchen in Charlotte is a small white stool that I remember well from childhood, its only significance being that it is the same stool on which she and her sister, Jane, as children, would set out my grandmother's potato yeast rolls to rise while dinner was being prepared. "That was one of our little tasks: to place the rolls on the stool, cover them with a tea cloth, watch them from time to time, and let Mama know when they were puffy. Lord, I can still smell the aroma of those yeast rolls."

2 medium-size boiling potatoes, peeled and quartered
2 envelopes active dry yeast
2 tablespoons plus 1 teaspoon sugar
½ cup (1 stick) butter, melted
¼ cup vegetable shortening, melted
2 large eggs, beaten
2 teaspoons salt
6½ cups all-purpose flour

Place the potatoes in a saucepan, cover with water, bring to a low boil over moderate heat, cover, and cook till tender, 15 to 20 minutes. Drain the potatoes in a colander, reserving 1 cup of the potato water.

Cool the potato water to lukewarm, combine with the yeast and 1 teaspoon of the sugar in a small bowl, and set aside.

Mash the potatoes to measure 1 cup and place in a mixing bowl. Add the butter, shortening, 2 tablespoons sugar, eggs, salt, yeast mixture, and 2½ cups of the flour and beat with an electric mixer for 2 minutes. Gradually stir in enough of the remaining flour to make a soft dough, then turn the dough out onto a lightly floured surface, and knead till smooth and elastic, 8 to 10 minutes. Place the dough in a well-greased bowl, turn to coat all sides, cover with a clean towel, and let rise in a warm place till doubled in bulk, 1 to 1½ hours.

Punch the dough down, shape into 1½-inch balls, and place the balls in three 9-inch cake pans. Cover with clean towels and let rise in a warm area till doubled in bulk, about 1 hour.

Preheat the oven to 400°F.

Bake the rolls till golden brown on top, about 25 minutes.

Yield: About 30 rolls

Skillet Cornbread

It was almost a religious law in Mother's family that anytime vegetables were placed on the table, some form of cornbread had to be served (and usually biscuits to boot). When it was not being slathered with country butter, it was crumbled into bowls of pot likker from the vegetables and eaten with a spoon; and when any was left over in the pan, it was kept to be used to make stuffings. The custom persisted throughout my youth, and still today when we're planning to serve string beans, collards, black-eyed peas, or any other vegetable simmered slowly with streak-o'-lean, Mother will invariably ask "Don't you think we'd better make a little cornbread?"

1½ cups white cornmeal
3 tablespoons all-purpose flour

1 teaspoon baking soda
1 teaspoon salt
1¾ cups buttermilk
1 large egg
2 tablespoons vegetable shortening
1 tablespoon bacon grease

Preheat the oven to 475°F.

In a mixing bowl, combine the dry ingredients and mix well. In another bowl, combine the buttermilk and egg and beat till well blended, then add it to the dry ingredients and mix the batter till blended thoroughly.

Place the shortening and bacon grease in a 9-inch iron skillet and heat till the shortening melts. Pour the hot fats into the batter, stir well, and pour the batter back into the skillet. Bake in the oven till the cornbread is golden brown, about 20 minutes.

To serve, turn the skillet upside down on a big plate, remove, and cut the cornbread into wedges.

(To make corn sticks, pour the batter into greased corn stick pans and bake till golden brown, about 10 minutes.)

Yield: 4 to 6 servings

Center Pier Hush Puppies

Often it seems like members of the Villas and Pierson families have spent half their lives trying to track down the ultimate recipes for dishes we truly relish, and, to be sure, hush puppies are no exception. These round or oblong little fried corn dodgers are almost indigenous to the Carolina coastal areas, and tempers can flare at barbecue and fish houses when cooks debate what does and does not constitute a great hush puppy. Suffice it that, to date, the ultimate example for Mother and me are the perfectly seasoned, perfectly mixed, perfectly fried nuggets we discovered at the Center Pier restaurant at Carolina Beach, North Carolina, the recipe for which we quickly jotted down on a paper napkin as the black cook rattled off her ingredients and technique. Be warned that people devour these hush puppies as if they were peanuts.

2 cups all-purpose flour
1½ cups cornmeal
3 tablespoons sugar
1 teaspoon baking powder
1 teaspoon salt
½ cup finely minced onions
1⅓ cups milk
1 cup water
⅓ cup vegetable oil
1 large egg, beaten
Corn or vegetable oil for deep-frying

Sift together the flour, cornmeal, sugar, baking powder, and salt in a large mixing bowl. Add the onion, milk, water, oil, and egg and stir just long enough to blend the ingredients.

In a deep-fat fryer or deep cast-iron skillet, heat about 2½ inches of oil to 375°F. Drop the batter in batches by tablespoons into the fat, making sure not to crowd the pan, and fry the hush puppies till golden brown. Drain briefly on paper towels and serve immediately.

Yield: At least 40 hush puppies

Martha Pearl Says:

"There's nothing, repeat nothing, worse than a heavy, poorly seasoned, warmed-over hush puppy that's been fried in old fat. I use nothing but fresh Crisco, and, although it means staying in the kitchen till the last minute, I serve them almost from the fat. As for the cornmeal, Jimmy uses yellow, but I prefer white."

Poppy Seed Muffins

½ cup (1 stick) butter, at room temperature
¾ cup sugar
2 large eggs
¾ cup sour cream
1½ teaspoons pure vanilla extract
2 cups all-purpose flour
½ teaspoon baking soda
1 teaspoon salt
¼ cup poppy seeds

Preheat the oven to 400°F.

In a mixing bowl, cream together the butter and sugar with an electric mixer, then add the eggs one at a time, beating well after each addition. Add the sour cream and vanilla and continue beating till well blended. Add the flour, baking soda, salt, and poppy seeds and stir till well blended and smooth.

Grease the cups of a 12-cup muffin tin, fill each cup two thirds full, and bake till the muffins are browned, 15 to 20 minutes. Let cool on a rack.

Yield: 12 muffins

Martha Pearl Says:

"For an altogether different but delicious muffin, I sometimes omit the poppy seeds in this recipe and add 1 mashed ripe banana and ½ cup finely chopped nuts to the batter."

Tommy's Orange Muffins

A couple of summers ago, just as Mother and Aunt Dee were packing the car to return to Charlotte after one of their extended stays in East Hampton, up drove our friend Tom Bernstein with a tin of these orange muffins for the two ladies "just in case there might be a hunger attack." Within the week, Mother had called to get the recipe, and already they've become a staple at the breakfast table and on brunch buffets.

1 large orange
$1/3$ cup orange juice
6 tablespoons ($3/4$ stick) butter, at room temperature and cut into chunks
1 large egg
$1/2$ cup seedless golden raisins
1 tablespoon light rum
$1 1/2$ cups all-purpose flour
$3/4$ cup sugar
1 teaspoon baking powder
1 teaspoon baking soda
1 teaspoon salt

Grate the rind of the orange onto a small plate and reserve. Remove and discard the white orange pith, cut the orange into quarters, and remove the seeds.

Preheat the oven to 400°F.

In a blender, combine the rind, orange quarters, orange juice, butter, egg, raisins, and rum, blend 5 seconds, and transfer to a large mixing bowl. In another bowl, sift together the dry ingredients, then add it to the orange mixture and stir till just blended (do not overstir).

Spoon the mixture into a buttered and floured 12-cup muffin tin, fill each cup two thirds full, and bake till the muffins are golden, 15 to 20 minutes.

Yield: 12 muffins

Blueberry Muffins with Streusel Topping

Although it was my sister who originally got this recipe from a friend in Wilmington, North Carolina, it didn't take Mother long to determine what a nice gift the muffins would make to friends in the hospital or confined to the house with illness. Otherwise, both she and Hootie like to serve them for breakfast or on breakfast and brunch buffets in place of Danish pastries.

For the topping

2 tablespoons butter
2 tablespoons firmly packed light brown sugar
¼ teaspoon ground cinnamon
¼ cup finely chopped nuts

For the muffins

1½ cups all-purpose flour
2 teaspoons baking powder
½ teaspoon salt
¼ cup (½ stick) butter, at room temperature
½ cup sugar
1 large egg
1 teaspoon pure vanilla extract
½ cup milk
1½ cups fresh blueberries, picked over and rinsed

To prepare the topping, melt the butter in a small saucepan, then add the sugar and stir over low heat till dissolved. Add the cinnamon and nuts, stir well, and set aside.

Preheat the oven to 400°F.

To make the muffins, sift the flour, baking powder, and salt together in a bowl. In a large mixing bowl, combine the butter and sugar and cream together with an electric mixer till fluffy. Add the egg and vanilla and continue beating till well blended. Alternately, stir in the flour mixture and milk, mix well, then fold in the blueberries.

Grease a 12-cup muffin tin. Fill each cup two thirds full with batter, spoon a little streusel topping on each, and bake till golden, about 20 minutes.

Yield: 12 muffins

11

Desserts

*My sister, Hootie, at home in Charlotte, and already, at age 19, she has
mastered Mother's technique of baking the rich, luscious cakes that
will become her lifelong passion. Today she and Mother love
nothing more than to bake cakes together.*

If there is another area of the country (or indeed another place in the world besides England) where elaborate, rich, sinful desserts are as popular and beloved as in the South, I'd like to be informed. Since I'm that rare Southerner who has learned to control the sweet tooth, it never ceases to amaze me how utterly obsessed people like my mother, sister, and aunt are with complex frosted cakes oozing with butter, cream, sugar, and chocolate; puffy fruit, nut, and custard pies with double crusts and mountains of whipped cream; hot sticky cobblers practically lost in floes of melting ice cream; and large ceremonial fruitcakes reeking of whiskey. The number of cakes and pies and cobblers and dumplings and fresh fruit concoctions in Mother's black recipe book seems to double from year to year as she continues to gather new ideas from friends, from her various social and charity clubs, and from restaurants we visit. And if, in deference to my waistline, I usually irritate her by announcing defiantly that I want no more than a couple of spoonfuls of her luscious peach cobbler or just a thin slice of pound cake, less-disciplined guests at the table always do full justice to whatever dessert is placed before them.

Admonition Coconut Cake (Aunt Dee)
2 cups sugar
2 cups sour cream (2 ½ pt cartons)
2 pkgs. (6 oz ea.) frozen coconut
1 pkg. (2 layer size) yellow cake mix

The night before baking cake, combine
sugar, sour cream, + coconut - store in
refrigerator
    next morning, prepare cake + bake
in 2 layers, by pkg. directions.

Mother's sister, whom I've called "Aunt Dee" my entire life, is a devout Methodist with a tendency to invoke shades of morality when she names one of her many rich, sinful cakes and takes the recipe over for Mother to try.

Peach Cobbler

It's almost ridiculous the amount of peach cobbler we serve at both Mother's and my homes, but, for many of our friends, a Southern meal is simply not Southern without Mother's inimitable peach cobbler—hot or cold—topped with vanilla ice cream—preferably fresh from the churn. For years, she would use nothing but the sweet Elbertas that she hauls up in the car from South Carolina orchards to East Hampton to preserve, pickle, and churn into ice cream, but now she's almost convinced that peaches grown on the North Fork of eastern Long Island do have their merits. Back in Charlotte, of course, she freezes plenty of Elbertas every summer, which means that in her home there's also peach cobbler all during the winter. Do notice that the procedures for making peach and blackberry cobblers are altogether different.

4 pounds fresh peaches, peeled, pitted, and cut into $\frac{1}{2}$-inch slices
$\frac{2}{3}$ cup plus 2 teaspoons sugar
2 tablespoons butter
2 cups all-purpose flour
1 tablespoon baking powder
1 teaspoon salt
$\frac{1}{4}$ cup cold vegetable shortening
1 cup heavy cream
Vanilla ice cream

In a large bowl, combine the peaches with $\frac{2}{3}$ cup of the sugar, toss well, spoon the fruit into a shallow 10-cup baking dish, and dot with the butter.

Preheat the oven to 400°F.

Sift together the flour, baking powder, salt, and the remaining 2 teaspoons sugar in a mixing bowl and cut in the shortening with a pastry cutter or two knives till the mixture resembles coarse meal. Add the cream and stir till the dough forms a ball. Turn out the dough on a floured surface, roll out $\frac{1}{4}$ inch thick, and trim as necessary to fit the baking dish. Place the dough over the fruit, crimp the edges, and bake till the pastry is golden brown, about 30 minutes.

Let the cobbler cool about 15 minutes and serve warm topped with vanilla ice cream.

Yield: 6 to 8 servings

Blackberry Cobbler

It seems only yesterday when I would hear Henry clanging on his bucket, rush out the back screen door with Mother, and watch as she and the cheerful old black farmer chatted while measuring out tin cans of freshly picked blackberries. For lunch, we'd eat those luscious berries with fresh cream, and for supper there'd be this lattice cobbler topped with vanilla ice cream, and never was there anything so good. Eventually, of course, Henry went to his reward, and when Henry stopped coming, and I could no longer pluck those warm, sweet, seedy berries from his bucket one by one while he and Mother talked and laughed, I thought all the blackberries of the world had disappeared. Today, I often think the same when scouring the summer markets, but when Mother and I do find fresh blackberries (at a price!), you can be sure that this cobbler will be on the menu.

Double recipe Basic Pie Shell (page 234), unbaked
6 cups ripe fresh blackberries
1¼ cups sugar
1 cup water
2 tablespoons all-purpose flour
3 tablespoons butter

Preheat the oven to 375°F.

Divide the pastry in half and roll out one half with a floured rolling pin to fit a deep baking dish measuring approximately 11 x 8 x 2 inches. Roll out the remaining pastry very thin and cut into 1-inch-wide strips. Place half of the strips on an ungreased baking sheet and bake until partially cooked and slightly browned.

Increase the oven temperature to 425°F.

In a large saucepan, combine the berries, 1 cup of the sugar, and the water, bring to a boil, reduce the heat to moderate, and cook just till the berries are soft. In a bowl, combine the flour and remaining sugar, stir, add to the berry mixture, and cook till the mixture has thickened slightly, stirring constantly. Spoon a layer of berries into the pastry-lined pan, arrange a layer of the partially cooked pastry strips over the berries, and continue layering berries and pastry strips, ending with berries on top. Dot with the butter, arrange the remaining uncooked strips in a lattice formation across the top, and bake till nicely browned, about 25 minutes.

Yield: 6 to 8 servings

Basic Pie Shell

2 cups all-purpose flour
¼ teaspoon salt
⅔ cup vegetable shortening
¼ cup ice water

In a mixing bowl, combine the flour and salt, then cut in the shortening with a pastry cutter or two knives until the mixture resembles coarse meal. Stirring with a spoon, gradually add the water till a ball of dough is formed. Wrap the dough in plastic wrap and chill till ready to use.

To bake the pie shell, preheat the oven to 425°F, place the dough on a lightly floured surface, and roll it out from the center (not to and fro) with a lightly floured rolling pin to a ⅛-inch thickness. Carefully fold the pastry in half, lay the fold across the center of a greased pie plate or pan, unfold it, and press it loosely on the bottom and sides of the plate. Prick the bottom and sides with a fork, place the plate on a heavy baking sheet, and bake till the shell browns evenly, 12 to 15 minutes.

Yield: One 9- or 10-inch pie shell

Martha Pearl Says:

"I've never understood all this nonsense about scattering tacks and beans and Lord knows what else over foil-lined pastry to keep it from bulking. Pricking the shell evenly with a fork has always worked just fine for me, and, besides, we Southerners like our pie shells to look homemade."

Southern Pecan Pie

Mother can get very touchy when it comes to the correct way to make genuine Southern pecan pie, and I don't think I ever saw her so enraged as the time I "destroyed" a pie by not including any sugar, adding both corn syrup *and* molasses, and having pecans on the top instead of throughout the filling. "Why do you have to fool around with a simple recipe that's been in the family for generations?" she asked in total frustration.

4 large eggs
1 cup sugar
1 cup light corn syrup
1½ teaspoons all-purpose flour
¼ teaspoon salt
1 teaspoon pure vanilla extract
¼ cup (½ stick) butter, melted
2 cups pecan halves
One 9-inch Basic Pie Shell (facing page), unbaked
Whipped cream

Preheat the oven to 350°F.

In a large bowl, beat the eggs with an electric mixer, then add the sugar, corn syrup, flour, salt, and vanilla and beat till well blended. Stir in the butter and pecans and mix well. Turn the mixture into the pie shell and bake till the filling is soft in the center when the pie is gently shaken, 50 to 60 minutes. Cool the pie completely on a rack, chill slightly, and serve with dollops of whipped cream.

Yield: One 9-inch pie; 6 servings

Martha Pearl Says:

"The only real secret to any great pecan pie is fresh nuts—and by fresh I don't mean those half-rancid pecans sold in cans and cellophane packages. Anybody who truly loves pecan pie will buy the nuts when they're in season, shell them, and freeze whatever's left over in tightly sealed plastic bags. I've kept frozen pecans up to a year with no problem."

Kress' Pecan Chiffon Pie

Up till the early sixties, Kress' was a simple dime store smack in the center of downtown Charlotte, but so popular was the Southern food turned out in the basement lunchroom by black cooks that people always had to wait in line to be seated. I remember my granddaddy Paw Paw taking me down to Kress' on Saturday mornings for a big breakfast, but Mother's memories extend much further back when she and other students at Central High School would walk to the store at least once a week just to have a slice of this pie. The cost: ten cents.

½ cup coarsely chopped pecans
½ cup firmly packed dark brown sugar
⅔ cup water
2 tablespoons cornstarch mixed with 2 tablespoons water
2 medium-size egg whites, at room temperature
2 tablespoons granulated sugar
One 9-inch Basic Pie Shell (page 234), prebaked
¾ cup heavy cream
¼ cup finely chopped pecans for garnish

Preheat the oven to 275°F.

Spread the coarsely chopped pecans on a baking sheet and toast in the oven till barely browned, 10 to 15 minutes. Set aside.

In a saucepan, combine the brown sugar and water and bring to a boil. Using a whisk, stir in the cornstarch and stir constantly till the mixture becomes clear and has the consistency of a thick pudding. Remove from the heat.

In a bowl, beat the egg whites with an electric mixer till peaks form, then gradually add the white sugar, and beat till the peaks are stiff. With the mixer on low speed, gradually add the pecans and the brown sugar mixture but do not overmix. Pile the filling into the pie shell. Whip the cream till stiff peaks form, spread over the top of the pie, and sprinkle the chopped pecans on top.

Yield: One 9-inch pie, 6 servings

S & W Custard Pie

During and shortly after World War II, much of the South's claim to restaurant fame were the S & W cafeterias located in various major cities, vast, rather spiffy halls where, for a couple of bucks, people could select from elaborate displays of country-style steak, fried chicken, rare roast beef custom-carved from a gigantic round, fried shrimp, corn muffins, and other such wholesome dishes. Yes, the food was good, honest, and very Southern, and my sister and I always looked forward to being taken to the S & W every Friday night, followed by a movie at the nearby theater. Mother seems to remember every dish ever served at the S & W, but never was she so happy as when the recipe for the cafeteria's famous custard pie appeared in the *Charlotte Observer.*

1¼ cups sugar
2 tablespoons butter, at room temperature
½ teaspoon salt
4 large eggs, beaten
2 cups milk
1 teaspoon pure vanilla extract
One 10-inch Basic Pie Shell (page 234), unbaked

Preheat the oven to 425°F.

In a mixing bowl, combine the sugar, butter, and salt and beat with an electric mixer till smooth. Add the eggs and mix till well blended. Add the milk and vanilla and beat till smooth.

Turn the mixture into the pie shell, flute the shell high around the edges, and bake 15 minutes. Reduce heat to 350°F and bake till the pie begins to set around the edges and the middle is still jiggly, 12 to 15 minutes longer. Let the pie cool, then chill slightly.

Yield: One 10-inch pie; 6 servings

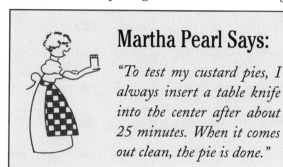

Martha Pearl Says:

"To test my custard pies, I always insert a table knife into the center after about 25 minutes. When it comes out clean, the pie is done."

Lemon Meringue Pie

Even my father, who generally abhorred lemon meringue pie since he said so many were made with that awful condensed milk, couldn't get his fill of Mother's classic wonder. Once, when I took a pie that she had baked in East Hampton to the editor-in-chief of *Town & Country*, he was so taken by the flavor and texture that he consumed the entire pie in a single sitting—and wondered why he tossed and turned all night!

1 cup plus 6 tablespoons sugar
¼ cup cornstarch
¼ teaspoon salt
1½ cups boiling water
2 teaspoons grated lemon rind
⅓ cup fresh lemon juice
3 large eggs, separated
2 tablespoons butter
One 9-inch Basic Pie Shell (page 234), prebaked

Preheat the oven to 325°F.

In a heavy saucepan, combine 1 cup of the sugar, the cornstarch, and salt and mix till well blended. Gradually add the boiling water, stirring constantly, and cook over moderate heat till the mixture thickens, stirring. Add the lemon rind and juice and stir. In a small bowl, beat the egg yolks, add a small amount of the lemon mixture, stirring constantly, and pour the egg mixture into the lemon mixture. Add the butter and continue cooking till the mixture is very thick, stirring, then pour into the baked pie shell.

In a bowl, beat the egg whites with an electric mixer till thickened, then gradually add the remaining 6 tablespoons sugar and beat till stiff peaks form. With a spatula, cover the pie with the meringue, sealing all the edges. With a spoon, make a few peaks in the meringue, bake just till the top has browned slightly, and cool the pie before serving.

Yield: One 9-inch pie; 6 servings

Martha Pearl Says:

"In making any meringue, always use 2 tablespoons of sugar to each egg white to assure a high, fluffy topping. Also, to keep it from shrinking while baking, make sure that the meringue is spread to the very edges of the pie."

Butterscotch Pie

Honey, you got any butterscotch pie?" my Unca' Nalle used to ask perplexed waitresses in restaurants, knowing full well that the only human being on earth who still made the effort to make the pie was Mother. After we all had a good laugh, of course, she'd promise to fix her brother the pie the next time he and Aunt Mary Frances came for dinner, and, as usual, he'd end up taking home whatever was left over.

One 13-ounce can evaporated milk
1 cup milk
1 cup firmly packed light brown sugar
5 tablespoons all-purpose flour
½ teaspoon salt
1 teaspoon pure vanilla extract
3 tablespoons butter
3 large eggs, separated
One 9-inch Basic Pie Shell (page 234), prebaked
6 tablespoons granulated sugar

In a bowl, combine the two milks and stir till well blended.

In the top of a double boiler, combine the brown sugar, flour, and salt, place over simmering water, and add the milks, vanilla, and butter. Stir constantly till the mixture thickens, cover, and cook 10 minutes, stirring occasionally.

In a small bowl, beat the egg yolks, then gradually add about 3 tablespoons of the hot mixture, stirring constantly, return the egg mixture to the hot mixture, and cook 2 to 3 minutes, stirring constantly. Remove from the heat and let cool. When thoroughly cooled, pour the mixture into the pie shell.

Preheat the oven to 325°F.

In a bowl, beat the egg whites with an electric mixer till firm peaks form. Gradually add 5 tablespoons of the sugar, beating steadily till the whites are stiff. Spoon the meringue over top of the pie and spread to seal the edges completely. Sprinkle the remaining sugar over the top and bake just till the meringue is slightly browned.

Yield: One 9-inch pie; 6 servings

Fried Peach Pies

F ried fruit pies were one of my grandmother Maw Maw's well-known special-ties, and none was so popular with relatives, friends, and neighbors as the ones made with the dried peaches she always bought in bulk. Making the unusual pies does require a little time and patience, but whenever Mother and I serve them with a little vanilla ice cream, guests rave.

2 cups all-purpose flour
1 teaspoon baking powder
½ teaspoon salt
½ cup (1 stick) butter, softened
6 to 8 tablespoons ice water
One 8-ounce package dried peaches
½ cup granulated sugar
½ teaspoon ground cinnamon
¼ teaspoon ground nutmeg
Vegetable oil for frying
½ cup confectioners' sugar

In a large bowl, combine the flour, baking powder, and salt, then add the butter and cut in with a pastry cutter or two knives till the mixture resembles coarse meal. Add 6 tablespoons of the ice water, toss lightly, and gather the dough into a ball, adding more ice water a few drops at a time if the dough is too crumbly. Wrap in waxed paper and refrigerate at least 1 hour before using.

Place the dried peaches in a saucepan with enough water to cover, add the sugar, cinnamon, and nutmeg, bring to a boil, reduce the heat to low, and simmer till the peaches are tender. Remove from the heat and cool to room temperature.

Place part of the chilled dough on a lightly floured surface and roll out about to ⅛ inch thick. Place a saucer about 6 inches in diameter over the dough, cut out one round, and place the round on a plate. Gather up the scraps, add more dough to the scraps, and continue rolling out and cutting more rounds till all the dough is used up.

To shape the pies, place about 3 tablespoons of the peach mixture on the lower third of each round, fold the round in half, press the edges together, and, using a fork dipped in flour, score the edges by pressing down firmly.

Pour enough oil into a heavy skillet to measure about 1 inch deep and heat till a small piece of bread tossed in is quickly browned. Fry the pies a few at a time on both sides till golden and crisp. Drain on paper towels and keep warm till served dusted with the confectioners' sugar.

Yield: 10 to 12 pies

Martha Pearl Says:

"Never use fresh peaches in this recipe; they're just too juicy and will ruin the texture of the pies. Dried apricots and apples also make delicious fillings."

Mrs. Sherrill's Old-Fashioned Pound Cake

This traditional pound cake (1 pound each of butter, sugar, and flour) was first served to Mother when she was a young bride by the mother of one of Daddy's closest friends, and, to this day, Mother has never tampered with the recipe. I've complained that the pound cake never has a "sad streak" (an under-cooked, sweet "streak" running down the middle that some Southerners love), but no amount of pleading coaxes Mother to alter her sacred method of baking.

1 pound (4 sticks) butter
1 pound (2 cups) sugar
9 large eggs
1 pound (4 cups) all-purpose flour
Dash of salt
2 teaspoons pure vanilla extract
Juice of 1 lemon

Preheat the oven to 325°F.

In a large bowl, cream the butter with an electric mixer, then gradually add the sugar, continuing to beat till well creamed and smooth. Add the eggs one at a time, beating well after each addition. Gradually add the flour and salt, beating constantly. Add the vanilla and lemon juice and continue beating till well blended.

Grease and flour a 10-inch tube pan, pour in the batter, and "spank" the bottom of the pan to distribute the batter evenly. Bake till a straw inserted into the cake comes out clean, about 1¼ hours, taking care not to overcook. Turn the cake out on a rack and let cool.

Yield: One 10-inch cake; 12 servings

Martha Pearl Says:

"One day I asked Mrs. Sherrill why the cake was so delicious, and she said 'Dear, the secret is the fresh lemon juice: its stablizing effect acts the same as cream of tartar.' I never forgot this principle."

Chocolate Pound Cake

My sister's chocolate pound cake, which is altogether different from Mother's traditional classic, is undoubtedly one of the greatest chocolate creations I've ever known and one of the few pound cakes other than her own that Mother has endorsed. Note that the baking time is reduced just enough to produce the slightly uncooked "sad streak" I so relish. Personally, I prefer the cake without a glaze, but since most guests love a rich chocolate icing, Mother and I usually gild the lily.

For the cake

1 cup (2 sticks) butter
½ cup Crisco vegetable shortening
3 cups granulated sugar
5 large eggs
3 cups all-purpose flour
½ teaspoon baking powder
½ teaspoon salt
¼ cup unsweetened cocoa powder
1 cup milk
1 teaspoon pure vanilla extract

For the glaze

One 5-ounce bar German chocolate
1 tablespoon butter
¼ cup water
1 cup confectioners' sugar
Dash salt

Preheat the oven to 325°F.

To make the cake, cream the butter and shortening together in a large bowl with an electric mixer till light and smooth. Add the sugar and continue beating till well blended. Add the eggs one at a time, beating after each addition till well blended. In a bowl, sift together the flour, baking powder, salt, and cocoa and add alternately with the milk to the batter, beating well. Add the vanilla and beat till well blended.

Grease and flour a 10-inch tube or Bundt pan, pour in the batter, and "spank" the bottom of the pan to distribute the batter evenly. Bake 1 hour and 10 minutes, let the cake cool in the pan, and turn out onto a cake plate.

While the cake is baking, make the glaze by melting the chocolate and butter in the water over low heat. Sift the sugar over the mixture, add the salt, and stir till well blended and smooth. Keep warm.

When the cake is finished baking and has been positioned on the cake plate, drizzle the glaze over the top, allowing some to drip down the sides. Let the glaze cool completely before serving the cake.

Yield: One 10-inch cake; 12 servings

Hummingbird Cake

Southerners love big, rich, complex cakes, and none exemplifies the passion more than this spicy, sinful, dramatic confection that Mother adopted from my sister not too long ago. Needless to say, neither can explain its connection to a hummingbird.

For the cake

3 cups all-purpose flour
2 cups granulated sugar
1 teaspoon baking soda
1 teaspoon ground cinnamon
1 teaspoon salt
3 large eggs, beaten
1½ cups vegetable oil
1½ teaspoons pure vanilla extract
One 8-ounce can crushed pineapple, undrained
2 cups chopped nuts (pecans, walnuts, or hazelnuts)
2 cups chopped bananas

For the frosting

Two 8-ounce packages cream cheese, at room temperature
1 cup (2 sticks) butter, at room temperature
Two 16-ounce boxes confectioners' sugar, sifted
2 teaspoons pure vanilla extract

To make the cake, preheat the oven to 350°F and combine the flour, sugar, baking soda, cinnamon, and salt in a large bowl. Add the eggs and oil and stir till the dry ingredients are moistened, taking care not to beat. Stir in the vanilla, pineapple, 1 cup of the nuts, and the bananas.

Grease and flour three 9-inch cake pans and divide the batter among them. Bake till a straw inserted into the middle of the cakes comes our clean, 25 to 30 minutes. Let the cakes cool in the pans 10 minutes, then turn out onto a rack to cool completely.

To make the frosting, combine the cream cheese and butter in a large bowl and cream with an electric mixer till smooth. Add the sugar, beat till light and fluffy, and stir in the vanilla.

Spread the frosting between the cakes stacked on a cake plate, frost the top and sides of the cake, and sprinkle the remaining nuts over the top.

Yield: One 9-inch cake; 12 servings

Mississippi Mud Cake

When Mother and the members of her Charity League workshop meet to make items for their annual bazaar, each lady usually brings something for lunch. Once a member showed up with this rich classic from her home state of Mississippi, and Mother says that "We girls ate so much that all we could do after lunch was go home and take a good nap."

For the cake

2 cups all-purpose flour
2 cups granulated sugar
½ cup (1 stick) margarine or butter, cut up
3½ tablespoons unsweetened cocoa powder
½ cup vegetable shortening
1 cup water
1 teaspoon ground cinnamon
½ cup buttermilk
2 large eggs, beaten
1 teaspoon baking soda
1 teaspoon pure vanilla extract

For the icing

½ cup (1 stick) margarine or butter
3 tablespoons unsweetened cocoa powder
⅓ cup milk
One 16-ounce box confectioners' sugar, sifted
1 teaspoon pure vanilla extract
1 cup chopped walnuts

Preheat the oven to 400°F.

To make the cake, combine the flour and sugar in a bowl and set aside.

In a saucepan, combine the margarine, cocoa, shortening, and water, bring to a boil, and remove from the heat. Add the cinnamon and flour mixture and mix well. Add the buttermilk, eggs, soda, and vanilla and mix well. Scrape the batter into a greased and floured 16 x 11-inch baking pan and bake till a straw inserted into the cake comes out clean, about 20 minutes.

Meanwhile, to make the icing, combine the margarine, cocoa, and milk in a saucepan and bring almost to a boil, stirring. Add the sugar, vanilla, and walnuts and stir till the sugar is fully dissolved and well blended.

Remove the cake from the oven and let cool slightly. Pour the icing over the top, smooth with a rubber spatula, and let cool completely.

To serve, cut the cake into 24 squares.

Yield: At least 12 servings

Italian Cream Cake

Mother got this recipe from her sister, my Aunt Dee, who, every Christmas, makes a cake for each of her three daughters and their families. An amusing but typical curiosity is that the directions for making the cake in Mother's black recipe book are given in exactly two short sentences. "Once they have the ingredients," she scoffs, "everybody knows how to make a cake."

For the cake

½ cup (1 stick) butter
½ cup vegetable shortening

2 cups granulated sugar
5 large eggs, separated
2 cups all-purpose flour
1 teaspoon baking soda
¼ teaspoon salt
1 cup buttermilk
1 teaspoon pure vanilla extract
One 3½-ounce can Angel Flake coconut

For the icing

¼ cup (½ stick) butter, at room temperature
One 8-ounce package cream cheese, at room temperature
One 16-ounce box confectioners' sugar, sifted
1 teaspoon pure vanilla extract
1 cup chopped pecans

Preheat the oven to 350°F.

To make the cake, combine the butter, shortening, and sugar in a large bowl and cream with an electric mixer till smooth. Add the egg yolks one at a time, beating after each addition till well blended. In a bowl, sift together the flour, baking soda, and salt and add alternately with the milk to the egg mixture, beating. Add the vanilla and coconut and stir till well blended. In a bowl, beat the egg whites with an electric mixer till stiff peaks form, then fold into the batter.

Grease and flour three 9-inch cake pans, divide the batter equally among the pans, and bake till a straw inserted in the middles comes out clean, 25 to 30 minutes. Cool the cakes in the pans on a rack.

Meanwhile, to make the icing, cream together the butter and cream cheese in a large bowl with an electric mixer and gradually add the sugar and vanilla, mixing well till the icing is smooth.

When the cake layers are cooled, remove from the pans, place one layer on a cake plate, and spread one third of the icing on the layer. Place the second cake layer over the icing and spread with more icing. Top with the third layer and spread icing over the top and around the sides. Sprinkle the top with the chopped pecans.

Yield: One 9-inch cake; 10 to 12 servings

Original Kentucky Whiskey Cake

Although Mother has no recollection where she got the recipe for this spectac-
ular cake (perhaps from a close Kentucky friend of Daddy's who attended
their wedding?), only her dark fruitcake illustrates better her art as a master cake
baker. Yes, it takes time and a bit of effort to make the cake correctly, but, in her
own words, "people turn flips when they taste it." Do notice that the cake should
be made about a week in advance.

1 pound candied cherries, halved
$\frac{1}{2}$ pound seedless golden raisins
2 cups bourbon
$1\frac{1}{2}$ cups (3 sticks) butter, at room temperature
2 cups granulated sugar
1 cup firmly packed light brown sugar
6 large eggs, separated
5 cups all-purpose flour
1 pound chopped pecans
2 teaspoons ground nutmeg
1 teaspoon baking powder

In a bowl, combine the cherries, raisins, and bourbon and let soak overnight.
   Preheat the oven to 275°F.
   In a large bowl, cream the butter and two sugars together with an electric mixer
till fluffy, then add the egg yolks and beat well. Stir in the soaked fruit and bourbon. In a bowl, combine $\frac{1}{2}$ cup of the flour with the pecans and set aside. Add the
remaining flour, nutmeg, and baking powder to the creamed mixture and mix
well. In a bowl, beat the egg whites with an electric mixer till stiff peaks form and
fold them into the mixture. Add the floured pecans and fold gently.
   Grease a 10-inch tube pan and line it with greased brown paper or waxed
paper. Pour the batter into the pan, "spank" the bottom to distribute the batter
evenly, and bake till a straw inserted into the cake comes out clean, 3 to $3\frac{1}{2}$ hours.
Cool the cake, turn it out of the pan, peel off the brown paper, and store in a
tightly covered container about 1 week before serving.

Yield: One 10-inch cake; 10 to 12 servings

Martha Pearl Says:

"I often substitute chopped dates for the raisins. Also, a good way to maintain the moisture and flavor of this cake while it is mellowing is to stuff the center hole with cheesecloth soaked in bourbon."

Maw Maw's 1-2-3-4 Cake With Caramel Icing

Of all the birthday cakes my sister and I enjoyed as children, we loved none more than our grandmother's 1-2-3-4 cake (so-called, quaintly, because of the numerical progression of the first four cake ingredients) with luscious caramel icing. Mother remembers that Maw Maw used to make the same cake with different icings (chocolate, coconut, vanilla, or strawberry) for her, Aunt Dee, and Unca' Nalle when they were young, and after my sister got married and began raising a family, the tradition continued with my nephew and niece. And what cake did I ask Mother to bake for my fiftieth birthday fling? You guessed it.

For the cake

1 cup (2 sticks) butter
2 cups granulated sugar
4 large eggs, well beaten
3 cups all-purpose flour
3 teaspoons baking powder
1 cup milk
1 teaspoon pure vanilla extract

For the icing

½ cup (1 stick) butter
1 cup firmly packed dark brown sugar
¼ cup milk
2 cups sifted confectioners' sugar

Preheat the oven to 350°F.

In a large mixing bowl, cream the butter and sugar together with an electric mixer till smooth, add the eggs, and continue beating till smooth. In a bowl, mix the flour and baking powder together and add alternately with the milk to the butter mixture, beating steadily till smooth. Add the vanilla and beat till well blended.

Grease and flour three 9-inch cake pans, divide the batter evenly among the pans, "spank" the bottoms of the pans to distribute the batter evenly, and bake till a straw inserted in centers comes out clean, 25 to 30 minutes. Let cool.

Meanwhile, to make the icing, melt the butter over low heat in a saucepan, add the brown sugar and milk, bring to a boil, and remove from the heat to cool. Add the confectioners' sugar and mix till well blended.

When the cake layers are cooled, remove from the pans, place one layer on a cake plate, and spread one third of the icing on the layer. Place a second cake layer over the icing and spread with more icing. Top with the third layer and spread icing over the top and around the sides.

Yield: One 9-inch cake; 10 to 12 servings

Fresh Apple Cake

Although my daddy could hardly fry bacon, he was obsessed with good food and forever on the lookout for dishes that Mother might reproduce at home. This recipe, for example, he got from the wife of one of his buddies at the health club where he kept fit, an utterly delicious cake that Mother wasted no time testing with great success on ten members of her book club.

2 cups sugar
3 large eggs
1 teaspoon pure vanilla extract
1½ cups vegetable oil
3 cups all-purpose flour
1 teaspoon baking soda
1 teaspoon ground cinnamon
1 teaspoon ground nutmeg

1 teaspoon salt
3 cups cored, peeled, and chopped Granny Smith apples
1 cup seedless golden raisins
1 cup chopped walnuts

Preheat the oven to 350°F.

In a large mixing bowl, combine the sugar, eggs, vanilla, and oil and mix till well blended. In another bowl, combine the flour, soda, cinnamon, nutmeg, and salt, add it to the sugar mixture, and stir till well blended. Fold in the apples, raisins, and walnuts.

Grease and flour a 13 x 9 x 2-inch baking pan, scrape in the apple mixture, and bake till a straw inserted into the middle comes out clean, about 1 hour. Do not overcook.

To serve, cut the cake into squares.

Yield: 12 servings

Heirloom Dark Fruitcake

Although Mother figures that the origins of the elegant fruitcakes she bakes every year can be traced back at least three generations in her family, her most vivid memory is of the "spend-the-day" parties that my grandmother and three close friends would have in the fall when each would help the others prepare fruit-cakes for the upcoming holidays. Typically, the ladies would cut up all the fruit and prepare the pans while the menfolk and children shelled the pecans, after which the great mounds of batter would be mixed, the cakes baked, and the fin-ished products wrapped carefully in cheesecloth soaked in bourbon or wine before being stored in tins to mellow for months, even years. (I still have one heirloom cake that's been aging in the refrigerator twenty-six years!) Today, there're not many Southern ladies like Mother left who make fruitcake in this age-old tradi-tion, and how sad our many relatives and friends would be each Christmas if they could not depend on her to supply them with at least one small truly homemade cake to grace the holiday table. Despite the rather dubious reputation of fruitcake that has evolved in this country (due mostly to all those wretched commercial products), rest assured that nobody ever makes jokes about Mother's aromatic, moist, colorful masterpieces that have even been featured on national television and that one day will be part of her proud kitchen legacy. Doused periodically with bourbon or brandy and kept tightly covered in the bottom of the refrigerator, this fruitcake will keep literally for decades and only improve with age.

1 pound seedless golden raisins
1 pound seedless dark raisins
½ pound crystallized citron, coarsely chopped
¼ pound crystallized orange peel, coarsely chopped
¼ pound crystallized lemon peel, coarsely chopped
1 pound crystallized pineapple, coarsely chopped
1 pound dates, pitted and coarsely chopped
1 pound crystallized cherries, cut in half
2 pounds pecans, coarsely broken up
4 cups sifted all-purpose flour
1 pound (4 sticks) butter, at room temperature
2 cups sugar
1 dozen large eggs
1 teaspoon ground cinnamon
½ teaspoon ground cloves
½ teaspoon ground nutmeg
¼ teaspoon ground ginger
1 teaspoon salt
2 teaspoons pure vanilla extract
2 teaspoons pure almond extract
¾ cup bourbon or brandy
Bourbon for sprinkling and soaking
Clear corn syrup
Crystallized cherries, pineapple, and pecan halves for decoration

In a large mixing bowl, combine the raisins, citron, orange peel, lemon peel, pineapple, dates, cherries, and pecans, add half the flour, and mix well. In another very large bowl, cream the butter with an electric mixer, add the sugar, and beat till light and fluffy. Add the eggs one at a time, beating well after each addition. Add the remaining flour, the spices, salt, and extracts, and mix with a wooden spoon till well blended. Add the fruit-and-nut mixture along with the bourbon and, using your hands, mix the batter well.

Preheat the oven to 250°F.

Grease and lightly flour the bottom and sides of one 10 x 4-inch tube pan and two 8 x 4½ x 2½-inch loaf pans and line each with heavy brown paper, letting the paper extend 1 inch above the pans. Grease the brown paper, scrape the batter into the pans, and, using your hands, pack the batter firmly to ½ inch below the tops of the pans. Cover the tops with sheets of waxed paper, place a shallow pan of water on the lower rack of the oven, place the cake pans on the middle rack, and bake the small cakes about 3½ hours and the large cake about 4 hours, till a straw inserted in the middles comes out clean, removing the waxed paper during the final 15 minutes of baking. (Do not overcook the cakes; watch the timing of each and check doneness periodically with the straw.)

Remove the cakes from the oven, immediately sprinkle each with bourbon, and let cool in the pans. Soak three double-thick pieces of cheesecloth large enough to envelop each cake in bourbon and squeeze the excess bourbon from the cheesecloth. Remove the cakes from the pans by lifting up the brown paper, and discard the paper. Brush the tops of the cakes with corn syrup, decorate with crystallized cherries, pineapple, and pecans, and let dry. Wrap the cakes securely in the cheesecloth and store in airtight containers at least 1 month before cutting. (To age cakes longer, wrap tightly in aluminum foil, place in containers, and store in the refrigerator, sprinkling the cheesecloth with bourbon every 6 months.)

Yield: One 5½-pound and two 2½-pound fruitcakes

Apple Dumplings With Brandy Hard Sauce

My grandmother would have snickered contemptuously at the "modern" way that her daughter makes the hard sauce for these dumplings, for I can see Maw Maw now: taking a big saucer shortly before the dumplings had finished baking, plopping down a chunk of fresh butter in the saucer, and, while gradually adding sugar, a little boiling water, and either brandy or fruit juice, mashing the mixture with a heavy fork till the sauce formed. Exactly how she did it so successfully we'll never know, but to this day I've never tasted a hard sauce quite like hers.

For the dumplings

¼ cup firmly packed light brown sugar
½ teaspoon ground cinnamon
½ teaspoon ground nutmeg
¼ cup seedless golden raisins
Double recipe Basic Pie Shell (page 234), unbaked
4 medium-size Granny Smith apples, cored and peeled
4 teaspoons butter

For the sauce

¼ cup (½ stick) butter, at room temperature
1 cup sifted confectioners' sugar
1 teaspoon boiling water
3 tablespoons brandy

Preheat the oven to 400°F.

To make the dumplings, combine the sugar, cinnamon, nutmeg, and raisins in a bowl and set aside.

On a lightly floured surface, roll out the dough to form a 14-inch square and cut the square into quarters. Place an apple in the center of each quarter, stuff the apples with equal amounts of the raisin mixture, and dot each with a teaspoon of butter. Dipping your fingertips in water, moisten the edges of each pastry quarter, bring the edges of the pastry up over each apple, and pinch the edges to seal. Place the dumplings in a 9-inch-square baking dish and bake till the apples are tender and the crusts browned, 35 to 40 minutes.

Meanwhile, to make the hard sauce, cream the butter and sugar together in a bowl with an electric mixer, then add the boiling water and beat till smooth. Add the brandy and continue beating till the mixture is a fluffy sauce.

Serve the sauce over the hot dumplings.

Yield: 4 servings

Ambrosia

It is literally inconceivable that Mother might serve her elaborate Christmas dinner without including a cut-crystal bowl of ambrosia to be served with all the fruitcake, cookies, and Lord knows what other desserts. After once researching this Greek "food of the gods" and tracing its evolution through the Roman Empire to England and the American South, I began adding grapefruit to my ambrosia, only to have Mother hit the ceiling and lecture me that "no real Southerner would ever corrupt this sacred formula with . . . grapefruit!"

6 large oranges
½ cup sugar
2 cups freshly grated coconut
¼ cup freshly squeezed orange juice

Peel the oranges, cutting away all white pith, and carefully remove the orange sections from the membranes that surround them. In a crystal bowl, arrange a layer of orange sections across the bottom and sprinkle a little of the sugar and coconut on top. Repeat the layers till the ingredients are used up, ending with a layer of coconut. Drizzle the orange juice over the top, cover the bowl with plastic wrap, and chill well before serving in crystal compote dishes.

Yield: 6 servings

Martha Pearl Says:

"This is the original recipe for the ambrosia that I grew up eating. My grandmother made it all the time, and although she never measured anything, the ambrosia was always perfect. Today a lot of people add pineapple, grapes, and other fruits, but that is not true ambrosia. You can add a little orange liqueur to give it zip if you like."

Harold J. Villas
4211 Dumbarton Place
Charlotte, North Carolina 28211

MA-MA'S DARK FRUITCAKE

2 cups sugar
1 lb. butter, *softened*
1 ~~18~~ eggs (10-12)
4 cups sifted all-purpose flour
1 teasp. *ground* cinnamon
½ teasp. *ground* cloves
½ teasp. *ground* nutmeg
1 teasp. salt

} *Baking powder? stop.?*

> 2 tsp. vanilla
  2 tsp. almond extract

1 lb white seedless raisins }
1 lb. dark seedless raisins } *or 2 lb dark raisins*
½ lb. crystalized citron, *come & chopped*
¼ lb crystalized orange peel, "
¼ lb. crystalized lemon peel, "
1 lb. crystalized cherries, *cut in half*
1 lb. crystalized pineapple, "
1 lb. dates (pitted) "
1½ lbs. shelled pecans , *come & broken up*
3/4 cup Bourbon or sweet wine — *1½ cups?*

Chop uo the citron, orange peel, lemon peel, pineapple and dates,
leaving the cherries and nuts whole.(You can break the nuts up
if desired). Mix well with 2 cups of the above flour.

Cream butter, add sugar and blend until light and fluffy. Add
the eggs, one at a time, beating well. Add the remaining 2 cups
of flour, cinnamon, cloves, nutmeg and salt. Mix well.

Using hands, in a very large bowl, add the nuts and fruits to
the mixture, along with the bourbon or wine. Mix well

Grease *+ flour* and line pan or pans with heavy brown paper and extend
1 inch above pans. Grease paper. Pack batter firmly into pans
with hands to ⅜ inch below top of pan. Cover tops with waxed
paper and place pan of water in oven on stove shelf under cakes.
Bake at 250 degrees for the following length of time: For 1 lb.
cakes, 2 to 2½ hours; 2 lb. cakes 3 to 3½ hours; 3 lb cakes or
larger, 4 hours. Remove waxed paper from top of cakes during last
15 minutes of baking. Test for doneness(a straw will be dry
when stuck in center of cake) before removing from oven. Do not
overcook ! Pour a little bourbon or wine over hot cake after
removing from oven and still hot. Let cool in pans, wrap in
cheese cloth soaked in bourbon or wine and store in tins until
ready to use. Cut with very sharp knife.
(you can also use brandy or fruit juice instead of wine or bourbon)

To decorate tops of cakes, brush with ~~white~~ *clear corn* Karo ~~jay~~ syrup and
place whole cherries, pineapple and nuts on tops in desired
pattern. Let dry before storing.

5-6 lb. cake — 1 large 10 x 4-inch tube cake pan
2 2½ lb. cakes — 2 small 8 x 4½ x 2½ loaf pans

*I once asked Mother to send me the definitive, detailed, failproof recipe for her
mother's heirloom fruitcake so I could publish it in* Town & Country. *When the
recipe arrived on a piece of her stationery, I had to do a bit of editing.*

Fresh Doughnuts

These homemade doughnuts, which were one of my father's passions, were first served by one of our neighbors during World War II when Mother and other ladies would hold sewing bees at Priscilla's home to make doll clothes for Santa Claus. Mother remembers with horror that the doughnuts were served religiously with ginger ale, "but, after all, what could you expect since Priscilla was from Boston."

¼ cup sugar
¼ cup (½ stick) butter, at room temperature
2 large eggs
2½ cups all-purpose flour
2 teaspoons baking powder
1 teaspoon baking soda
½ cup firmly packed light brown sugar
½ teaspoon ground cinnamon
¼ teaspoon ground nutmeg
½ teaspoon salt
¾ cup buttermilk
Vegetable oil for deep-frying

In a large mixing bowl, cream the sugar and butter together with an electric mixer, then add the eggs and beat till well blended. In another bowl, combine the flour, baking powder, baking soda, brown sugar, cinnamon, nutmeg, and salt and mix well. Add to the egg mixture, stirring with a wooden spoon till well blended. Gradually add the buttermilk and stir till the dough is soft and sticky.

On a lightly floured surface, roll out the dough ½ inch thick and cut out doughnuts with a doughnut cutter. Gather up the scraps of dough, reroll, and cut out more doughnuts.

In a large pot, heat about 1½ inches of oil to 350°F or till a bread cube dropped in browns. Add the doughnuts three or four at a time, fry till golden, about 1½ minutes on each side, and drain on paper towels.

Yield: About 16 doughnuts

12
Cookies and Confections

Pecan Pralines

3 day

3/4 cup unsalt butter
1 cup gran. sugar
1 " lt brwn sugar
1/2 " heavy cream
1 " milk
1 " chopped pecans
2 tbsp. vanilla
2 cup whole pecan halves

Melt butter over high heat.
Add sugars & heavy cream.
Cook 1 minute, whisking
constantly. Add milk, chop
pecans & van. Cook 4 more
minutes, whisking constantly.
Reduce heat to medium, cont.
cooking & whisking 5 minutes,
Add pecan halves & cont.
Whisking & cooking until
done, about 15 to 20 minutes

Years ago, Mother jotted this recipe on a paper napkin in a New Orleans restaurant while chatting with the cook, then added it to her black recipe book later on. She insists this is the one and only way to make authentic Creole pralines.

I may demonstrate admirable willpower when it comes to partaking of Mother's outrageously delicious regular desserts, but all defenses collapse when she decides to bake off a batch of benne cookies, jelly treats, nutty fingers, or any of the other small confections to which I've been virtually addicted my whole life. I can truthfully say that I don't recall ever so much as sampling a storebought cookie—not as a child, not in college or while studying in France, and certainly not as an adult—and never is there a time when the large cedar working table in my East Hampton kitchen is not lined with tins of the goodies that Mother made during her most recent visit. If my Aunt Dee (Mother's sister) happens to have come along, there's usually also a supply of her inimitable fudge, and when I spend Christmas with the family in Charlotte, special treats are always Mother's hand-dipped chocolate candy and the feathery mints that she and my sister have laboriously pulled weeks in advance. Suffice it that homemade cookies and confections are taken as seriously today in my family as when my Georgia grandfather used to help make the pecan chocolate chip cookies and my mother helped her mother pull the Christmas mints.

Benne Cookies

B enne (sesame seed) cookies are as indigenous to Charleston, South Carolina, as hot red pepper vinegar and without doubt one of the finest confections ever created. Mother has no idea where she got this recipe many years ago, but she insists that it's the only one that really works perfectly for her. The cookies are a bit tricky to make, so pay careful attention to what you're doing. I keep "bennes" in a tightly sealed tin up to a month.

1 cup benne (sesame) seeds
¾ cup (1½ sticks) butter, melted
1½ cups firmly packed light brown sugar
1¼ cups all-purpose flour
¼ teaspoon baking powder
¼ teaspoon salt
1 teaspoon pure vanilla extract
1 large egg

Preheat the oven to 300°F. Toast the benne seeds on a baking sheet till golden, 10 to 15 minutes, stirring. Remove from the oven and increase the heat to 325°F. Let the seeds cool.

In a large mixing bowl, combine all the ingredients and mix thoroughly with a wooden spoon. Drop the first batch of batter by ½ teaspoons onto a well-greased aluminum foil-lined baking sheet about 1½ inches apart and bake till evenly browned (if pale in the center and puffed, the cookies are not ready), 15 to 20 minutes, watching constantly to avoid burning. Remove from the oven, allow the cookies to cool a few minutes, carefully peel them from the foil, and cool on a wire rack. Repeat with the remaining batter after regreasing the cooled foil. When completely cooled, store the cookies in airtight containers.

Yield: About 85 cookies

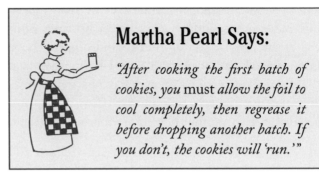

Martha Pearl Says:

"After cooking the first batch of cookies, you must *allow the foil to cool completely, then regrease it before dropping another batch. If you don't, the cookies will 'run.'"*

Peanut Butter Cookies

My strongest advice about these classic Southern cookies is to make sure they do not overcook and become hard, meaning they must be watched carefully while baking. As with gingersnaps, chocolate chip cookies, and any oatmeal cookie, these peanut butter cookies tend to lose their wonderful chewiness after only a few days in a sealed container. Once again, Mother's trick is simply to restore the moisture by placing a slice of fresh bread in the container.

1 cup (2 sticks) butter, at room temperature
1 cup granulated sugar
1 cup firmly packed dark brown sugar
1 teaspoon pure vanilla extract
2 large eggs, beaten
1 cup smooth peanut butter

2 cups all-purpose flour
1½ cups quick-cooking rolled oats
2 teaspoons baking soda
1 teaspoon salt

Preheat the oven to 350°F.

   In a mixing bowl, cream the butter, sugars, and vanilla together with an electric mixer, then add the eggs and beat till well blended. Stir in the peanut butter and mix well. Add the flour, oatmeal, baking soda, and salt and mix till well blended and the batter is smooth.

   Drop the batter by rounded teaspoons onto a greased baking sheet, press each round with the back of a floured fork to make crisscrosses, and bake till just lightly browned, about 10 minutes.

Yield: About 6 dozen cookies

Toffee Cookies

M other calls these her "bridge cookies" since whenever the club meets at her home, it's almost expected by the other members that, even with another dessert, there'll be a few toffee cookies to nibble on with coffee.

1 cup (2 sticks) butter
1 cup firmly packed brown sugar
1 large egg yolk
1 cup all-purpose flour
Six 1.05-ounce plain milk chocolate Hershey bars
⅔ cup crushed pecans

Preheat the oven to 350°F.

   In a large bowl, cream the butter and sugar together with an electric mixer, then add the egg yolk and beat till well blended. Gradually add the flour, stirring till well blended.

   Spread the mixture evenly in a greased 15½ x 10½-inch jelly-roll pan and bake till medium brown, 15 to 20 minutes. Remove from the oven and arrange the chocolate bars over the top. When the bars are melted, spread the chocolate evenly and sprinkle the crushed pecans over the top. When cool, cut into small bars or diamonds.

Yield: About 75 cookies

Pecan Chocolate Chip Cookies

¾ cup (1½ sticks) butter, at room temperature
1¼ cups firmly packed dark brown sugar
2 tablespoons milk
1 tablespoon pure vanilla extract
1 large egg
1¾ cups all-purpose flour
¾ teaspoon baking soda
1 teaspoon salt
1¼ cups semisweet chocolate chips
1¼ cups pecan or walnut pieces

Preheat the oven to 375°F.

In a large bowl, combine the butter, sugar, milk and vanilla and beat with an electric mixer till well blended. Add the egg and beat till well blended. In another bowl, combine the flour, soda, and salt, then add to the creamed mixture and stir till just blended. Stir in the chocolate chips and nuts.

Place well-rounded teaspoons of batter on ungreased baking sheets about 1 inch apart. Bake 8 minutes, allow to cool slightly on the baking sheets, then transfer to wire racks to cool completely. Store the cookies in airtight containers.

Yield: About 6 dozen cookies

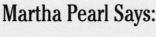

Martha Pearl Says:

"Since Jimmy can't stand my chocolate chip cookies the least bit crisp, I always try to slightly undercook them. If you prefer a bit more of a bite, bake them a minute or two longer. These cookies don't last long around our houses, but if you do store them in airtight containers, remember that the pecans can turn slightly rancid after only a week or so. And if you like your cookies to remain soft the way Jimmy does, be sure to store them with a slice of fresh bread."

Nutty Fingers

Mother has been making these addictive holiday cookies since before she was married, and for many friends and relatives, Christmas just wouldn't be Christmas if a few nutty fingers were not included in the gift boxes of confections she sends far and wide. Since pecans can turn rancid after a few weeks even when tightly sealed, I suggest you make no more of these cookies than you plan to consume fairly quickly or give away.

2 cups (4 sticks) butter, at room temperature
½ cup plus 2 tablespoons sifted confectioners' sugar
5 cups all-purpose flour
2 cups finely chopped pecans
2 teaspoons pure vanilla extract
Dash of salt
Sifted confectioners' sugar for rolling

Preheat the oven to 350°F.

In a large mixing bowl, cream the butter and sugar together with an electric mixer, then gradually blend in the flour with a wooden spoon. Add the nuts, vanilla, and salt and mix thoroughly.

Take small pieces of dough, form into finger shapes, and place them on one or two ungreased baking sheets about ½ inch apart, and bake till lightly browned, about 30 minutes. Let the fingers cool, then roll them in confectioners' sugar.

Yield: About 75 fingers

Creole Kisses

On one of our trips to Savannah, my parents and I once had occasion to be invited to the palatial home of one of the city's most gracious grandes dames, a lady who had been born in New Orleans. After a splendid lunch of tiny boiled river shrimp, chicken pilau, pole beans, and cornbread, the black cook placed on the polished mahogany table a platter of these small pecan disks to be nibbled with coffee. Later, when Mother asked our hostess what her favorite Southern dishes were, she pronounced without hesitating, "Corn pudding, my dear, and these Creole kisses we're eating."

3 large egg whites
1 cup superfine sugar
½ teaspoon cream of tartar
1 teaspoon pure vanilla extract
1 cup chopped pecans

Preheat the oven to 250°F.

In a bowl, beat the egg whites with an electric mixer till frothy, then add the sugar, cream of tartar, and vanilla and beat till stiff peaks form. Fold in the pecans, then drop by teaspoons on a well-buttered, brown paper-lined baking sheet. Bake till golden, about 30 minutes. Cool the kisses completely and store in an airtight container.

Yield: 100 kisses

Pecan Tassies

Popular at teas, church socials, weddings, and various country club receptions, pecan tassies have always been considered a "stylish" confection throughout the South and an item no caterer would fail to include on a silver cookie tray. Mother makes them primarily for her altar guild meetings, but when she's visiting me in East Hampton, it's not unusual for the small cups to appear on one of our luncheon buffets.

½ cup (1 stick) butter, at room temperature
One 3-ounce package cream cheese, at room temperature
1 cup all-purpose flour
1 large egg
1 cup firmly packed light brown sugar
⅛ teaspoon salt
½ cup finely chopped pecans
¼ teaspoon pure vanilla extract

In a mixing bowl, combine the butter, cream cheese, and flour and mix with your hands till the dough can be formed into a ball. Pinch off twenty-four pieces of dough and press each piece firmly onto the bottom and sides of two greased 12-cup muffin tins.

Preheat the oven to 350°F.

In a small bowl, beat the egg with the sugar and salt and stir in the pecans and vanilla. Spoon the filling into the lined cups and bake till the pastry is golden, about 25 minutes. Let the tassies cool and carefully unmold on a large plate.

Yield: 24 tassies

Oaten Biscuits

This is the very latest addition to Mother's vast cookie repertoire, the result of my tasting the "biscuits" on a recent trip to Donegal, Ireland, and her interpreting the sketchy recipe I jotted down while talking with the lady cook in the tiny restaurant of a local folk museum. Mother had to make about three batches before she was totally satisfied, but I can assure you that these are some of the most delicious cookies you'll ever put in your mouth—ideal with afternoon tea or coffee.

½ cup (1 stick) butter, at room temperature
½ cup sugar
1 cup all-purpose flour
½ teaspoon baking soda
Pinch of salt
1½ cups quick-cooking rolled oats

Preheat the oven to 350°F.

In a bowl, cream the butter and sugar together with an electric mixer, then add the flour, baking soda, and salt and beat till well blended. Add the oats and, using your hands, blend till the mixture is very sticky. Transfer the dough to a lightly floured surface and roll or pat out about ¼ inch thick. Using a 2½-inch biscuit cutter or small juice glass, cut out the biscuits and place on an ungreased baking sheet. Gather up the scraps of dough and cut out more biscuits. Bake the biscuits till slightly browned, 18 to 20 minutes.

Yield: 25 to 30 biscuits

Fruitcake Cookies

Don't think for a minute that these cookies are made simply with leftover batter from Mother's large fruitcakes. One key ingredient that makes the cookies different, for example, is the sherry extract, a product that's often difficult to find these days and that Mother orders special from her grocer. "McCormick puts it out," she huffs, "but, for some reason, lots of grocers just don't stock it." In any case, make every effort to acquire the extract, for people do love these cookies (we eat them not only over the holidays but throughout the year) and they make a delightful gift. (Sprinkled periodically with sherry or brandy, the cookies keep up to a year in tightly closed containers.)

1½ cups all-purpose flour
¼ teaspoon baking soda
½ teaspoon salt
½ teaspoon ground cinnamon
¼ cup (½ stick) butter, at room temperature
½ cup firmly packed light brown sugar
2 large eggs
¼ cup dry sherry
1 teaspoon sherry extract
3½ cups chopped pecans or walnuts
3 slices candied pineapple, chopped
1 cup candied cherries, chopped
1 cup chopped dates
¼ pound seedless golden raisins
¼ cup mixed chopped crystallized orange and lemon peel

Preheat the oven to 300°F.

In a small bowl, combine the flour, baking soda, salt, and cinnamon and set aside.

In a large mixing bowl, cream the butter and sugar together with an electric mixer. Add the eggs and beat till well blended. Add the dry ingredients and sherry alternately to the butter mixture, then add the sherry extract, stir in the nuts and fruit, and mix well. Drop the mixture by heaping teaspoons onto a greased baking sheet about 1½ inches apart and bake till slightly browned, about 20 minutes.

Yield: About 85 cookies

Christmas Sugar Cookies

Friends around the country to whom Mother sends a tin of goodies for Christmas are almost guaranteed to find a small batch of these delicate sugar cookies among the cheese biscuits, fruitcake cookies, nutty fingers, and other confections. She got the recipe originally from her old friend Bunny Foster, whom Mother has known since she was two years old when they were next-door neighbors.

2 cups (4 sticks) butter
1½ cups sugar
4 cups all-purpose flour
½ teaspoon salt
1 large egg
1 teaspoon pure vanilla extract
1 teaspoon pure almond extract
Candied cherries, cut in half
Pecan halves

Preheat the oven to 350°F.

In a large bowl, cream the butter and sugar together with an electric mixer, then add the flour, salt, egg, and extracts and mix till well blended.

Drop small bits of batter by teaspoons onto an ungreased baking sheet and press cherry or pecan halves into the middle of each bit. Bake till just slightly browned, about 15 minutes, making sure not to overcook (the cookies should be crisp on the outside with a slightly soft interior). With a spatula, transfer to paper towels and let cool completely. Repeat with the remaining batter, cherries, and pecans till all the batter is used up. Store in airtight containers.

Yield: About 100 cookies

Jelly Treats

Since, over the years, I have literally *never* been without a tin of Mother's jelly treats in my college dorm, apartments in New York and France, country house, and various other abodes, some members of the family (my nephew, Charles Royal, in particular) often refer to these wonderful confections as "Jimbo cookies." Ironically (and embarrassingly), it was only a few years ago that I finally mastered baking the treats, one problem being that I tended to overcook them. Ideally, the color should be just barely golden and the texture almost like firm cake, so watch the cookies very carefully during the first 10 minutes of baking. We've kept jelly treats in tightly closed containers up to two months, but if you're not as passionate about cookies as we are, you might want to halve this recipe.

1½ cups (3 sticks) butter, at room temperature
1 cup sugar
4 large egg yolks
4 cups all-purpose flour
Currant or mint jelly or orange marmalade

Preheat the oven to 325°F.

In a large mixing bowl, cream the butter and sugar together with an electric mixer, then add the egg yolks and beat thoroughly. Gradually add the flour and mix till well blended and the batter is firm.

Roll pieces of the batter into small balls about the size of a large marble in the palms of the hands, then place them on ungreased baking sheets about 1½ inches apart, press a thimble or fingertip in the center of each, and bake until dull in color, about 10 minutes. Remove the cookies from the oven, place a dollop of jelly in the depressions, and continue baking till the cookies are just slightly browned, about 10 minutes. Let cool till the jelly is hard and store in airtight containers.

Yield: About 100 treats

Martha Pearl Says:

"At Christmastime, I use red currant and mint jelly for these cookies, but strawberry and peach preserves also make delicious treats."

Gingersnaps

¾ cup vegetable shortening
1 cup granulated sugar
1 large egg
¼ cup dark molasses
2 cups all-purpose flour
2 teaspoons baking soda
½ teaspoon salt
1 tablespoon confectioners' sugar
1 teaspoon gound cinnamon
1 teaspoon ground ginger
Granulated sugar for coating

Preheat the oven to 350°F.

In a large bowl, cream the shortening and sugar together with an electric mixer till fluffy, then add the egg and molasses and stir till well blended. In another bowl, combine the flour, baking soda, salt, confectioners' sugar, cinnamon, and ginger, then gradually fold it into the molasses mixture.

Pinch off a small amount of the mixture and, using the palms of your hands, roll into a ball about the size of a large marble. Repeat the procedure till all the dough is used up. Roll the balls lightly in sugar, place on a greased baking sheet, and bake till golden, 10 to 12 minutes, taking care not to overcook. Cool the gingersnaps on a wire rack and store in an airtight container.

Yield: About 55 to 60 gingersnaps

Martha Pearl Says:

"If the cookies start drying out and getting hard, place a slice of fresh bread in the container and close tightly. Almost miraculously, the cookies absorb every trace of moisture from the bread and soften beautifully."

Lemon Bars

My sister began making these delectably tart bars shortly after she was married, and they've since become a staple in Mother's large cookie repertory. Since the confections tend to be extremely soft and difficult to negotiate with the fingers, we usually allow them to "firm up" for about an hour in the open air before serving.

For the cake layer

1 cup all-purpose flour
$\frac{1}{2}$ cup (1 stick) butter, at room temperature
$\frac{1}{4}$ cup confectioners' sugar
$\frac{1}{8}$ teaspoon salt

For the topping

1 cup granulated sugar
3 tablespoons fresh lemon juice
2 large eggs, slightly beaten
$\frac{1}{2}$ teaspoon baking powder
$\frac{1}{8}$ teaspoon salt

Confectioners' sugar

Preheat the oven to 350°F.

To make the cake layer, combine all the ingredients in a mixing bowl, stir till well blended, and scrape the mixture into a greased 9-inch-square pan. Press the mixture down with your fingers and bake 20 minutes.

Meanwhile, to make the topping, combine all the ingredients in another bowl and stir till well blended and thick. When the cake layer has finished baking, pour the topping over the hot layer and spread evenly with a rubber spatula. Return to the oven and bake 20 minutes longer. Cool, dust with confectioners' sugar, and cut into 2 x 1-inch rectangles.

Yield: About 50 bars

Caramel Brownies

½ cup (1 stick) butter
One 16-ounce box light brown sugar
2 large eggs, beaten
1 teaspoon pure vanilla extract
2 cups self-rising flour
1 cup coarsely chopped nuts (pecans, walnuts, or hazelnuts)

Preheat the oven to 325°F.

In a large saucepan, melt the butter, then add the sugar and stir over moderate heat till it dissolves. Remove the pan from the heat and, stirring constantly, add the eggs. Add the vanilla, flour, and nuts and stir till well blended. Pour the mixture into a greased shallow 20 x 9 x 3-inch pan and bake till firm, about 35 minutes. Let cool and cut into 2-inch-square brownies.

Yield: About 45 brownies

Aunt Dee's Chocolate Fudge

Mother's sister, Jane Theiling (my Aunt Dee), is the world's most hopeless chocoholic, a lady who literally cannot get through a day (in Charlotte, in East Hampton, traveling in Europe, anywhere) without eating chocolate in one form or another. It's no surprise, therefore, that her fudge (the same fudge that was always placed in my Christmas stocking as a child) is the richest, sweetest, smoothest, most addictive ever created—so addictive, in fact, that when she once worked at Merrill Lynch in Charlotte and took a batch to the office that hadn't "made" correctly because of the weather, her co-workers simply ate the chocolate with a spoon! Curiously, in all those years Aunt Dee had never written down the recipe or even formulated the ingredients, so when Mother and I asked her to share the secret for this book, all she could do was simply tell us generally how she makes the fudge. After following her directions the best we could, Mother could only say "This takes great patience."

3 cups sugar
5 to 6 tablespoons unsweetened cocoa powder

Dash of cream of tartar
Dash of salt
3 tablespoons dark Karo syrup
1 cup milk
1 teaspoon pure vanilla extract
6 tablespoons (¾ stick) butter

In a large saucepan, combine the sugar, cocoa, cream of tartar, salt, and syrup and mix well. Gradually add the milk, stirring till well blended. Place the pan over moderate heat and stir till the mixture just boils, taking care not to scrape the sides of the pan or stir after it boils. Continue to boil till the mixture reaches the soft ball stage (238°F on a candy thermometer), tested by dropping a small amount of it into a cup of cold water and seeing whether it is firm when rolled between your fingers.

Remove the pan from the heat, add the vanilla and butter, stir till well blended, and place in a larger pan of cold water to cool slightly. Begin beating on low speed with an electric mixer and gradually increase the speed till the fudge loses its shine and becomes very thick. Place a large sheet of waxed paper on a counter, pour the fudge onto the paper, and spread evenly with a rubber spatula about ½ inch thick. Let cool and cut into 1½-inch squares.

Yield: About 25 squares

Hand-Dipped Chocolate Candy

Regardless of the moral implications, family deaths and funerals in the South can still inspire an almost gastronomic occasion when relatives and friends bring all sorts of foods to be shared with those paying respects. When my Swedish grandmother died, for instance, a customer of my father's printing firm showed up at the house with a decorated tin full of this candy, the recipe for which Mother acquired at a later date. Ever since, the candy has become part of her large array of Christmas confections.

½ cup (1 stick) butter, at room temperature
One 14-ounce can sweetened condensed milk
Two 16-ounce boxes confectioners' sugar
1 teaspoon pure vanilla extract
2 cups finely chopped pecans
½ pound bitter chocolate
½ block paraffin
Pecan halves for decoration

In a large bowl, combine the butter, condensed milk, confectioners' sugar, vanilla, and chopped pecans till well blended, then chill about 30 minutes in the refrigerator. Using the palms of your hands, roll the mixture into small balls about the size of large marbles.

In a saucepan, melt the chocolate and paraffin together over low heat. Using a toothpick or small fork, dip each ball into the chocolate mixture, place the balls on a sheet of waxed paper, and place a pecan half over the hole made by the toothpick. When completely dry, place the balls in individual candy paper cups.

Yield: About 100 pieces

Pulled Mints

When I was barely two years old, two old-maid neighbors gave my grandmother a heavy marble slab and showed her how to make these mints. Maw Maw, in turn, taught Mother, and eventually they had my sister and me pulling mints to be placed in tiny crepe paper baskets and used for birthday parties when no candy was available during World War II but there were some rations of sugar. Today, Mother still has that same old marble slab, but because of her bursitis, she usually has to depend on Hootie to pull the mints at Christmas. I confess that I've never mastered the intricate and dying art (and the procedure is difficult), but, thanks to Mother and Hootie, we're one of the few Southern families left who can serve homemade mints during the holidays. If you fail at first pulling these mints, try, try again.

2 cups sugar
1 cup water
½ cup (1 stick) butter
4 drops oil of peppermint (available in drugstores and some supermarkets)
Any food coloring

In a large pot, combine the sugar and water, bring to a boil, and stir till the sugar dissolves. Reduce the heat to moderate, add the butter, and cook, uncovered and *without stirring,* till a candy thermometer reaches 260°F, the hard ball stage, when a drop of the mixture dropped in cold water forms a hard ball.

Pour the mixture onto a well-buttered cold marble slab or other such hard surface, making sure not to scrape the pot. Sprinkle on the oil of peppermint plus a few drops of the desired food coloring and, when cool enough to handle, begin pulling and stretching the mixture back and forth with buttered hands, pulling out with the right hand and bringing back to the left hand to overlap till the mints are dull and small ridges form lengthwise on the surface. (The food coloring and oil are distributed as the mixture is pulled back and forth.) Twist the pulling mixture into a rope about ½ inch wide and cut with buttered kitchen shears into ¼-inch pieces. Place the mints on waxed paper and, when cooled completely, store in airtight containers to cream up and ripen. (They will keep up to 2 months.)

Yield: 1 pound of mints

13

Pickles, Relishes, and Preserves

Mother putting up my favorite bread and butter pickle—enough jars to last us an entire year.

Not long ago while shopping in a supermarket, Mother gasped in excitement when she spied pickling Kirbys on sale for 49 cents a pound and proceeded to buy the entire box.

The second Mother tasted my sister's cranberry chutney, she asked Hootie for the recipe. Needless to say, neither lady needs detailed cooking instructions.

Cape Fear Cranberry Chutney
(Hootie)
1 cup fresh orange sections
¼ c. orange juice
4 cups fresh cranberries
2 c. sugar
1 c apple, unpeeled & chopped
½ c. raisins (I use white)
¼ c. chopped walnuts
1 TAB vinegar
½ tsp ground ginger
½ tsp cinnamon)
Combine & bring to boil —

Of all the great Southern culinary traditions, none is more sacred and respected than that of canning virtually any edible that can be successfully preserved in a jar. Putting up food seems to be an increasingly dead art in most other areas of the country, but to Southern cooks like my mother, the annual activity of pickling, preserving, and jelly-making remains as important as it was to their parents and grandparents. One of my sharpest childhood memories is sitting around the kitchen table in summer with my father, sister, and grandparents peeling fresh fruit and vegetables for Mother to process in the large canning pot before packing them into Mason jars, a communal, joyful labor that not only guaranteed us yet another year of delectable peach and pear preserves, chow chows, relishes, watermelon-rind pickle, and marmalades but provided Mother with additional goodies to include in her Christmas food baskets.

Although Mother still prefers to put up certain items in Charlotte where she has ready access to Elberta peaches, thick-skin watermelons, and damson plums, much of her canning is now done in my East Hampton kitchen when she comes to visit each summer. Week after week, we scour the roadside markets for the finest yellow squash, okra, and prickly Kirbys; we drive to the North Fork of Long Island just to pick our own plump strawberries, blueberries, and raspberries; and, come August, hardly a day passes that we're not out asking some farmer when he expects to have the first yellow Tuxedo corn, or the first speckled Twice-As-Nice, or the first glorious white Snowbelle or Silver Queen. Then, back at the house, out come the giant sterilizing pot, the jars saved over the past year, the new lids, the pectin and paraffin, and vinegar and spices and ten-pound bags of sugar. Mother and I strap on our heavy aprons, friends drop by to watch all the action, and, as the kitchen aromas intensify and the hot filled jars on the counter gradually ping and seal themselves, I'm always aware that Mother is passing on a custom that is as old as the South itself.

TO STERILIZE AND SEAL JARS FOR CANNING

Unscrew the ring bands from the canning jars, remove the lids, and wash both thoroughly with soap and hot water. Arrange the jars in a large pot or baking pan and cover with water. Bring the water to a boil, cover, and sterilize the jars for 10 minutes.

Remove the jars from the water with tongs and pack with the food to be canned, taking care not to touch the insides of the jars once they have been sterilized. Wipe the rims very clean with moist paper towels, then use tongs to dip the sealing lids into the water used for sterilizing the jars, fit the lids on top of the jars, and screw the ring bands on tightly.

Place the filled jars in a draft-free area till the lids ping and remain down when pushed with a finger (these are signs they are sealed). Store any jars whose lids remain convex in the refrigerator and use first.

Crystal Pickle

It is none other than Craig Claiborne who has pronounced Mother's crystal pickle to be one of the finest delicacies he's ever tasted, and well he should considering the time, effort, and love involved in putting them up. So far, I've refused to go to all the trouble, but not a year passes that she doesn't make at least two batches of these wondrous pickle to be included in her "Goodies from Martha's Kitchen" Christmas gift bags.

2 cups pickling lime (available in Southern supermarkets and by special order from Ball in other markets)
8 quarts cold water
8 pounds unpeeled Kirby cucumbers, scrubbed under running water
3 tablespoons mixed pickling spices
9 cups sugar
2 quarts 5% white vinegar
¼ cup salt

In a large 10 to 12-quart pot (not aluminum or cast-iron), combine the pickling lime and water and stir till well blended. Trim the ends from the cucumbers, cut the cucumbers into ¼-inch slices, add the slices to the lime water (making sure they are covered with liquid), and let stand undisturbed 24 hours.

The next day, drain the slices in the sink and rinse under cold running water to remove all traces of lime water. Wash the pot to remove all traces of lime water and refill with fresh cold water. Add the cucumber slices and let soak 3 hours to remove any possible last traces of chemical residue. Drain the slices in the sink and wash the pot again.

Tie the pickling spices in a piece of cheesecloth loosely enough so that they can move around. Place the spice bag in the pot, add the sugar, vinegar, and salt, heat just to the boiling point, remove the pot from the heat, and add the cucumber slices. Let stand 24 hours, stirring often.

On the third day, bring the mixture to a boil, reduce the heat to moderately low, and simmer till the cucumbers begin to look clear, 10 to 15 minutes. With a slotted spoon, fill hot, sterilized jars with the slices and fill the jars with hot liquid to within ⅛ inch from the top. Seal, allow the pickle to stand several weeks, and serve ice cold.

Yield: 10 pints

Martha Pearl Says:

"It is very *important that every trace of pickling lime be rinsed off the cucumber slices and their container after the initial soak. Actually, what I do is place the slices in a clean sink and, with the water running steadily, pick them up again and again with my hands till they are thoroughly rinsed."*

Bread and Butter Pickle

These are the homemade pickle that I eat literally every day of my life when I'm at home, explanation for why I don't recall ever even tasting commercial bread and butter pickle. Since the pickle can never be made with those huge, waxy, seedy, overly soft specimens that fill the supermarkets, we not only grow our own small, firm Kirbys but stay on eternal watch for those selling for less than forty-nine cents a pound. Mother says that I'm "stingy" about giving away our bread and butters, but I confess that if the supply on my basement shelves slips under about ten jars, I do panic. Once you acquire the Kirbys, these are very simple pickle to put up—a cinch compared to crystal or watermelon-rind pickle.

6 pounds pickling cucumbers (Kirbys), scrubbed and sliced into ¼-inch rounds
6 medium-size onions, thinly sliced
⅓ cup salt
4½ cups sugar
1½ teaspoons turmeric
1½ teaspoons celery seeds
2 tablespoons mustard seeds
3 cups 5% cider vinegar

In a large mixing bowl, arrange alternate layers of cucumber rounds and sliced onions, sprinkling each layer with the salt. Cover the top of the mixture with ice cubes or crushed ice, mix the ice thoroughly with the cucumbers and onions, and let stand 3 hours. Drain thoroughly.

In a large enameled or stainless-steel pot, combine the sugar, turmeric, celery seeds, mustard seeds, and vinegar and bring to a boil. Add the cucumbers and onions and return to a boil. Pack the cucumbers and onions into hot, sterilized jars, fill the jars with hot liquid to ¼ inch from the tops, seal, and store in a cool area. Refrigerate after opening.

Yield: Eight 1-pint jars

Martha Pearl Says:

"Some people might think this is a lot of onions, but Jimmy and I both like lots of onions in our bread and butter pickle. If you don't, use just three to four onions instead. Also, I can't emphasize enough the importance of wiping the edges of the jars totally clean to assure perfect sealing."

Watermelon-Rind Pickle

These elegant pickle that friends clamor for represent for many the height of Mother's art of canning and preserving, and since we wouldn't touch a jar (much less give any away as gifts) that hadn't been allowed to age at least six months, those resting on shelves in my basement are as sacred as certain bottles of fine wine. I remember as a child my father having to stop the car at watermelon stands every ten miles or so on our way to the summer beach cottage so that Mother could check the rinds of melons for thickness; and even today the fur flies if a vendor refuses to let her "plug" one as a potential candidate for her precious watermelon-rind pickle. The process is time-consuming but basically easy, and once you've tasted these beauties (with pit-cooked pork barbecue, fried chicken, or baked spareribs), you'll be nothing less than insulted by those commercial pickle that fetch eight dollars or more a jar. Do remember that every trace of pink flesh must be removed from the rind, and be sure not to overpack the jars before sealing.

6 pounds thick watermelon rind
2 cups pickling lime (available in Southern supermarkets and by special order from Ball in other markets)
1 tablespoon alum (available in spice section of supermarkets)
$\frac{1}{2}$ pound fresh ginger, peeled and cut into quarters
6 cups of sugar
6 cups 5% white vinegar
1 tablespoon whole allspice
1 tablespoon cloves
Two 3-inch-long sticks cinnamon

Remove all the dark green outer rind and all pink flesh from the watermelon rind, discard, and cut the trimmed pale rind into 2-inch fingers. Place the fingers in a large glass or enameled container. Dissolve the lime in 2 gallons of cold water, pour over the rind, cover with plastic wrap, and let soak overnight.

The next day, combine the alum with 1 gallon of cold water in a large container, transfer the drained rind fingers to the solution, and let soak 5 minutes. Drain the rind.

In a large enameled pot, combine the ginger with 1 gallon of cold water, add the rind, bring to a boil, reduce the heat to moderately low, and simmer 30 minutes. Drain, remove the ginger, and rinse the rind thoroughly under cold running water for exactly 5 minutes. Rinse out the pot.

In the pot, combine the sugar, vinegar, 3 cups water, allspice, cloves, and cinnamon. Bring the liquid to a boil and add the rind. Return the liquid to a boil, reduce the heat to low, and simmer slowly, uncovered, for 3 hours.

Pack the fingers into hot, sterilized jars, fill each jar with hot liquid to ¼ inch from the top, seal, and store in a cool area at least 4 months before serving. Refrigerate after opening.

Yield: About seven 1-pint jars

Mustard Chow Chow

"Cha" is the Mandarin Chinese word for "mixed," and while the term "chow chow" was being used around 1840 in California to describe any of the chopped vegetable dishes prepared by Chinese laborers, nobody has yet to explain how this relish became a staple of the Old South. Mother got this recipe many years ago from her old friend Blanche Walker, who was raised in the country in a big family who produced the relish in massive quantities to serve with virtually everything they ate. Mother still follows the original recipe that makes fifteen to sixteen one-pint jars of chow chow, but since the sheer quantity of ingredients is hard to deal with, and since few people own a big enough pot, she halves the recipe here. Chow chow is awfully good served with roasted meats and fried chicken.

3 cups chopped green cabbage
3 cups chopped green tomatoes
⅓ cup salt
3 cups seeded and chopped red bell peppers
3 cups seeded and chopped green bell peppers
3 cups chopped onions
1 large bunch celery, chopped
½ head cauliflower, chopped
3 cups 5% white vinegar

One 16-ounce box light brown sugar
$\frac{1}{4}$ cup all-purpose flour
$1\frac{1}{2}$ tablespoons dry mustard
2 teaspoons turmeric
$4\frac{1}{2}$ teaspoons water

In a large bowl, combine the cabbage, tomatoes, and salt, add enough cold water to cover, and soak overnight.

Drain the mixture thoroughly and transfer to a large pot. Add the peppers, onions, celery, cauliflower, vinegar, and brown sugar and bring almost to a boil. In a small bowl, combine the flour, mustard, and turmeric, add the water, mix well to make a paste, and add the paste to the pot. Gradually bring the liquid to a roaring boil, stirring constantly. Remove the pot from the heat, spoon the chowchow into hot, sterilized jars, seal, and store in a cool area. Refrigerate after opening.

Yield: Eight 1-pint jars

Squash Relish

Throughout most of the South, where there is an abundance of yellow crook-neck squash during the warm months, you see this relish being served all the time with cold meats and poultry, grilled fish, and sandwiches. Mother has been putting it up for years and years, and she is very particular about using small squash with the tiniest seeds possible.

10 small or 7 medium-size yellow squash, stems removed and cut into chunks
4 medium-size onions, chopped
1 medium-size green bell pepper, seeded and chopped
1 medium-size red bell pepper, seeded and chopped
$\frac{1}{4}$ cup salt
3 cups sugar
2 cups 5% white vinegar
2 teaspoons celery seeds
2 teaspoons turmeric

In a blender, combine the vegetables in batches and blend till coarsely chopped. Transfer to a large mixing bowl, add the salt plus enough water to cover, and let stand 1 hour. Place the vegetables in a colander, rinse quickly under cold running water, and drain well.

In a large saucepan, combine the sugar, vinegar, celery seeds, and turmeric, bring to a boil, and let boil for 3 minutes. Add the vegetable mixture, stir, return to a boil, reduce heat to moderately low, and simmer 4 to 5 minutes.

Spoon the relish into hot, sterilized jars, seal, and store in a cool area. Refrigerate after opening.

Yield: Six 1-pint jars

Martha Pearl Says:

"Sometimes I drain the relish completely, add a little mayonnaise, and use it to make small tea sandwiches for lunch or tea."

Cranberry Conserve

Some years ago, my sister showed up for Thanksgiving in East Hampton suggesting that we try her cranberry conserve in place of traditional cranberry sauce with the big turkey dinner. Everyone was so taken by the conserve that Mother now puts it up every year between Thanksgiving and Christmas and serves it well through the summer with roasted poultry and pork. (Unpreserved, the conserve keeps well under refrigeration about 2 weeks.)

1 pound fresh cranberries, picked over and rinsed
1½ cups water
1 cup sugar
½ cup seedless golden raisins
2 oranges, cleanly peeled, seeded, and cut into small chunks
¾ cup chopped pecans

Place the cranberries in a large saucepan, add the water, and bring to a boil. Reduce the heat to moderately low and simmer till the berries just pop open, 3 to

5 minutes. Add the sugar, raisins, and orange chunks, stir, and simmer about 15 minutes longer. Stir in the nuts, simmer 2 minutes longer, remove the pan from the heat, and let cool slightly.

Spoon the conserve into hot, sterilized jars, seal, and store in a cool area. Or spoon the mixture into jars, cover lightly with lids, and refrigerate till ready to serve. Refrigerate after opening.

Yield: About five ½-pint jars

Green Tomato and Apple Chutney

The time to put up chutney is late summer and early fall, when fruits and vegetables are in such abundance and offer limitless possibilities for experiment. Here is a good, honest, not-too-sweet, not-too-sharp chutney that Mother serves with curries and any number of cold meat dishes.

2 cups 5% cider vinegar
3 pounds green tomatoes, cored and cut into ½-inch cubes
1 pound green tart apples, peeled, cored, and cut into ½-inch cubes
3 medium-size onions, coarsely chopped
½ cup seedless golden raisins
1 cup firmly packed dark brown sugar
1 tablespoon peeled and grated fresh ginger
1 tablespoon ground cloves
1 tablespoon crushed mustard seeds
3 garlic cloves, minced
1½ teaspoons red pepper flakes
2 tablespoons salt

In a large pot, combine all the ingredients and bring to a boil. Reduce the heat to moderately low, cover, and simmer till soft, thick, and well blended, about 1 hour, adding a little more vinegar if the chutney becomes too stiff and dry.

Spoon the chutney into hot, sterilized jars, seal, and allow to mellow at least 2 months in a cool area before serving. Refrigerate after opening.

Yield: Four 1-pint jars

Grandmother Holmes's Apple Chutney

When Mother was very young, there were no legitimate restaurants in Charlotte, so when the family ate out, it was either at friends' homes, in hotels or boarding houses, or in public "dining rooms" that served home-cooked meals. One such rather exclusive dining room in a large Colonial house was run by the grandmother of one of Mother's closest friends, Florence Holmes, who eventually got this century-old recipe for the apple chutney that Grandmother Holmes never failed to put on the table. Today, both Flossie and Mother still make the chutney to be given as birthday and Christmas gifts, and I'm rarely without a jar to serve with various pork dishes and grilled hamburger steaks.

7 large Granny Smith apples, cored and cut into pieces
4 cups sugar
2 cups currants
2 to 3 oranges, cleanly peeled, seeded, and finely chopped
½ cup 5% white vinegar
⅓ teaspoon ground cloves
1 cup coarsely chopped pecans

In a large pot, combine the apples and sugar and mix till well blended. Add the currants, oranges, vinegar, cloves, and pecans, bring to a boil, reduce the heat to moderately low, cover, and simmer till the nuts are tender, about 30 minutes.

Ladle the mixture into hot, sterilized jars, seal, and store a few weeks to mellow before using. Refrigerate after opening.

Yield: Nine ½-pint jars

Pickled Okra

If you think that Mother is fastidious about buying okra for her okra and tomatoes, you should watch her picking it out pod by pod at the farmers' market for her pickled okra. Each piece has to be perfect: the color, texture, length (no more than two inches), and width; and if she so much as suspects that the okra is more than a few days old, she simply walks away in a huff. This is the one pickle of Mother's that rarely crosses the Mason-Dixon Line. "I've tried to give it to non-Southerners, but they just don't seem to care for it." All I can say is that some of my Yankee friends would give her a good argument.

4 teaspoons dill seeds
3½ pounds small fresh okra, rinsed thoroughly and stems trimmed
4 small fresh hot red peppers
4 small fresh hot green peppers
8 garlic cloves, peeled
4 cups 5% white vinegar
1 cup water
6 tablespoons salt

Sterilize four 1-pint jars and place ½ teaspoon of dill seeds in the bottom of each. Pack okra into the jars, taking care not to bruise them, add another ½ teaspoon of dill seeds to each jar, and add one of each hot pepper and two garlic cloves to each jar.

In a large saucepan (not aluminum or cast-iron), combine the vinegar, water, and salt, bring to a boil, and pour equal amounts of the liquid over the okra to ¼ inch from the tops of the jars. Seal and store in a cool area at least 1 month before serving. Serve the okra chilled. Refrigerate after opening.

Yield: Four 1-pint jars

Martha Pearl Says:

"The reason I buy only small pods is because they're much more tender than the large ones and not stringy. Remember also that bad okra bends and is dull in color. To prevent okra from 'running,' never cut off the entire stems and into the body of the pods."

Pickled Peaches

This is the same recipe for pickled peaches that my grandmother and great-grandmother used when relatives would send bushels of fresh Elbertas and Southern Belles from Georgia up to Charlotte. A lot of Southerners use cling-stone peaches since they're the first of the season and hold their shape well; Mother prefers to pickle freestones—preferably those about the size of a golf ball—since their texture is more fibrous. By no means overcook these peaches: they're done when they can be stuck easily with a toothpick. For ideal flavor and texture, the peaches should be stored at least four months and preferably six before using.

3 cups 5% white vinegar
2 pounds sugar
Three to four 3-inch-long sticks cinnamon
6 pounds small, firm fresh peaches
Whole cloves

In a large saucepan (not aluminum or cast-iron), combine the vinegar, sugar, and cinnamon and bring to a boil. Stir well, reduce the heat slightly, and cook till a medium thick syrup forms, about 20 minutes.

Meanwhile, bring a large kettle of water to a boil, dip the peaches in the water in batches, and remove their skins as the peaches are withdrawn from the water. Stud each peeled peach with two cloves.

Add the peaches in batches to the hot syrup, increase the heat slightly, and cook

Martha Pearl Says:

"When shopping for peaches, make absolutely sure that they have plenty of fuzz—proof that they've not been commercially processed. I really prefer to peel my peaches by hand since dipping them in hot water can make them too soft. It takes more time and energy to hand-peel, but after you've practiced a few times, there's really nothing to it."

just till tender, 5 to 10 minutes. Pack the peaches in hot, sterilized jars, add syrup to within ¼ inch of the tops, seal, and store in a cool area. Refrigerate after opening.

Yield: Five 1-pint jars

Peach Preserves

Frankly stated, most people familiar with Mother's pickle and preserves agree that there are no peach preserves on earth that can touch the ones she makes with Southern Elbertas each and every summer. They are undoubtedly my favorite of all her preserves, and there's never a time when my basement shelves in East Hampton are not loaded with jars aging up to nine months. As I have learned by making the preserves repeatedly with her, the secret is impeccably fresh, firm, sweet peaches that are allowed to cook very slowly in syrup that must be watched carefully for just the right thickness.

3 pounds fresh, firm peaches, peeled, pitted, and sliced ¼ inch thick
6 cups sugar

In a large pot, combine the peaches and sugar, cover, and let stand overnight to allow the peaches to leach out and moisten the sugar.

The next day, bring the mixture slowly to a boil, stirring frequently, then reduce the heat slightly and cook till the fruit is clear and the syrup is thick, about 40 minutes. Spoon the peaches into hot, sterilized jars, seal, and store in a cool area. Refrigerate after opening.

Yield: Seven 1-pint jars

Martha Pearl Says:

"To test the thickness of the syrup in these preserves, I spoon about a tablespoon of the hot liquid onto a saucer and place it in the freezer about 5 minutes. If the syrup is not ready, it will be thin and runny."

THINGS TO DO TODAY

DATE _____ COMPLETED

1. Strawberry Preserves - ☐
2. 2 qt Strawberries ☐
3. 8 cups sugar ☐
4. 4 teas lemon juice ☐
5. mash + bring boil berries ☐
6. + 4 cups sugar. Boil 5 min ☐
7. add remaining 4 cups sugar ☐
8. + boil 10 min - add lemon juice ☐
9. before removing from fire - add ☐
10. 1 pkg (30z.) Certo at same time ☐
11. Pour in crock or bowl + let ☐
12. stand 24 hours or overnite ☐
    Pour in jars cold + cover paraffin

Printcrafters
of the Carolinas, Inc.

220 E. PETERSON DR. / CHARLOTTE, NORTH CAROLINA 28210 / (704) 527-4912

Strawberry Preserves

Mother has been making these preserves ever since the recipe appeared forty years ago in the *Charlotte Charity League Cookbook,* and, along with her peach, the strawberry are her most popular with relatives and friends. The trick here is never to overcook the berries, which should remain firm and plump; and, ideally, the preserves should be aged about six months for optimum flavor and texture. Do note that since the berries are put up cold, they must be sealed with hot paraffin by tilting the jars and filling all the edges.

1 quart fresh strawberries, hulled and washed
4 cups sugar
2 teaspoons fresh lemon juice
2 tablespoons pectin (Certo)

If the strawberries are large, cut them in half. In a large saucepan, combine the strawberries and 2 cups of the sugar, bring slowly to a boil, and cook rapidly at a boil 5 minutes, stirring. Add the remaining sugar, return to a boil, and cook 10 minutes longer, stirring in the lemon juice 2 minutes before removing the pan from the heat. Add the pectin and stir well. Pour the mixture into a large mixing bowl, skim off the foam, cover, and let stand 24 hours, stirring occasionally.

Spoon the strawberries into hot, sterilized jars, seal with hot melted paraffin, and store in a cool area to age. Refrigerate after opening.

Yield: Four ½-pint jars

Martha Pearl Says:

"From what I read and hear, nobody these days recommends sealing preserves with paraffin, frightened that it might not work. Well, besides the fact that the large amount of sugar acts as a preservative, all I can say is that I've been using paraffin for the past forty years and have never once lost a jar from spoilage. Just make sure that you seal every edge by slowly tilting the jar till the paraffin begins to set."

Pear Preserves

In the South, hard, speckled "horse pears" collected on farms are used to make the most delicious preserves imaginable. Unfortunately, the only commercial pears outside the region that bear any resemblance are Bosc and Anjou, and even these varieties are not that easy to find. Never use Bartlett, Comice, or other such soft eating pears found in supermarkets to make these preserves, and if you're really determined to produce a few treasured jars, keep a sharp eye open at farmers' markets in late fall and winter for what are often simply labeled "cooking pears."

3 cups sugar
3 cups water
9 medium-size hard pears (about 3 pounds), cored, peeled, and cut into eighths
1 lemon, thinly sliced
5 pieces preserved ginger (available in specialty food shops)

In a large saucepan, combine half the sugar and the water, bring to a boil, and cook 2 minutes, stirring. Add the pears, reduce the heat slightly, and boil gently 15 minutes. Add the remaining sugar and the lemon slices, stir till the sugar has dissolved, and cook rapidly till the fruit is clear, about 25 minutes. Cover and let stand overnight.

Pack the fruit into hot, sterilized jars and add a piece of ginger to each jar. Cook the syrup about 5 minutes and pour over the pears, leaving about ¼ inch at the top of jars. Seal and store in a cool area at least 2 months before serving. Refrigerate after opening.

Yield: Five ½-pint jars

Damson Plum Preserves

Cultivated extensively in England before being introduced into the Colonial American South, the dark, tart damson plum has long been prized as one of the most ideal fruits for preserving. When I was young, hardly a week went by in midsummer that some farmer didn't drop by the house to sell Mother a bucket of damsons, but today "they've become scarce as hens' teeth and I have to scour the outdoor markets to find just a few baskets." If you're unable to locate damsons, you might try preserving either greengages or extremely bitter sloes, but remember that the purple, sweet plums that flood the supermarkets in July and August are not for cooking.

6 cups sugar
1 cup water
3 pounds damson plums, pitted and coarsely chopped (about 6 cups)

In a large pot, combine the sugar and water and stir till the sugar dissolves. Bring to a boil, add the plums, and return to a boil. Reduce the heat to moderately low and simmer the plums gently, uncovered, till the fruit is clear and the syrup thick, 30 to 40 minutes. Ladle into hot, sterilized jars, filling to the top, seal, and store in a cool area at least 2 months before serving. Refrigerate after opening.

Yield: Six 1-pint jars

Three-Fruit Marmalade

My English friend Mary Homi is a master at preserving and pickling, and nothing illustrates her fine art like this unusual marmalade she told Mother how to make some years ago. Ideally, Seville oranges should be used, but, given their scarcity in this country, we've found that firm temples yield almost as good marmalade.

2 medium-size grapefruits
2 temple oranges
4 lemons
12 cups water
12 cups sugar

Wash the three fruits thoroughly, remove the rind, and cut the rind into shreds. Remove all pithy white membrane from the fruits, cut the fruits into chunks, and tie all the membrane and seeds in a cheesecloth bag. Combine the shredded rind, cut-up fruits, and cheesecloth bag in a large pot, add the water, and let soak overnight.

Bring the liquid to a boil, reduce to moderately low heat, cover, and simmer till the peel is just soft, about 1½ hours. Remove the cheesecloth bag and, when cool enough to handle, squeeze its juices back into the pot. Add the sugar to the pot, stir till well dissolved, bring the mixture to a boil, and boil rapidly 5 to 10 minutes, till the desired consistency is achieved, tested by dropping a small amount on a chilled plate. Scrape the marmalade into hot, sterilized jars, seal, and store in a cool area. Refrigerate after opening.

Yield: Twelve ½-pint jars

Hot Pepper Jelly

Nothing is more Southern at cocktail parties and large buffets than to spread hot pepper jelly over a few eight-ounce blocks of cream cheese and serve it with crackers. Although the first mention I know of this regional specialty is in a very early edition of *Charleston Receipts,* Mother's recipe comes from an old friend in Texas whose family would never dream of serving any cold ham or pork dish without the jelly on the side.

2 medium-size red bell pep-
    pers, seeded and chopped
3 hot green peppers, seeded
    and finely chopped
1½ cups 5% cider vinegar
6½ cups sugar
One 6-ounce bottle pectin
    (Certo)

Martha Pearl Says:

"When handling these or any hot peppers, be sure to wear rubber gloves to avoid burning your hands."

In a blender, combine the two types of peppers and 1 cup of the vinegar and blend till the peppers are finely minced. Transfer the mixture to a stainless-steel or enameled saucepan, add the sugar and remaining vinegar, and bring to a boil. Stir, remove the pan from the heat, and skim the surface. Stir in the pectin, return the pan to the heat, and boil hard 1 minute. Remove the pan from the heat and skim again.

Pour the jelly into hot, sterilized jars, seal, and store in a cool area. Refrigerate after opening.

Yield: Six ½-pint jars

Lemon Curd

My English friend Mary Homi first prepared this delectable curd for Mother and me years ago, and ever since it's been a staple for breakfast and at tea time with toast, biscuits, and scones. Mary also fills tiny tarts with the curd mixed with whipped cream, and she even spoons it directly onto ice cream as a dessert.

2 lemons
½ cup (1 stick) butter, at room temperature
1¼ cups superfine sugar
2 large eggs, beaten

Grate the rind of both lemons and set aside. Cut the lemons in half, squeeze the juice from both through a sieve into a small bowl, and set aside.

In a saucepan, cream the butter and sugar together with an electric mixer and cook over low heat till about the consistency of honey, about 10 minutes, stirring. Add the grated lemon rind and juice, stir well, remove the pan from the heat, and let cool 10 minutes. Add the eggs, stir well, and cook over low heat till the mixture is custardlike, about 10 minutes. Scrape into two ½-pint jars, cover with lids, and store in the refrigerator at least 2 weeks before serving. (Kept refrigerated, the curd keeps well 2 to 3 months.)

Yield: Two ½-pint jars

14

Sauces and Dressings

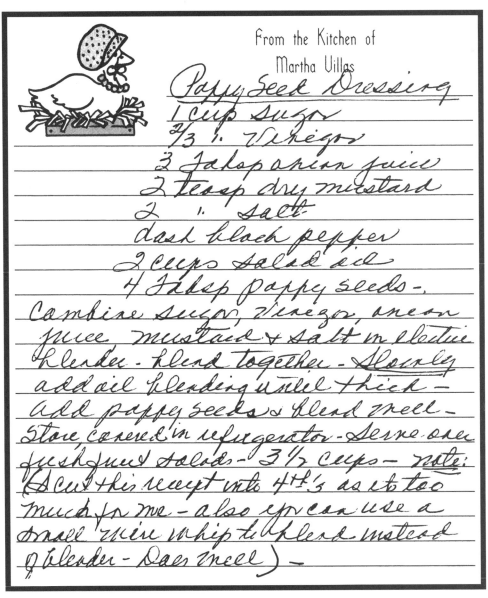

From the Kitchen of
Martha Villas

Poppy Seed Dressing

1 cup sugar
2/3 c. Vinegar
3 Tablsp onion juice
2 teasp dry mustard
2 " salt
dash black pepper
2 cups salad oil
4 Tablsp poppy seeds –

Combine sugar, Vinegar, onion
juice, mustard & salt in electric
blender. blend together. Slowly
add oil blending until thick –
add poppy seeds & blend well –
Store, covered in refrigerator. Serve over
fresh fruit salads – 3 1/2 cups – note:
(I cut this receipt into 4th's as its too
much for me – also you can use a
small "wire whip" to blend instead
of blender – Does well) –

As can be seen on the original recipe, Mother not only uses onion juice in this dressing (despite my objection) but really prefers a wire whisk to a blender for mixing—better texture, she says.

Although Mother is as adept at making classic sauces as the best trained chef, just about the only time she whips one up while "cooking Southern" is when she has reason to dramatize some vegetable dish like broccoli or cauliflower for an elaborate buffet. "Southerners like food to taste of what it is," she's forever lecturing, "so we basically don't care for fancy sauces on things like fish, meat, and vegetables." Natural gravies made with pan drippings and perhaps a little flour, of course, are another story, as are the various tangy barbecue sauces used to baste age-old specialties like pit-cooked pork barbecue, baked spareribs, oven-barbecued brisket of beef, and chicken barbecued in a paper bag. It also stands to reason that since salads are so popular in the South, a number of clever salad dressings would be as important to Mother's repertory as to that of any other housewife.

Dill Dressing

2 cups sour cream
1 tablespoon fresh lemon juice
1 teaspoon grated onion
2 tablespoons chopped fresh dill
Salt and black pepper to taste
Pinch of sugar

In a bowl, combine all the ingredients, mix till well blended, and chill in a covered bowl or jar at least 1 hour before using.

Serve over seafood salads, fish croquettes, and cold poached fish. Keeps 1 week in the refrigerator.

Yield: About 2 cups

Celery Seed Dressing

1 cup vegetable oil
⅓ cup cider vinegar
1 tablespoon prepared mustard
1 tablespoon grated onion
1 teaspoon celery seeds
1 teaspoon paprika
1 teaspoon salt
Freshly ground black pepper to taste

In a small bowl, combine the oil, vinegar, and mustard and whisk till well blended and frothy. Add the remaining ingredients and whisk till well blended. Pour the dressing into a jar, cover, and chill several hours before using.

    Serve over poultry salads. Keeps 1 week in the refrigerator.

Yield: About 1½ cups

Poppy Seed Dressing

1 cup sugar
⅔ cup cider vinegar
2 tablespoons minced onion
2 teaspoons dry mustard
2 teaspoons salt
Black pepper to taste
2 cups vegetable oil
2 to 4 tablespoons poppy seeds, according to your taste

In the container of a blender, combine the sugar, vinegar, onion, mustard, salt, and pepper and blend momentarily. Gradually add the oil and blend till the mixture is thick. Add the poppy seeds and blend just to mix well. Transfer the mixture to a jar and store covered in the refrigerator till ready to use.

    Serve over fresh fruit salads. Keeps up to 2 weeks.

Yield: About 3½ cups

Blue Cheese Buttermilk Dressing

1 cup homemade (below) or Hellmann's mayonnaise
1 cup buttermilk
¼ teaspoon minced garlic
3 ounces blue cheese

In a bowl, combine the mayonnaise, buttermilk, and garlic and mix till well blended. Crumble the blue cheese into the mixture, stir well, chill thoroughly, and serve over any mixed green salad. Keeps 1 week in the refrigerator.

Yield: About 2¼ cups

Mustard Buttermilk Dressing

½ cup buttermilk
½ cup homemade (below) or Hellmann's mayonnaise
1 tablespoon prepared mustard
¼ teaspoon Worcestershire sauce
Freshly ground black pepper to taste

In a small bowl, combine all the ingredients and stir till well blended. If not used immediately, store in a covered jar in the refrigerator.

Serve over meat, seafood, and potato salads and use to make coleslaw. Keeps 1 week in the refrigerator.

Yield: 1 cup

Mayonnaise

2 extra large egg yolks
2 teaspoons Dijon mustard
2 teaspoons white vinegar or fresh lemon juice
2 cups vegetable or peanut oil

Place the yolks in a mixing bowl, add the mustard and vinegar, and beat vigorously with a whisk or electric mixer till frothy.

Begin adding the oil drop by drop, beating continuously. Gradually add the remaining oil in a slow stream, beating all the time, till the oil is used up. Do not continue beating after all the oil has been added.

Yield: About 2 cups

Martha Pearl Says:

"If you don't plan to use the mayonnaise immediately, beat in a tablespoon of water to stabilize the emulsion while stored in the refrigerator. The mayonnaise keeps, chilled, about 1 week."

Herb Mayonnaise

1 cup homemade (page 305) or Hellmann's mayonnaise
¼ cup finely chopped fresh parsley
2 tablespoons minced fresh chives
½ teaspoon fresh lemon juice
¼ teaspoon paprika
¼ teaspoon salt
Freshly ground black pepper to taste
Dash of Worcestershire sauce
½ cup sour cream

In a bowl, combine all the ingredients but the sour cream and stir till well blended. Fold in the sour cream, cover, and keep refrigerated till ready to use.

Serve over any congealed seafood, poultry, or vegetable salad. Keeps 1 week in the refrigerator.

Yield: About 1½ cups

Curried Cucumber Mayonnaise

1 cup homemade (page 305) or Hellmann's mayonnaise
3 tablespoons fresh lemon juice
1/4 teaspoon curry powder
Dash of Tabasco sauce
1/2 cup finely chopped peeled and seeded cucumber, well drained

In a mixing bowl, combine the mayonnaise, lemon juice, curry powder, and Tabasco and stir till well blended. Add the cucumber, stir till well blended, cover with plastic wrap, and chill well before serving.

Serve over fish salads or fresh ripe tomatoes. Keeps 1 week in the refrigerator.

Yield: About 1½ cups

Horseradish Sauce

1/2 cup homemade (page 305) or Hellmann's mayonnaise
1/2 cup sour cream
3 tablespoons prepared horseradish
2 tablespoons fresh lemon juice
1 tablespoon chopped fresh chives
1 teaspoon chopped fresh dill
1/4 teaspoon dry mustard

In a small bowl, combine all the ingredients and mix till well blended. Cover and chill several hours before serving with roast beef or broiled fish. Keeps 3 to 4 days in the refrigerator.

Yield: About 1 cup

Tartar Sauce

1 cup homemade (page 305) or Hellmann's mayonnaise
3 tablespoons finely chopped dill pickles
2 tablespoons finely chopped fresh parsley
1 tablespoon chopped capers
2 teaspoons finely chopped onion
1 teaspoon Dijon mustard

In a bowl, combine all the ingredients, mix till well blended, and chill well before serving with seafood. Keeps 2 weeks in the refrigerator.

Yield: About 1 cup

Cocktail Sauce

1 cup catsup
2 tablespoons prepared horseradish
1 tablespoon fresh lemon juice
1 tablespoon Worcestershire sauce
2 to 3 dashes of Tabasco sauce

In a small bowl, combine all the ingredients and stir till well blended. Cover and chill well before serving with boiled shrimp and other seafood. Keeps 2 to 3 days in the refrigerator.

Yield: About 1 cup

Raisin Sauce

$^1/_2$ cup firmly packed light brown sugar
2 tablespoons cornstarch
1 teaspoon dry mustard
$1^1/_2$ cups water
2 tablespoons fresh lemon juice
1 tablespoon cider vinegar

1 cup seedless raisins
½ teaspoon grated lemon rind

In a saucepan, combine the sugar, cornstarch, and mustard. Stirring, gradually add the water, lemon juice, and vinegar, bring to a boil, reduce the heat to moderate, and stir till the sugar is completely dissolved and the mixture smooth and not lumpy. Add the raisins and lemon rind and continue stirring till the sauce is thickened and bubbly, about 10 minutes.

Serve hot with baked ham or pork dishes. Keeps 1 week in the refrigerator.

Yield: About 3 cups

All-Purpose Barbecue Sauce

1 cup cider vinegar
1 cup warm water
3 tablespoons firmly packed brown sugar
2 tablespoons dry mustard
4½ teaspoons salt
2 teaspoons black pepper
1 cup (2 sticks) butter
½ cup catsup
¼ cup bottled chili sauce
3 tablespoons Worcestershire sauce
1 garlic clove, minced
1 large onion, finely chopped
Tabasco sauce to taste

In a large bowl, combine the vinegar, water, sugar, mustard, salt, and pepper, stir well, and let steep about 15 minutes.

In a large saucepan, melt the butter, then add the remaining ingredients and stir well over moderate heat. Add the steeped vinegar mixture, stir well, reduce the heat to low, and simmer about 1 hour, stirring periodically. Let the sauce cool and store in a large jar in the refrigerator till ready to use. Keeps 1 week in the refrigerator.

Yield: About 3½ cups

15

Beverages

```
              HOT BUTTERED RUM
1 pound butter, suftened
1 pound light brown sugar
1 pound powdered sugar
2 teaspoons ground cinnamon
2 teaspoons ground nutmeg
1 quart vanilla ice cream, softened
light rum
Whipped cream
Cinnamon sticks.
Combine butter, sugar, and spices; beat until light and
fluffy.  Add ice cream, stirring until well blended.
Spoon mixture into a 2 quart freezer container; freeze.
To serve, thaw slightly.  Place 3 tablespoons butter
mixture and 1 jigger rum in a large mug; fill with
boiling water. Stir well. (Any unused butter mixture can
be refrozen.) Top with whipped cream, and serve with
cinnamon stick stirrers.  Yiels; about 25 cups.
```

Recipe for: Eggnog - (for Christmas)

6 eggs - separated
1 cup sugar
1 pint Jack Daniels
1 pint of half & half -
Beat egg yolks + ½ cup sugar till lemon
colored. Gradually add whiskey. Beat
well. Beat egg white till stiff -
sugar. Add to yolks with ½ + ½
Chill - Serve with nutmeg.

After struggling for years to decipher Mother's recipes scratched on cards,
paper napkins, stationery, the backs of envelopes, and Lord knows what else,
the family once begged her to type out all the recipes in her black book. The
project at the typewriter lasted no more than one agonizing week.

Contrary to popular belief, Southerners do not quench their thirst exclusively with iced tea, Coke, and bourbon and branch. Yes, we do indeed drink a considerable amount of iced tea (one logical reason being that it goes so well with our basically plain style of food), and no, table wine has not yet gained the same prominence in the South as elsewhere in the country (most likely because so little genuine Southern food—like so little Mexican and Asian cuisine—pairs well with wine). What is often overlooked, however, are the remarkable number of cocktails, toddies, and punches that originated in the South and are still very much a part of our culture. The mint julep, of course, is legend, but equally beloved in my family have always been the Ramos gin fizzes that my father liked to concoct before lunch at our beach cottage, the smooth milk punches that we sip while opening presents on Christmas morning, the elegant syllabub spooned into crystal glasses at tea time, and the many party punches that Mother serves at large gatherings. And what, you might ask, is Martha Pearl Villas's favorite year-round, all-purpose, life-sustaining libation? Three fingers of Jack Daniel's sour mash on the rocks.

Ramos Gin Fizz

I remember distinctly the evening at the old Hotel Roosevelt in New Orleans when, perched at the bar with a pencil and paper napkin, Daddy copied down the formula for this delicious local cocktail as the bartender held forth on the one and only way to make it correctly. Today either Mother or I make our drinks in exactly the same way and usually serve them before small, sit-down lunches.

6 ounces gin
2 cups half-and-half
4 large egg whites
Juice of 2 lemons
4 teaspoons sugar
4 teaspoons orange flower water (available in specialty food shops)
Crushed ice

In a large cocktail shaker, combine all the basic ingredients plus plenty of crushed ice, shake well, and strain into highball glasses.

Yield: 4 servings

Mint Julep

One of my most prized possessions is a collection of eight silver monogrammed julep cups given to me as gifts over eight consecutive birthdays by my sister and used exclusively to serve mint juleps. Needless to say, Southerners can spend hours debating the proper way to prepare this famous libation, but all agree that each drink must be made separately, that the ice must be shaved and never in chunks, and that the sides of the cups should never be touched once they've been frosted. Mother got this recipe from our old Greek friend Stanley Demos, who for decades operated the reputed Coach House in Lexington, Kentucky. It is true that not even iced tea tastes as wonderful as a good mint julep on a sweltering summer day, and if you don't have the proper cups, well, so what?

5 fresh mint leaves plus 1 sprig fresh mint
2 teaspoons superfine sugar
1 tablespoon cold water
Finely shaved ice
4 ounces bourbon (preferably Jack Daniel's sour mash)

In a silver julep cup, place the mint leaves, sugar, and water. Crush the leaves well with a pestle or heavy spoon and stir till the sugar dissolves. Fill the cup with shaved ice, packing it down firmly, then add the bourbon and carefully mix the ice and whiskey together, cutting through the ice instead of stirring. Wipe the outside of the cup with a clean towel and place in the freezer till the cup is frosted, about 15 minutes. Carefully remove the cup from the freezer, being careful not to wipe off the frost, garnish the drink with the mint sprig, and serve at once with a party straw.

Yield: 1 serving

Planters Punch

I don't know how many summers our entire family spent at the beach cottage in South Carolina trying to determine the perfect formula for the Planters Punches that we enjoyed sipping on the deck after a full morning of boating and fishing, but once we all agreed on the proportions, the recipe remained fixed to this day. Typically, Mother keeps a huge pitcher of the fruit mixture in the refrigerator and adds the rum only when the drinks are made and according to how much of a buzz each person wants to experience.

4 ounces light rum
4 ounces amber rum
4 ounces dark rum
8 ounces pineapple juice
8 ounces orange juice
6 ounces fresh or bottled lime juice
¼ cup grenadine

Pour 1 ounce of each rum into each of four tall, narrow highball glasses and fill each glass with ice cubes. In a large pitcher or jar, combine the three fruit juices, add the grenadine, stir well, fill each glass to the top with the fruit juice mixture, and stir well.

Yield: 4 servings

Milk Punch

My father was always the bartender in the family, and never was he so fastidious about his many concoctions as when going through the ritual of mixing in his tall glass and silver shaker the Milk Punch we always drank on Christmas morning while opening gifts. Of course we were all half smashed by the time Mother got the cheese and eggs, country ham, and biscuits on the breakfast table, but Christmas simply was not Christmas without Daddy's smooth, potent Milk Punch. And the tradition continues to this day, no matter where Mother and I celebrate the holiday.

12 ounces bourbon
3 cups milk
5 teaspoons confectioners' sugar
5 drops pure vanilla extract
Cracked ice
Ground nutmeg

In a tall cocktail shaker, combine all the ingredients except the nutmeg and shake till icy cold and frothy. Pour the punch into Old-Fashioned glasses and sprinkle each drink lightly with nutmeg.

Yield: 8 servings

Coffee Punch

This is the rather smart punch that Mother created for my sister's large wedding reception and served those guests who, for one reason or another, didn't care for Champagne. Since then, she's prepared it for numerous other such festive occasions, and while I admittedly have never tasted the rich libation, Mother says that there's never a drop left in the punch bowl.

1 gallon strong coffee
1 quart heavy cream
6 tablespoons sugar
2 teaspoons pure vanilla extract
1/2 gallon vanilla ice cream

Place the coffee in a large container, let cool, and chill at least 2 hours.

In a large bowl, whip the cream till thickened, then add the sugar and vanilla and whip till very thick (be careful not to whip it to butter). Scrape the whipped cream into a large punch bowl, add the ice cream, pour on the chilled coffee, and stir till well blended.

Yield: 50 to 60 punch cups

Cranberry Party Punch

Southerners are legendary drinkers, and the amount of hard liquor still consumed at big cocktail parties is enough to startle those of the Perrier generation. To accommodate the teetotalers at their annual Christmas fling, Mother and Daddy once devised this nonalcoholic punch served in a large crystal punch bowl, and the libation was so attractive and delicious that even the heavy boozers would ask to try a cup.

Three 12-ounce cans frozen lemonade concentrate, thawed and diluted according to directions
4 cups cranberry juice cocktail
1 cup frozen orange juice concentrate, thawed and diluted according to directions
One 2-liter bottle ginger ale, chilled
1 orange, thinly sliced and seeded

In a large container, combine the juices and chill. Pour into a punch bowl, add the ginger ale just before serving, and float the orange slices on top.

Yield: 1½ gallons or 30 to 35 punch cups

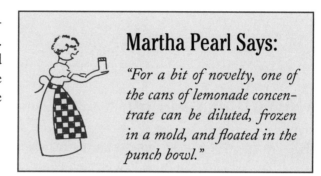

Martha Pearl Says:

"For a bit of novelty, one of the cans of lemonade concentrate can be diluted, frozen in a mold, and floated in the punch bowl."

Hot Buttered Rum

Just as Mother and I and the friends with whom we celebrate Christmas continue to sip Milk Punch around the fire while opening presents, so has it become a holiday tradition in my sister's family to serve mugs of hot buttered rum. When Mother fixes this drink for casual social get-togethers during the winter, she freezes the ice cream mixture in a large plastic container; Hootie prefers to use ice-cube trays.

1 pound (4 sticks) butter, at room temperature
One 16-ounce box light brown sugar
One 16-ounce box confectioners' sugar
2 teaspoons ground cinnamon
2 teaspoons ground nutmeg
1 quart vanilla ice cream, softened
Light rum
Boiling water
Whipped cream
Cinnamon sticks

In a large container, combine the butter, sugars, and spices, beating till light and fluffy with an electric mixer. Add the ice cream and stir till well blended. Spoon the mixture into a 2-quart plastic freezer container and freeze till firm.

To serve the drinks, thaw the butter mixture slightly, then place 3 tablespoons of the mixture into each mug or cup, add 1 jigger of rum, fill with boiling water, and stir. Top each drink with a dollop of whipped cream and serve with a cinnamon stick stirrer. (Any unused butter mixture can be refrozen.)

Yield: About 15 mugs or 25 punch cups

Christmas Eggnog

Nobody loved eggnog more than my maternal grandmother, and even when Maw Maw was confined to a nursing home at age ninety-three, the one thing she always asked Mother to bring at Christmastime was a jar of this spirited concoction ("with plenty of whiskey!") that she had sipped for nearly a century. Traditionally in the South, eggnog is served primarily when relatives and friends drop by to "visit" and leave Christmas presents, and today during the holidays, Mother is still never without a large pitcher of eggnog in the refrigerator to serve with slices of fruitcake and cookies.

6 large eggs, separated
1 cup sugar
2 cups blended whiskey or bourbon
2 cups half-and-half
Ground nutmeg

In a large bowl, combine the egg yolks and ½ cup of the sugar, whisking till light and lemon-colored. Gradually add the whiskey, whisking constantly.

In another large bowl, whisk (or beat with an electric mixer) the egg whites till thick, then add the remaining sugar and whisk till stiff. Add the half-and-half to the whiskey mixture and fold in the egg whites. Chill the eggnog thoroughly and serve either in a punch bowl sprinkled with nutmeg or in individual crystal glasses sprinkled with nutmeg.

Yield: About 6 cups, or 8 to 10 servings

Sweet Maa's Syllabub

Since North Carolina was a totally dry state when Mother was growing up, every summer her mother and grandmother would make big crocks of potent scuppernong and blackberry wine, store it in the cellar, and use it not only for drinking and all-purpose cooking but for making this delicate drink called syllabub. Little did they know, I'm sure, that syllabub, prepared as a much more dense, puddinglike dessert, had been a part of English gastronomy for centuries before evolving in the American South as a drink served with various tea cakes. In any event, Southerners have always relished the subtle drink spiked with wine, Madeira, or sherry, and Mother says she never saw my grandmother so furious as when Maw Maw once placed her syllabub on the back porch to cool, only to have the family cat lap every last ounce from the bowl.

¼ cup fresh lemon juice, strained
2 cups sweet white wine or Madeira
½ cup superfine sugar
2 teaspoons finely grated lemon rind
3 cups half-and-half

In a large, stainless-steel bowl, combine the lemon juice, wine, and sugar and stir till the sugar is completely dissolved. Add the lemon rind and stir till well blended. Add the half-and-half and beat with an electric mixer till the half-and-half forms still peaks on the blades when lifted from the bowl.

Cover the syllabub with plastic wrap, chill for 30 minutes, pour into a cut-glass bowl, and ladle into punch cups.

Yield: 6 to 8 punch cups

Russian Tea

This spicy winter concoction has been popular for decades throughout the South and is often served by hostesses in the afternoon in place of regular tea. Mother likes to serve Russian Tea with small tea sandwiches and cookies before one of her guild or book club meetings.

Juice of 3 oranges, strained
Juice of 2 lemons, strained
1 cup sugar
3 quarts water
4 tea bags
1 teaspoon whole cloves
One 3-inch-long stick cinnamon

In a medium-size container, combine the orange and lemon juices and sugar, stir well, and set aside.

In a large saucepan, bring the water to a rolling boil, remove from the heat, add the tea bags, cloves, and cinnamon, cover, and let steep 5 minutes. Remove and discard the tea bags and spices, add the fruit juice and sugar mixture, bring to a boil, and serve in teacups.

Yield: 25 cups

Hot Chocolate

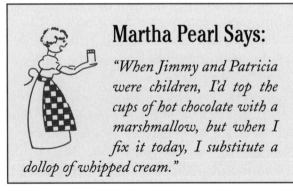

Martha Pearl Says:

"When Jimmy and Patricia were children, I'd top the cups of hot chocolate with a marshmallow, but when I fix it today, I substitute a dollop of whipped cream."

Today I don't drink much hot chocolate aside from the occasional cup at breakfast, but when my sister and I were young, a real treat was the cups of hot chocolate and cookies that Mother would have waiting on cold winter afternoons when we got home from school.

¹/₄ cup unsweetened cocoa powder
¹/₄ cup sugar
Dash of salt
4 cups milk

In a saucepan, combine the cocoa, sugar, and salt and, stirring, add a small amount of the milk to dissolve the dry ingredients. Increase the heat and gradually add the remaining milk, heating to just below the boiling point and stirring constantly. Serve in coffee cups.

Yield: 4 servings

Index